BLACK LIKE YOU

ALSO BY JOHN STRAUSBAUGH

The Drug User: Documents 1840–1960
(coedited with Donald Blaise)

Alone with the President

E: Reflections on the Birth of the Elvis Faith

Rock Til You Drop:
The Decline from Rebellion to Nostalgia

JEREMY P. TARCHER/PENGUIN

a member of

Penguin Group (USA) Inc.

New York

BLACK LIKE YOU

BLACKFACE, WHITEFACE, INSULT & IMITATION IN AMERICAN POPULAR CULTURE

JOHN STRAUSBAUGH

JEREMY P. TARCHER/PENGUIN
Published by the Penguin Group
Penguin Group (USA) Inc., 375 Hudson Street, New York, New York 10014, USA • Penguin
Group (Canada), 90 Eglinton Avenue East, Suite 700, Toronto, Ontario M4P 2Y3, Canada
(a division of Pearson Penguin Canada Inc.) • Penguin Books Ltd, 80 Strand, London WC2R 0RL,
England • Penguin Ireland, 25 St Stephen's Green, Dublin 2, Ireland (a division of Penguin
Books Ltd) • Penguin Group (Australia), 250 Camberwell Road, Camberwell, Victoria 3124,
Australia (a division of Pearson Australia Group Pty Ltd) • Penguin Books India Pvt Ltd,
11 Community Centre, Panchsheel Park, New Delhi–110 017, India • Penguin Group (NZ),
Cnr Airborne and Rosedale Roads, Albany, Auckland 1310, New Zealand (a division of Pearson
New Zealand Ltd) • Penguin Books (South Africa) (Pty) Ltd, 24 Sturdee Avenue,
Rosebank, Johannesburg 2196, South Africa

Penguin Books Ltd, Registered Offices: 80 Strand, London WC2R 0RL, England

A list of permissions can be found on page 371, which is a continuation of this copyright page.

Most Tarcher/Penguin books are available at special quantity discounts for bulk purchase for
sales promotions, premiums, fund-raising, and educational needs. Special books or book
excerpts also can be created to fit specific needs. For details, write Penguin Group (USA) Inc.
Special Markets, 375 Hudson Street, New York, New York 10014.

Library of Congress Cataloging-in-Publication Data
Strausbaugh, John.
Black like you : blackface, whiteface, insult & imitation in American popular culture /
John Strausbaugh.
p.   cm.
Includes bibliographical references.
ISBN 1-58542-498-6
1. African Americans in popular culture. 2. Racism in popular culture—United States.
3. Blackface entertainers—United States. 4. Imitation. 5. Stereotype (Psychology)—United States.
6. African Americans—Race identity. 7. Whites—Race identity—United States.
8. United States—Race relations. 9. Popular culture—United States. I. Title.
E185.625.S77   2006   2006040940
305.896'0973—dc22

Printed in the United States of America
1   3   5   7   9   10   8   6   4   2

BOOK DESIGN BY MEIGHAN CAVANAUGH

While the author has made every effort to provide accurate telephone numbers and Internet
addresses at the time of publication, neither the publisher nor the author assumes any
responsibility for errors, or for changes that occur after publication. Further, the publisher does
not have any control over and does not assume any responsibility for author or third-party
websites or their content.

ACKNOWLEDGMENTS

First, many thanks to Darius James for his smart and funny words, and for his encouragement and advice.

A number of friends, colleagues and experts helped in the research and writing of this book. Two erudite bibliophiles did the heaviest lifting and deserve special mention: Kurt Thometz of Jumel Terrace Books and Lauri Bortz of Abaton Book Company. But I am indebted to all of the following for their help: Brian Berger, William Bryk, Carole Carroll, D. B. Doghouse, Celia Farber, Scott Huffines, Lisa Kearns, Norman Kelley, Jim Knipfel, Kathleen Kotcher, Don McLeod, Philip Jackson Merrill, Diane Ramo, Rasha Refaie, William Repsher, Ken Swezey, James Taylor, Tony Trachta and Christine Walker.

Thanks to my fantastic editor, Ken Siman, to Joel Fotinos, and to everyone else at Tarcher/Penguin.

A big shout-out to Laura Lindgren for the beautiful jacket design, and to Meighan Cavanaugh for designing the interior. Thanks to Anna Jardine for her precise and astute copyediting.

I am not an academic scholar. In these pages I cite historians, musicologists, linguists and other professional scholars whose work inspired and informed this book. I refer you to the bibliography for further reading.

For helping me keep the rent paid and the lights on while I was writing, I'm very grateful to Chris Calhoun, Laurie Liss, Sam Sifton and Scott Veale.

If I've forgotten anyone, let the insults fly.

CONTENTS

LIST OF ILLUSTRATIONS

1

A PESTILENCE OF IGNUNCE

Blackface in the Twenty-first Century

Methinks there is need of a Society for the Diffusion of Useful Ignorance, what we will call Beautiful Knowledge, a knowledge useful in a higher sense: for what is most of our boasted so-called knowledge but a conceit that we know something, which robs us of the advantage of our actual ignorance? —HENRY DAVID THOREAU

There may be people more racist, misogynist and classist than me. But I'm certainly the most ignunt. —SHIRLEY Q. LIQUOR

It was brutally cold on the streets of lower Manhattan the night of February 14, 2004. The city had been frozen for weeks in the mean heart of an uncommonly vicious winter, making everything from the pavement to the air itself feel even harder and more unyielding than usual. But it was the night of Valentine's Day, so all over the city people were darting into clubs and restaurants to celebrate.

On the Bowery, outside a gay club called the Marquee, a dozen or so young people, shivering and stamping their feet, had formed two lines facing each other on the sidewalk—a narrow gauntlet through which patrons had to pass to reach the stairs down to the basement-level entrance.

"Shirley Q. Liquor is racist and misogynist," a shivering young female informed me, thrusting a small yellow flyer into my hand.

Shirley Q. Liquor Is Not a Cabaret Act, the flyer declared. *It Is A Racist, Classist, Misogynist Attack.*

The back of the sheet bore an "OPEN LETTER TO LGBTST COMMUNITIES" (Lesbian, Gay, Bisexual, Two-Spirit and Transgendered), exhorting them to "Help End Shirley Q. Liquor's Gay Exploitation of Racism, Sexism & Poverty for Profit." It was signed by several organizations representing gays and lesbians of color.

I stood at the bottom of the stairs for a while and watched other

Flyer distributed by protesters at
Shirley Q. Liquor performance, 2004.

patrons run the gauntlet. A chic young Black couple followed me down the stairs.

"They said this show is racist," the young woman fretted.

"Why don't we make up our own minds?" the man replied, pushing the flyer into a coat pocket.

If the protesters were hoping to shame patrons away from the club, it wasn't working. In fact, it's likely that their presence was enhancing the thrill ticket-holders derived from doing something they knew was naughty and politically incorrect. The last time Shirley Q. Liquor had come to Manhattan, a year and a half earlier, a larger, more vocal group of protesters had succeeded in shutting down a club in Chelsea, and scheduled performances in other Northeastern cities were subsequently canceled by skittish promoters. Indeed, very few of Shirley Q. Liquor's scheduled performances ever seemed to happen. Tonight's return visit to Manhattan had not been openly advertised; it was sold out by word of mouth. Running the gauntlet of protesters, descending to the basement-level entrance, entering a club with a somewhat risqué reputation to see a performer who had literally been banned in Boston—it all added to the sense that one was engaged in a titillatingly underground activity.

The small club—a dance floor with a stage at the front and a bar in the back—was packed with a capacity crowd of maybe 150. The audience was almost entirely White males. I counted no more than a dozen females, and no more than a dozen non-White faces, who included that young couple I'd seen, a scattering of young Black men and a few Asians. On the left and the right, two nearly naked Black go-go dancers, a male and a female, ground their hips. Their physiques were almost cartoons of stereotyped Black sexuality—his prodigious endowment bulging in tiny briefs, her huge breasts and rump straining to burst out of a gaudy bikini. It was open to interpretation whether the stereotypes the dancers evoked were being ironically subverted or merely flaunted.

The opening act, a standard drag queen, was politely received.

The next act parted the curtains on the small stage to a warmer response. "Betty Butterfield" was a corpulent, doughy-faced man costumed as a trailer park diva, like an overweight Tammy Faye Bakker. A bad red wig teetered precariously on his head; large plastic jewelry adorned his fingers and ears; his cheeks were clownishly rouged, his mouth made twice its size with shiny orange lipstick, and oversized sunglasses hid the upper portion of his face. Drawled in a whispery sigh, Betty's act satirized Southern White womanhood as a drunken, drug-addled, TV-addicted mess of shallow Christianity and self-pitying confusion.

There was another intermission, and then Shirley Q. Liquor shuffled into the spotlight. The crowd exploded in an uproar of applause and cheers. The mood was something like that at an intimate rock concert. Shirley Q. Liquor was obviously the same portly man who'd played Betty Butterfield—a man named Chuck Knipp—now wearing a bad pink wig, with his girth draped in a kind of housedress. Instead of the clownish White-woman makeup, his face, neck and hands were now coated a greasy chocolate brown, shiny and dark as shoe polish. His orange lips and eyes stood out garishly bright against the darkened skin, forming an old, yet instantly recognizable, icon: the blackface minstrel mask.

Like most of the audience, I had listened to Shirley Q. but never seen her. Knipp says the character began as a joke recording on his home telephone answering machine in the mid-1990s. This developed into radio spots syndicated by the American Comedy Network—which as of 2005 had reportedly been played on three hundred stations around the country—and CDs sold through a website, the Shirley Q. Liquor Store, which also vended Shirley Q. posters, T-shirts, mugs, bumper stickers and other merchandising. Downloads of Shirley's material topped the list of most-sold comedy at mp3.com for some time. A grassroots cult following grew as fans passed recordings around. Her following was particularly strong among gay males.

Listening to Knipp, a White man, impersonating Shirley Q. Liquor, a Black woman, was one thing. Actually *seeing* a White man in blackface drag on a stage in New York City in the twenty-first century was an entirely different experience. As a White male, my response to the iconic and taboo blackface mask was instant and visceral. I was shocked, shamed and a little revolted. Another White man I spoke to later said that his first glimpse of Knipp in blackface that night had actually made him feel sick to his stomach.

And yet, as Knipp began to reel off his jokes and skits, I found myself laughing, often uproariously, along with the rest of the mostly White, mostly gay audience. While it is certainly worth arguing whether or not Shirley Q. Liquor's act was "racist, classist, misogynist," what I think cannot be denied is that it was also funny, extremely daring satire, transgressing accepted boundaries of public discourse.

Knipp said in an interview on the Southern Decadence website that when he took Shirley Q.'s act onto the stage, "I had no idea how to do this character as a live performance the first time. Up until then, I had been on radio or in a recording studio. Then it hit me—if I am going to perform this character onstage, I'll have to get in drag and paint my face a different color. Some people ask me if I do blackface. I don't think that's it. I use regular African-American lady brown foundation and all kinds of eye shadows. And I really like the pink wig."

At the Marquee, Knipp made no effort to fool anyone that he was either Black or female. The effect was intentionally ridiculous, suggesting a self-mocking parody of both blackface and drag conventions. If Knipp was poking fun at women and Blacks, he also seemed to be mocking Whites and gay males. This became explicit when his jokes were directed as often at Whites, gays and lesbians (characterized as "homosexicals" and "bulldaggas") as at Black women. "Y'all need to be ashamed, White people," he admonished the crowd at one point. "You ain't right."

There is much about Shirley Q. Liquor that seems a calculated throwback to more openly racist times. Her character is an easily recognized stereotype from the 1970s and 1980s: the Black "welfare queen." She's a middle-aged single mother on government assistance, who claims she has never worked a day in her life. She speaks Ebonics with a broad Gulf States drawl, as in her signature greeting, "How you durrin?" She has nineteen "chirrun," so many she struggles to remember all their names—and those of their various absent fathers. In one of her routines most often cited by both fans and protesters, "Who Is My Baby Daddy?," she croons the children's names, including Cheetoh, Limbo, Curtis, Lemonjello (pronounced luh-MAHN-juh-lo), Orangejello (o-RAHN-juh-lo), Kmartina, Velveeta, Cocoa Puffs, Maybelline, Gingivitis, Brylcreem, Nyquil and Shithead (shee-THAYD). She drinks malt liquor, smokes too much, drives a Cadillac, shops at "Kmark," attends the Mount Holy Olive Second Baptist Zion Church of God, but mostly seems to while away her days with her friend Watusi, watching soap operas, gossiping about the neighbors, and commenting on the generally "ignunt" state of humanity.

At its best, Knipp's humor is inspired satire of an America seen from its lowest rung, poking equal fun at Blacks and Whites, rich and poor, its pop culture excesses and its silly pretensions. Shirley Q. is at times a truly insightful and empathetic portrait of the stranded Black single mother confronting chronic poverty and all that comes with it, from the uncaring welfare bureaucracy to rude shop clerks.

"Baby, we was extremely povertied this week," she announces in one routine. "My check had not came on time. Oo, we was stretchin' it, honey." Her electricity is shut off. "I ax them to cut my power on. I said, 'A woman have got to have some fans runnin' down here in this heat.' And they wouldn't do it. They gon' talk about a deposick. I said, 'Look, if I had the money for a deposick I woulda done paid the bill.' Now why they don't see that? See, who is workin' down there that's this ignunt? . . . You know, nothin' is really on sale anymore," she sighs. "Ninety-nine cent is not a bargain if you do not have ninety-nine cent."

"Who Is My Baby Daddy?" began to look a bit less scandalous in the fall of 2005 when media outlets around the world, from *The New Yorker* to TV news in China, reported with straight faces on "Marry Your Baby Daddy Day," a bizarre if ingenious publicity blitz whipped up by Brooklyn-based Black author Maryann Reid to promote her novel of the same name. Out of five hundred applicants, Reid chose ten Black couples who'd had children out of wedlock to participate in a mass wedding and reception, all expenses paid. I wonder if they played the Shirley Q. routine as the happy couples marched down the aisle.

The Shirley Q. routine "If I Was a White Lady," sung to the tune of "If I Were a Rich Man," from *Fiddler on the Roof*, includes the lines:

> *If I was a White lady,*
> *I would sit around and lounge around*
> *and watch The Price Is Right.*
> *All day long I'd sit up on the phone,*
> *Ordering stupid stuff from QVC.*
> *I wouldn't be on welfare,*
> *My ignunt-ass husband would have a job at DuPont,*
> *Maybe Chevron or Bayer aspirin,*
> *Something besides Taco Bell . . .*

Ignunce is a concept of deep importance to Shirley Q., as it has been for a long time in Southern culture. The word "ignunce" appears in Joel Chandler Harris' Uncle Remus stories. In Baltimore, where I grew up, both Black folks and crackers pronounced it "ignint," or the syllable-and-a-half "ign't," or sometimes "iggorant." (Whole books have been written about how Baltimoreans speak. It's been called Bawlmerese, but I prefer to think of it as Baltimoronics.) In dictionary English, *ignorance* is a value-neutral word, and simply means a lack of knowledge. But in Southern American vernacular, for both Blacks and Whites, to call a person "ignorant" is an insult that implies a person is not just unlearned but uncouth, stupid and rude. It's similar to the way Italians use *maleducato*—"poorly educated"—to mean rude and boorish.

So Shirley Q. reads from Proverbs 14:7: "'Leave the presence of the fool, for there you do not meet no word of knowledge.' . . . What I'm sayin' is, we are livin' in ignunt times. There seem like it's a pestilence of ignunce what have swepteded the land." In another skit, her sister is pulled over by a traffic cop and charged with DRI—"Drivin' Real Ignunt." Onstage at the Marquee, Shirley Q. gently chided the "protetsers" outside, wondering why they called her racist and "missogamuss." Then again, she admitted, "there may be people more racist, misogynist and classist than me. But I'm certainly the most ignunt."

At his worst, Knipp stoops to traffic in the lowest, most common racist jokes. His routine in which Shirley sings "The Twelve Days of Kwanzaa" was called "toxically politically incorrect" by *The Atlanta Journal-Constitution,* one of the few mainstream newspapers not to find the act too marginal to mention. (Virtually all media coverage has been in gay or alternative weeklies.) The brilliance of Shirley Q. Liquor's best material makes the slumming worst all the more troubling and mystifying. But it also, as we'll see, places the act securely within the American tradition of blackface performance, which has from its very inception displayed a tremendous emotional, sexual and political confusion. The question asked most often about Shirley Q. Liquor's oeuvre—Is it mocking Black culture, or celebrating it?—turns out to be a conundrum at the heart of blackface.

Knipp told the Southern Decadence website that he had studied up on the history of blackface minstrelsy, and rejects it as a model for his act. He likens Shirley Q. more to the comic impersonations of Tracey Ullman.

"It never occurred to me that doing Shirley Q. was in any way racist," he said. "To me, it's total character immersion. Is she a stereotype of a bygone day? Certainly. But she's just real enough to cause what I call an 'anxious giggle' in most everyone who hears her perspective. . . .

"I am a firm believer that comedy is a way to heal past injustices, prejudice and hate. Laughter is healing and in my attempt to make people laugh, I think I can work just as hard as any social activist to make this world just. I have seen prejudice and hatred and know it well. My hometown is in the heart of hatred. I commuted with black students to and from Lamar University [in Texas]. . . .

"My character Shirley Q. Liquor was created in celebration of, not to downgrade, black women. . . . My comedy isn't racist, nor am I. More than anything, my comedy makes fun of whites' views of blacks. My comedy pokes fun at everything, including myself. That's what comedy is about, making us escape [from] everyday life and seeing the funny side."

To Knipp's many detractors, this must sound like simply the excuses of a racist. But I think it's worth considering whether the shock value of an act like Shirley Q. Liquor might not serve some larger social purpose, much as Knipp claims. At this stage of American culture's development, a White comedian in blackface is the guiltiest of "guilty pleasures," the most shocking of "shock humor," the ultimate "naughty joke." Virtually all other forms of ethnic or identity jokes, while often frowned on, are permissible. Black comics routinely joke about White people, and about Black people. Latino comics can joke about Asians. Gay comics can joke about heterosexuals, and vice versa. Jewish jokes by anyone not Jewish are both risky and risqué, but permissible as long as they don't descend to "hate speech."

But White people's joking about Black people is almost automatically treated as hate speech. The blackface mask is utterly taboo, in a way no other comic impersonations of ethnicity or identity are. It may be considered tasteless and tactless for the Black hiphop artist Andre 3000 to dress up as a Native American for the Grammy Awards, but it is not forbidden. Black comics like Dave Chappelle and the Wayanses may upset some people with their whiteface routines, but whiteface is not taboo. But blackface *is* taboo, and a White comedian making jokes about Black people will be banned. The long and terrible history of Black and White relations in America almost ensures that this must be so.

Yet American humor has always been very rough-and-tumble. What strikes Americans as funny exists on a sliding scale from vulgar insult (blonde jokes, faggot jokes, Polack jokes) to what's most often judged hate speech today (nigger jokes, kike jokes). Ethnic/identity humor plays a huge role in American culture. It's part of the toughening-up process that leads to mutual tolerance (if not mutual admiration) in America's mongrel culture. Theoretically, all Americans are free to insult all other Americans. Theoretically, we are all fair game. Everybody has a right to be ignunt in America. There's a reason why insult is protected free speech in America, and not susceptible to libel litigation the way it is in the UK. In America, insult is not actionable. We are expected to be able to "give as good as we get," to "dish it out and take it."

One of the functions of humor is to serve as a forum where we Americans can say things about one another that we cannot say in polite conversation. In comic performance and jokes we say how we really feel about one another in ways we never do in public and with a straight face. In that sense, Shirley Q. Liquor's blackface mask is the ultimate in not-a-straight-face. It allows White people to laugh about Black people in public, in ways they normally would do only in private. By penetrating the surface of polite, politically correct discourse, Shirley Q. Liquor forces her audience to acknowledge feelings, attitudes and opinions that they have been well trained to hide and repress. One of the signal failures of politically correct social programming has been the notion that if Americans could be trained to speak and act *as if* they don't have any of these opinions or attitudes, these attitudes and opinions will disappear. Comedians like Shirley Q. Liquor, Dave Chappelle, Chris Rock, Carlos Mencia, and once upon a time Andrew Dice Clay, Richard Pryor and Lenny Bruce, have challenged this failed experiment in social engineering.

Not surprisingly, Knipp's detractors remain unconvinced, and as of 2005 were still managing to prevent his performances in most cities.

It is perhaps surprising that one of Knipp's most enthusiastic supporters is RuPaul, the Black drag queen, who invited Shirley Q. to record a few short intersong segments for his 2004 CD *Red Hot.* Writing on his weblog just after the 2002 protest that closed down Knipp's performances in Chelsea, RuPaul called the actions of the protesters a "witch hunt," by "a group of unsophisticated barbarians with misguided rage," a "self-righteous lynch mob." He went on to write that "these fascists believe that Mr. Knipp 'not only makes fun of black women, but re-enforces every racist stereotype.' that argument was valid 40 years ago, before there were black media moguls who make fun of black women and reinforce racist stereotypes. i guess the rap & hip hop community is exempt because they appear to be black." Shirley Q., RuPaul insisted, was "a loving homage to . . . southern black women."

It's worth noting that a number of Black comedians who are Knipp's contemporaries, and whose humor is quite similar to his, have also been accused of practicing a twenty-first-century version of minstrelsy—what *The New Republic* called "reactionary hipness." In a 2001 article, it charged the comics Chris Rock and Chris Tucker with "attempting to shuck, jive, grin, shout, and bulge their eyes all the way back to the days of minstrelsy." Chris Rock had by then outraged critics several times—by appearing in whiteface, and wearing minstrelish white gloves, in an Annie Leibovitz photo spread in *Vanity Fair* in 1998, and with his infamous routine distinguishing Black people from "niggers." *The New Republic* went on to accuse the four Black comedians in Spike Lee's 2000 documentary *The Original Kings of Comedy* of trafficking in racist stereotypes that revived the nineteenth-century "coon show." It also touched on the familiar critique that much hiphop and rap music was also new-model minstrelsy.

In the New York University newspaper *Washington Square News* shortly after Shirley Q.'s Valentine's Day performance, a young woman who'd been in the audience noted: "That's what makes it so hard to criticize Shirley Q.'s material: We've all heard it before and laughed. It may have been from a Wayans brother, an entertainer named Cedric or a friend, but it came from black faces, who allegedly were not in blackface. Surely no one can still be so hypocritical as to believe disrespectful stereotypes are acceptable from people who look like you, but insist it is racism when a member of another race finds humor in it. A show like Shirley Q. Liquor serves to challenge our usually unquestioned standards of entertainment."

Gays and lesbians of color point out that Knipp's large following among White gay men reveals a deep and long-standing rift in the community along racial lines. (Some feminists have argued that *all* drag performance is as insulting to women as blackface is to Blacks, and that both should be banned.) Knipp's White gay fans respond that there's an aspect of turnabout in this. Black American culture, they argue, is notoriously homophobic, and antigay sentiments are often and openly expressed in the jokes of Black comedians and the lyrics of Black rappers. If that's permitted, why not Knipp's blackface humor?

Isn't everybody allowed to be ignunt once in a while?

It's because of my exposure to Shirley Q. Liquor's act—and the complex feelings her act aroused in me—that I came to write this book. When I was growing up in the 1950s and 1960s, Baltimore was a chocolate and vanilla city, with the two flavors rarely mixing. I didn't have a Black friend until high school. I watched the events of the civil rights movement unfold on the same TV where I enjoyed reruns of *The Amos 'N' Andy Show*. I have friends my age who can remember their parents engaging in a little amateur blackface, but I saw none of that in my neighborhood. To me, as I suspect to many people, it was quizzical and embarrassing behavior some White folks had gotten up to in the past. Nigger jokes abounded, as did Polack jokes and other forms of ethnic insult humor. All of this was frowned on by my parents, who were good German-Irish Catholics and taught us values of tolerance, charity and equality. Of course, this also lent such humor a certain guilty, illicit thrill.

Seeing Shirley Q. Liquor in blackface in 2004 took me back to the racially segregated (de facto, if not always de jure) world of my childhood. I became intrigued about blackface's history and persistence, and what it says about how much has changed in American culture during the time I've lived—and what hasn't. This book is the result.

WHILE IT'S BEEN MOSTLY CONFINED WITHIN AN "UNDERground" and gay context, the controversy over Shirley Q. Liquor reflects tensions in American culture broadly defined. As a natural consequence of how much we like to insult and crack jokes at one another, we Americans often seem primed to take offense at the first hint that we are being made fun of. This touchiness seems to have increased in recent decades, rubbed raw by the growing stridency of "identity politics" and political correctness. Freedom of expression, even ignunt expression, is a cornerstone of our society, and we are justifiably proud of it. Nevertheless, we seem ever ready to censor or censure all manner of expression we find hateful, offensive, insulting or simply in bad taste. Free speech is a right we tend to defend more jealously when *we* are speaking than when our neighbor is.

Still and all, only a handful of words and symbols have been considered absolutely taboo in current American society, unreservedly banned and forbidden. The swastika is one. The word "nigger," uttered by anyone not Black, is another. Blackface is a third. There are numerous other words and signs that are generally abhorred, that are slander or slurs, that can provoke rage or revulsion, cause shock or scandal, start fights or end friendships. There is a burgeoning catalogue of what is considered hate speech, so called because it is believed to incite hatred, discrimination and potentially violent treatment of women, homosexuals, or ethnic and religious groups. But the swastika, the "N-word" and blackface, because of their special historical significance, are the ne plus ultra of hate speech, and therefore taboo.

Yet like all social conventions, even taboos can change over time, and the severity of how society reacts to them is influenced by context. In the 1970s, punk rockers in the UK and the United States wore the swastika as one element of their ironic shock-value fashions, and it was generally understood they were using it that way. But in 2005, when Prince Harry dressed like a Nazi for a costume party, he was roundly chastised. And a swastika spray-painted or scrawled anywhere is still widely counted as a "hate crime."

The word "nigger," which for decades was so taboo it could be rendered only as "the N-word," began to resurface in public discourse in the 1990s. While still extremely controversial and scandal-provoking, its ubiquity in rap lyrics created a social context in which some White Americans have felt emboldened to use it as well— insisting that they are deploying it not in its old-fashioned service as a racial slur, but in the newer role Black users have given it, in which it sometimes can be used as an insult, but just as often is not. Ten years earlier, Quentin Tarantino simply could not have made a film like his 1997 *Jackie Brown,* in which Samuel L. Jackson cannot seem to utter a line without the word "nigger" in it.

And blackface, unconditionally banned for decades as well, has crept back into the public arena. Black performer Ben Vereen was widely criticized for wearing blackface when presenting a musical tribute to the Black vaudevillian Bert Williams at Ronald Reagan's 1981 inaugural ceremonies. Critics said that Vereen's use of black-face was insensitive and inappropriate, even though it was historically accurate. (Williams, like virtually all Black performers in the early twentieth century, had routinely worn it.)

Whoopi Goldberg and her then lover Ted Danson may never live down the uproar that followed his appearance in blackface at her

1993 Friars Club roast. The roast is a private affair, at which comics try to top one another with outrageous and supremely tasteless gags they would never attempt in public. Danson's blackface was clearly intended as self-parody; as *The New York Times* later noted, the joke "delighted the subject and most guests, but seemed to offend those who read about it in the tabloids after Montel Williams stormed out in a huff." Blacks and liberals thundered against Danson and Goldberg in the media for weeks, and still cite the event as an unconscionable gaffe; New York City's Black mayor, David Dinkins, denounced them; some Black members quit the Friars; fellow performers abandoned Danson and Goldberg en masse. (Paragon of good taste Bobcat Goldthwait was reported to have remarked, "Jesus Christ, Ted, what were you thinking? Do you think black people think blackface is funny in 1993?") Goldberg's reputation was dented but survived the controversy; Danson's career never returned to its *Cheers* heights. They broke up not very long after the incident.

A decade later, Shirley Q. Liquor was not the only professional White comedian performing in blackface. In the summer of 2004, a Texas comic named Willie P. Richardson toured Southern arenas as an opening act for country-and-western legend Ray Price. Like Chuck Knipp, Richardson is known mostly for his radio skits and CDs, which are based on telephone prank calls à la *Crank Yankers*. Onstage, he performs in blackface—but confoundingly makes no real attempt to impersonate a Black person. He speaks in an East Texas drawl that could be Southern White or Black, and on tour he uttered only one joke that revolved around race, a live version of his best-known phone prank: "a mock phone call in which Richardson tells a nurse that there might have been a mixup at the hospital because his family was black and their newborn baby looked 'Mexican,'" as a Louisiana newspaper put it. "While the audience laughed, a midget wearing a diaper and sombrero strutted on stage, bringing even more laughter." Otherwise, Richardson performed as though unaware that he was even wearing blackface.

White audience members interviewed after a concert in Lafayette, Louisiana, said they'd seen nothing offensive in the act. Even Black viewers sounded more bemused than outraged:

> "I'm not sure what to think. In watching him, I'm not sure why he has to even wear the paint. He could do the show without it," said City-Parish Director of Community Development Melanie Lewis, who is black. Lewis said she came to monitor the show.
>
> "I thought he would be more stereotypical," she said, but added that by simply painting himself black, Richardson's show could potentially open some cultural wounds.
>
> "It hearkens back to a painful time in our history. I think there are still some wounds on both sides," Lewis said.

That's a far cry from the reaction Danson had gotten ten years earlier.

Tracey Ullman has generated almost no controversy performing in blackface on national TV. Ullman has based her entire career on comic impersonations of numerous races, ethnicities, ages and social classes, some of them gentle satire, while others—a swarthy Middle Eastern taxi driver, a leering Chinese woman who likes to eat cats— manifestly as "offensive" as anything Shirley Q. Liquor does. Ullman's blackface character is a lusty, wisecracking middle-aged woman who works airport security. In a sense, she's just Shirley Q. with a job.

Civil War reenactment groups go to extraordinary lengths in striving for authenticity. This includes the musicians who play at their events, whose efforts at realism extend "from constructing period instruments and donning near-perfect replicas of clothing from the era, to performing the old minstrel classics exactly as they originally were, sometimes even in blackface," according to a 2003 article in the *Houston Press*. With the groups using old-time minstrel names like Free and Accepted Minstrels of Old New Orleans, Amoskeag Players, Second South Carolina String Band, and Allendale Melodians ("who proudly declare themselves 'the only blackface minstrel troupe in America'"), "the endeavor is done so faithfully that, as one modern-day minstrel player put it, 'If you squint your eyes and your ears a little, you can travel right back to the 1840s.'"

The article goes on: "It should be noted that no minstrel musician interviewed for this article thought it should be played for general audiences; nor had any of the musicians performed in blackface in front of anything other than a controlled, closed audience, one that had first received ample historical context."

The reporter, who despite these measures clearly disapproves, reassures readers: "Written off by most mainstream historians and musicologists as nothing more than racist theatrics and overwrought melodrama, minstrelsy hasn't merited serious cultural study since its awkward birth in the 1830s." This is so far from correct that it seems willful ignunce, a not uncommon affliction in the field of blackface history.

In 1978, Bobby Berger, a Baltimore police officer, began performing an Al Jolson tribute in blackface at local parties, restaurants, and VFW and American Legion halls. Though he did it on his own time, his superiors ordered him to stop, after receiving complaints from the local NAACP. Berger refused, and was dismissed from the force in 1984. He sued, claiming that his First Amendment rights had been violated, and won.

Since 1997, Berger has been doing his Jolson routine, along with tributes to a number of other celebrities, at his own place, Bobby B's Palace & Supper Club, in the Baltimore suburbs. The NAACP has not complained.

In 2005, a surreal film called *What Is It?*, produced and directed by actor Crispin Glover, began making the independent film festival circuit. A man costumed as a blackface minstrel appears in it, but since the film is one long series of disturbing images calculated to shock and offend, the blackface was received in that context.

There is another way to contextualize contemporary blackface: It is far from the only form of ethnic drag or ethnic humor being used by professional entertainers, just the most controversial. Like Tracey Ullman, Eddie Murphy built a large part of his career on his uncanny impersonations of WASPs, Jews, Italians and entire families of obese, vulgar Black people. In one of his funniest skits from his *Saturday Night Live* era, he ventures out into the world in whiteface. "I studied for my role very carefully," he tells the TV audience. "I watched lots of *Dynasty*. See? See how they walk? Their butts are real tight when they walk. They keep their butts tight. I've gotta remember to keep my butt real tight when I walk." The Wayanses starred in full-body whiteface drag in their 2004 movie *White Chicks*.

At the 2004 Grammy Awards show, telecast by CBS, Andre 3000 of the Atlanta hiphop duo OutKast performed his megahit song "Hey Ya!" in gleeful Native American drag, complete with a recording of Navajo dance drums, a stylized tipi and a crew of dancers costumed as sexy squaws. There was an instant explosion of outrage from Native American organizations. One website fulminated: "OutKast Grammy Awards Performance Racist! How about a cute dance number featuring a 'Step 'N Fetch it' Uncle Tom character waiting on White folks? Not funny? Well neither is this!" CBS issued a standardly worded apology. Andre 3000 did not.

In all the public outcry, there was very little discussion of whether the young Black performer intended to mock Native American culture or celebrate it. Most commentators simply assumed the former. No one seems to have noticed that his routine was less evocative of American Indian culture than of another tradition altogether: Mardi Gras Indians, the Black groups in New Orleans who parade every year in elaborately stylized Native American costumes. These revelers clearly intend no disrespect to Native Americans; they celebrate the culture, and a sense of a shared history. Still, they have also met with disapproval from some Native American organizations.

Interestingly, the video for "Hey Ya!" which had been in constant rotation on music television stations the previous summer and fall, raised no eyebrows with its gentle spoof of Beatles-era White pop groups—or its chorus of three Black males (all Andre himself) dressed as lawn jockeys. (In 2005, the joke would be taken a step further in a very low-budget film, *The Rodnees: We Mod Like Dat,* about a struggling hiphop crew from Brooklyn who reinvent themselves as latter-day Black Beatles.) The video for OutKast's other hit of 2003, "The Way You Move," featured scantily clad black lovelies striding around an African plain like wild beasts, and this, too, was received without controversy.

The same nightclubs that ban Shirley Q. Liquor would likely jump at the chance to book Dave Chappelle, a Black comedian whose ethnic humor has been denounced as offensive by some Whites. In one funny routine, he plays a blind Black man who was raised among Whites and becomes a virulently racist KKK spokesman. In another, he seeks to answer the question "Is it true White people can't dance?" He postulates that White people *can* dance, but only if the right music is played. He proceeds to demonstrate that White people dance whenever they hear an electric guitar; Black people dance whenever they hear funky drums; and Latin people dance whenever they hear funky drums, an electric piano and a singer wailing "gibberish in Spanish." This is typical of Chappelle's strategy of rendering what would normally be called offensive and racially charged material both humorous and harmless by being an all-purpose and polyethnic offender. When you're offending every body's tribe, no one tribe can reasonably claim to be "more" offended than any other. Tracey Ullman and Eddie Murphy benefit from similar strategies.

BLACKFACE HAS ONE KIND OF MEANING WHEN USED BY A comedian like Chuck Knipp or Tracey Ullman. Then there's what we might call amateur blackface. It's easy to write off White students wearing blackface to frat parties as just ignunt asses. Certainly their use of blackface is offensive, and it may well be classified as hate speech. But again, these instances don't happen in a social vacuum. They usually seem to be consciously intended to provoke controversy and/or outrage—even when the practitioners profess innocence.

In the 2000s, blackface has appeared on a number of college campuses around the country. At Auburn University in Alabama, "several white members of two fraternities dressed up as KKK Klansmen and black gang members," the Syracuse University *Daily Orange* reported in 2003. "An Oklahoma State party went even further when students dressed as Klansmen and pretended to lynch students in blackface. At the University of Mississippi, pictures emerged from a party showing a student in a police costume holding a gun to the head of a student in blackface who was pretending to pick cotton."

At Syracuse, a blackfaced White student attended a Halloween party as Tiger Woods. White frat members attended a University of Louisville costume party in blackface, dressed as pimps and prisoners. White law students at Florida State University donned Afro wigs and fake gold jewelry to attend a "Pimps and Ho's" party. A group of blackfaced University of Tennessee students went to a party as the Jackson Five. At the University of Wisconsin, a student performing in a fraternity variety show appeared as NBA star Charles Barkley. At a University of Virginia frat party, one student "dressed as Uncle Sam in blackface with an Afro wig, while two others dressed as tennis champions Venus and Serena Williams." White Texas A&M students in blackface threw a "ghetto party" on Martin Luther King, Jr., Day. The University of Nebraska at Omaha student newspaper *The Gateway* had to apologize for an April Fool's parody issue, *The Ghettoway,* written in hiphop slang with bylines like "Ima Slapu" (I'm a-slap you) and "Donbee Trippen." Similar incidents occurred at Georgia State University, Penn State, Oklahoma State, Emory University and a number of other campuses in the years 2000–2005.

Blackface incidents and other expressions of racial tension on campus date back to the mid-1980s, as colleges and universities that had been all or nearly all White aggressively ramped up their ethnic and cultural diversity programs, actively wooed minority students and faculty, and poured funds into new Black and Asian studies departments and Black student unions. It wasn't long before White student groups began to complain that they were the "new minority" on campus and victims of "reverse discrimination" as students of other ethnicities received various kinds of what seemed to be preferential treatment. And as particularly strident variants of multicultural proselytizing spread through college campuses everywhere, some White students felt that they were being taught to feel only shame about their heritage, while minority students were strongly encouraged to feel pride about their own backgrounds.

These feelings were expressed not only by frat boys in the South; there were a number of incidents at the liberal Northern campuses that were most active in recruiting and promoting diversity. At the University of Wisconsin at Madison in 1986, for example, White students in blackface and Afro wigs threw a Harlem-themed party, complete with fried chicken and watermelon. This was followed the next year by a "Fiji Island" party, and the next by a "mock slave auction." Even Harvard was not immune; in 1992, two White medical students caused an uproar when they put on blackface and went to a Halloween party as Anita Hill and Clarence Thomas.

None of these incidents cited rises much above the level of a mean-spirited and intentionally provocative prank—the sort of behavior for which frat boys have long been infamous. But because they suggest a history of poisonous race relations, they routinely turn campuses and local communities upside down in paroxysms of anger, outrage and denunciation, involving student rallies to end the "hate crimes," public show-trials for both perpetrators and administrators, suspensions for individual students and their fraternities, widespread expressions of shame and guilt from White students, and editorials in local newspapers by community leaders. The more clever minority student groups exploit the occasion to present school administrators with long lists of "demands" for, among other things, increased funding for minority student groups, minority faculty and minority facilities. For their part, the perpetrators always seek to evade punishment by disingenuously declaring their innocence of any intent to offend, and even ignorance that their pranks might be insulting.

Adults have indulged in intentionally provocative blackface stunts as well. In the Broad Channel community of Queens, New York, a loose-knit group of local men (the community is largely White) were in the habit of entering a float in an annual Labor Day parade. The float usually parodied some recent movie or TV show, with an undisguised element of racial commentary, intended to show the community's unease on becoming integrated by other ethnic groups. Thus one year the men spoofed *The Dukes of Hazzard* with a "Gooks of Hazzard" theme, dressing up in Asian drag; another year they did *Jurassic Park* as "Hasidic Park" in Jewish costumes. In 1998 they went too far for Mayor Rudolph Giuliani, when they donned blackface and Afro wigs for a float called "Black to the Future," with props including the requisite Kentucky Fried Chicken and watermelons. For the pièce de résistance, one participant, who happened to be a New York City fireman, allowed himself to be dragged from the back of the float—a clear reference to the murder of James Byrd, a Black man in Texas, earlier that year. Local media had a field day with footage of the float, and the mayor insisted that the two firemen and one New York City police officer who participated be fired. The three men sued, claiming their First Amendment rights had been violated, and in 2003 a judge agreed.

In 1999, Missouri governor Mel Carnahan found himself in a public relations nightmare when evidence surfaced that as a young municipal judge in the mid-1960s he'd worn blackface in amateur minstrel shows. In 2004, a Louisiana judge was suspended for a year without pay for attending a Halloween party in blackface, wearing a prison outfit and handcuffs. He insisted that he'd not meant to insult or mock anyone. That same year, the president and the chairman of the board of trustees of the University of Central Florida appeared in public wearing large Afro wigs. They claimed they were doing so to honor one of the school's star basketball players, who happened to wear his hair that way. In 2005, a White high school teacher in Macon, Georgia, who apparently did not keep up with the news, was forced to resign after attending a school basketball game in blackface and an Afro wig.

Blackface is not unique to the United States—though practitioners in other cultures often seem genuinely clueless about its potential to provoke. In 1995, the Club Med in the Senegalese capital of Dakar hosted the Third African–African American Summit, attended by the Reverend Al Sharpton, U.S. commerce secretary Ron Brown and many other distinguished visitors. The resort's African managers, hoping to please their guests with a display of African-American culture, organized a show for them— a minstrel show, complete with blackfaced, white-gloved performers. The offended summit organizers threatened to sue.

At around the same time, Japanese girls who were ardent fans of hiphop began to braid their hair in cornrows and even darken their skin, through tanning salons or makeup, in emulation of Black American femininity. The term used is *ganguro*—literally, black face. Unsettling as the practice might be to Black Americans, these young women apparently mean no disrespect; in fact, their intentions are evidently the opposite of mockery. (This is not to say that there is no anti-Black attitude in Japan, as many Black Americans who've lived or visited there can attest.)

In Cape Town, South Africa, the local "Colored" (mixed-race) community has for more than a century celebrated New Year's Day with a parade derived directly from nineteenth-century minstrel shows. It's even called the Coon Carnival. Wearing minstrel-type outfits and blackface, people gambol in the streets to old-fashioned banjo tunes. They also claim that no disrespect to Blacks is intended; rather, they say they are celebrating their Black cultural roots.

SO WHAT IS BLACKFACE? WHERE DID IT COME FROM, AND when? What's its place in American popular culture?

Most of us would answer these questions quickly: Blackface is a form of racist caricature invented by White Americans in the minstrel-show days of the 1800s. It is a shameful reminder of White America's vicious hatred of Blacks. A part of America's past that is best forgotten in our more enlightened, polite era.

We might conjure a set handful of images: Al Jolson down on one knee, white-gloved hands outstretched, singing "My Mammy." A minstrel-show troupe in blackface and outlandish costumes, mugging ludicrously with banjos and tambourines. The self-mocking spectacle of a Black "coon show" performer like Bert Williams in the vaudeville years, or Mantan and Sleep 'n' Eat from Spike Lee's *Bamboozled*.

Blackface is most of those things, although it's incorrect that it first appeared in American minstrel shows, and I would argue that it's wrong to think that any history is best forgotten. But blackface is, or was, more than those things. However shameful we find it, blackface has played a large and integral role in the formation of American popular culture. It existed before the heyday of the minstrel show, and has persisted long after the minstrels faded away. Its influence or at least echoes can be seen in American music, theater, literature, film and TV, right through to today. Although it was certainly racist, it was sometimes something other than that, a reflection of the complex of neuroses and pathologies that mark relations between Whites and Blacks in America—a complicated web of love and hate, fear and guilt, attraction and repulsion, mockery and mimicry.

We know little of this today, because over the past half-century or so we've been busily forgetting it, erasing most of it from our history because it embarrasses and shames and enrages us. We've left ourselves only a handful of approved images to remember it all by—a set of stereotypes, if you will.

Blackface dancer doing "The Mammy," 1920s.

But the past does not cease to have an impact on us just because we choose to forget it. Historian W. T. Lhamon, Jr., who in recent years has done seminal work reconstructing the complex role of blackface in American culture, speaks of "lore cycles"—the funny way suppressed or apparently dead elements of folklore and popular culture pop back up years or even generations after they first appeared, often in new forms, wearing new disguises, behind new masks. There are no more minstrel shows, but many have argued that much about rock and hiphop smacks of minstrelsy. Jolson is long dead, but the Jolson impersonators continue to "black up." Joel Chandler Harris' Brer Rabbit is a largely forgotten bit of nineteenth-century Americana, but he lives on into the twenty-first century as Bugs Bunny. White Americans guiltily emptied their homes of racist memorabilia in the 1970s and 1980s—the mammy cookie jars, lawn jockeys and such—only to create a market for antique "Negrobilia," whose collectors today are mainly affluent Black Americans. And so on.

Lore recycles if it continues to serve some function in the culture. Blackface and other forms of ethnic humor persist because they continue to say something to us about relations among us below the polite surface of today's multicultural discourse.

In reconstructing blackface's role in American culture, it can be helpful to see how scholars thought about it in earlier times. In her landmark *American Humor* of 1931, Constance Rourke, a pioneer in what would later be called cultural studies, identified what she believed were three dominating figures of an "American type": the Yankee, the Frontiersman and the blackface Minstrel Man. They emerged at more or less the same time, in the 1820s and 1830s. This was a pivotal point in American history: the period when America began to move toward real democracy, the time when Americans became real Americans.

It was a classic generational turn-over. The Founding Fathers were landed gentry, and the nation they had created was run as an elite oligarchy. Things might have continued this way for a long time, had not the oligarchs so totally embarrassed themselves during the War of 1812. While James Madison and the Eastern policy wonks had abandoned Washington, leaving it to be sacked and burned, and the New England elite discussed secession and capitulation, it was the common American—untrained militiamen in Baltimore; a ragtag of Whites, Blacks, Creoles, mulattoes, even Indians, in New Orleans, under the command of frontiersman Andrew Jackson—who saved the young nation from reabsorption into the British empire. The common American did not forget or forgive, and it was the impetus for an entirely new and more democratic definition of the country. By the 1820s, the last of the Founding Fathers were passing away. Portentously, Thomas Jefferson and John Adams both died, and Stephen Foster was born, all on the fiftieth anniversary of the Declaration of Independence, July 4, 1826. What we might call second-generation Americans, the common man (and yes, it would be only the common man then), rose against the propertied elite. They demanded, for instance, the right to vote, which had previously been tied to land and wealth. And as soon as they got it, they started voting rough-hewn anti-elitists into office, like Jackson—Old Hick'ry—whom they elected president in 1828, and the frontiersman Davy Crockett, whom they sent to Congress.

There was radical upheaval in the cultural sphere as well. In theaters and music halls and on the printed page, the American rabble were starting to think and speak of themselves as a nation and a people, and first developing a recognizable American culture—a project that has turned out to be ongoing.

This is when Rourke's archetypes emerge. The Yankee was a New Englander, the clever, sharp-as-tacks traveling peddler, who camouflaged his intelligence behind a bland or taciturn exterior. A master horse-trader, he could sell ice to Eskimos, and never came out on the downside of a bargain. His humor was all the more wicked and cutting for being delivered in a clipped New England deadpan. Many attributes of the Yankee went into the image of Uncle Sam. The Frontiersman represented Americans' bottomless appetite for outrageous stories, tall tales and larger-than-life figures. He was Davy Crockett and Daniel Boone, John Henry and Paul Bunyan and Pecos Bill. He had the strength to lift mountains and bend rivers, and his sense of humor was as broad and wild as the continent. The blackfaced Minstrel Man, Rourke argued, brought the humor, songs and spirituality of the Southern Black into the mainstream of American culture.

These three figures dominated the emergent American culture of the 1820s and 1830s. They were everywhere—on the stages of "legitimate" theaters and in "low" farces, in numerous popular songs, in books and pamphlets and countless newspaper columns. Often they shared the stage or the page, in ways that they usually did not in life—one example of what I think is a common phenomenon in American history, that of popular culture's being out in front of social custom. As they did, their traits melded into a definable American "national character," as Rourke put it, one that was proudly claimed here and universally recognized, often with disdain, abroad. The American was brash, swaggering, bragging and brawling; a bold liar and teller of ridiculous tall tales, but also a nostalgic sentimentalist who could easily be reduced to tears by a sad song about his mother or his home; rough, untutored and rustic on the outside, disguising his canny and cunning wits; and always, everywhere, ready to scratch a fiddle, dance a jig or jump Jim Crow.

Many of Rourke's ideas have come to seem quaint and antique, and the flaws in her work have appeared with age. Certainly her list of archetypes needs to be expanded and updated, to include, for instance, the Outlaw/Gangster, the Preacher, the Celebrity. Rourke also had a tendency, common in her time, to overstate how much blackface minstrelsy was an accurate depiction of authentic Black life and culture.

But none of that is really what seems old-fashioned about Rourke's thesis today. It's her central belief in an "American type" and a "national character." That's a notion that today we are told to abhor as inherently racist, classist, sexist and various other *ist*s.

What happened was that between Rourke's time and ours, in the last quarter of the twentieth century, American culture came to a bedeviling hairpin turn on its road to becoming a truly "color-blind" democracy. It happened when the equal rights movements, which were all fundamentally based on traditional ideals of democracy and focused on the rights of individuals, mutated into multiculturalism, identity politics and diversity programs, which are collectivist and focused on the entitlements of tribal groups.

This is a profound ideological shift, from democracy to collectivism, from seeking to ensure that each individual American enjoys the full rights and benefits of citizenship, to vouchsafing that each identity group receives a share of benefits proportional to its demographic size relative to all other groups. Boston University anthropologist Peter Wood, the rare social studies scholar to take issue with the trend by the 2000s, gives a clear, cogent, contrarian description of its development in his book *Diversity: The Invention of a Concept.*

One impact of the multicultural/diversity movement was that Americans talked about race, ethnicity and so on more than ever before—and seemed more confused than ever about what these things meant. On the one hand, we were adjured, correctly, never to judge or treat one another on the basis of race, color, gender, religious affiliation, sexuality or other markers of "difference." At the same time, we were encouraged to explore, celebrate and even identify ourselves and everyone else by exactly these characteristics. We were told that the concept of race is a discarded scientific myth, that color is only skin-deep, that gender is an artificial social construct and sexuality is fluid and "performative." Then we were told that our race, our ethnicity, our gender and our sexual preferences define who we are. For two hundred years, we were told that the goal was to become full-fledged Americans, every citizen enjoying equal rights and equal opportunities along with every other citizen. We were now told that there can be no such thing as an "American," but instead only a balkanized patchwork of subgroups defined by race and color, ethnicity, sexuality, gender and a growing list of other characteristics.

Multiculturalism was founded on a postmodern, neo-Marxist interpretation of American history in which a dominant tribe—the White Heterosexual Northern European Christian Capitalist Male—had variously victimized a long list of "minority" tribes. In its original formation, there were only two basic minorities, Africans and Native Americans, but like Topsy in *Uncle Tom's Cabin,* the list "grow'd," until by the 1990s the system had developed into what has rightly been called a "victim culture." And "victimization," as cultural critic Shelby Steele notes, came to equal power. Rather than move society closer to the eradication of racist or sexist thinking, multiculturalism and the diversity movement made race, ethnicity and so on the focus of all attention. The irony was that extremist multiculturalism was racist to its core; no one believed more firmly or stridently than devout multicultists in distinct racial identities that distinguished one group of humans from all others. Even some of the movement's de facto spokespersons, like *Village Voice* writer Greg Tate, seemed to concede this point. "The prevalence of race as a concept—and its relationship to appearance, human status, and identity formation—is actually more significant today than it ever was," he wrote. "Our obsession with race is surpassed only by our seemingly polite and progressive neutrality regarding race."

And so theories like Rourke's fell out of favor. Which is all the more reason to dust them off and give them a read. When all the history you're taught comes from the same ideological bias, and opposing or contrary views are swept aside, you've entered the realm of Orwellian groupthink, and you owe it to yourself and your intellectual health to expand your reading list.

If you are able to. Another side effect of ideological groupthink is that history is not only rigidly interpreted, it is in fact rewritten or edited to fit the new paradigm. All sorts of historical and cultural materials have been, as the librarians say, "deaccessioned" over the last several decades, as Americans have become chronically embarrassed about their past. Any material from the historical record that is now determined to be "offensive" to any minority identity group is in danger of being censored, or disappeared altogether, made "unhistory." The best-known example is the protracted effort to have *The Adventures of Huckleberry Finn* removed from libraries and classrooms, or at the very least edited and censored, because some consider it racially insensitive. But whole segments of American popular culture from the past have been removed from general accessibility and general knowledge. Books, movies, television programs, songs, genres of plastic and graphic arts have been quietly hidden away. Sometimes the censoring is a voluntary act of goodwill, sometimes it's a response to pressure from an offended group. Always the result is that our general knowledge of American history, sketchy enough to begin with, is further diminished.

I'm not sure I'd argue that the disappearance of, say, lawn jockeys or *The Amos 'N' Andy Show* is a critical blow to American culture. Pop culture is ephemeral, and most of it is discarded and forgotten as soon as it's consumed anyway. I do think it's something else again to want to make *Huckleberry Finn* or *The Birth of a Nation* disappear because some people find either unsettling. But regardless of the perceived artistic value of the work under fire, I believe the impulse to censor cultural product that makes us uncomfortable is a fascist one that should always be resisted.

The people whom Wood in *Diversity* calls the diversiphiles, diversicrats and diversidacts did not achieve their dominance—or, to use a favorite buzzword, their hegemony—over American culture without opposition. In the so-called culture wars of the 1990s, the multicultists faced off against a new generation of old-fashioned, Eurocentric, anti-immigration nativists. This group was just as racist and divisive as the diversiphiles, and the two sides were fighting over a shared misconception of American culture. The nativists championed it as the American "core culture," the multiculturalists condemned it as the White Man's "monoculture," but they defined it the same way. The nativists argued that American culture was and always had been the culture the first Europeans had brought with them across the Atlantic—the Western European heritage of Protestantism, capitalism, representative government, the Great Books and the Great Works of Art all notoriously produced by Dead White Men. Traditionally, nativists have believed that this core culture, the very foundation of American Civilization, must be preserved at all costs against the erosions and mutations brought into America by later immigrants with their foreign ideas and customs.

Obviously, nativists and multiculturalists held precisely the same mistaken view of American culture. And both sides hated American culture. Nativists professed to love it, but their anti-immigrationist, Whites-only bigotry betrayed them. If they truly loved American culture, they would love it for what it is and has been from the start—an indigenous, internationalist mongrel, not a frontier outpost preserving the purity of Western European culture (which the Western Europeans have always done a fine job of preserving anyway, thank you very much). At least the multicultists never tried to disguise their hatred of American culture when they railed against the evil, imperialist, genocidal, sexist, racist, homophobic, exclusionist culture the Founding Fathers brought with them and transplanted here.

Maybe the Founding Fathers thought they were simply transplanting European culture here, but it hasn't worked out that way, and anyone who believes it has doesn't know much about American culture. American culture almost instantly started to mutate away from whatever models the Puritans and plantation owners brought over with them. It was inevitable. Nature and the landscape itself had a broadening, widening and democratizing effect from the very outset. Plus, there were already cultures here when the first Euros arrived, and those Euro settlers immediately started to be changed by their social, cultural and sexual intercourse with them. The Africans who were brought over as slaves had a most profound influence on the development of American culture. Successive waves of other immigrant-worker groups continued to add their own cultural influences—the Germans, Irish, Italians, Asians, Jews, Poles, Latin Americans, Caribbeans, Arabs and so on and so on. Even the so-called White culture was never so monolithic as both sides of the culture wars like to believe.

All those different cultural strains came together in America, influencing and altering one another, blending together to produce the unique, indigenous creature that is American culture. It is a mongrel, a mutt, a shaggy dog. It is, to give it a more scholarly term, syncretic. It outgrew the Dead White Men's silk britches a long time ago. American culture is a gumbo of African and Anglo-Saxon and Latino and Jewish and Celtic and Asian and Slavic and Islamic and French Creole and Pacific and many other flavors. It is neither a White monoculture, nor a multiculti patchwork quilt of separate and distinct subcultures. It is a blend, a mixing of many different cultural hues and fabrics to create an entirely new garment, in a color never before seen in the world. Not multicultural, but a mutt culture in which, Stanley Crouch observes, "no qualities of any sort that have to do with intelligence or will or spirit can be assumed on the basis of our favorite lines of demarcation. Color, sex, religion, class, and point of geographic origin are just more blanks that, even at close range, don't leave powder burns on the target board of Americana."

Imitation plays a large role in how American culture is formed. Black people who complain that Elvis or Eminem "stole" their music seem to be ignunt about how American popular culture is produced, disseminated, consumed and replicated. Why does Eminem sound Black? Why does Oprah wear her hair straight? Maybe they just *like* it. Americans are cultural magpies, and borrowing from one another is a big part of the creolizing that makes Americans and American culture unique.

Writing twenty years before the culture wars, Albert Murray described it this way: "Identity is best defined in terms of culture, and the culture of the nation over which the white Anglo-Saxon power elite exercises such exclusive political, economic, and social control [a control somewhat less omnipotent today than it was when Murray was writing] is not all-white by any measurement ever devised. *American culture, even in its most rigidly segregated precincts, is patently and irrevocably composite. It is, regardless of all the hysterical protestations of those who would have it otherwise, incontestably mulatto.* Indeed, for all their traditional antagonisms and obvious differences, the so-called black and so-called white people of the

United States resemble nobody else in the world so much as they resemble each other. And what is more, even their most extreme and
violent polarities represent nothing so much as the natural history
of pluralism in an open society" (emphasis in the original).

Elsewhere, Murray noted that "the United States is in actuality
not a nation of black people and white people. It is a nation of
multicolored people. There are white Americans so to speak and
black Americans. But any fool can see that the white people are not
really white, and that black people are not black. They are all inter-
related one way or another."

Murray coined a term for us all: Omni-Americans. Murray happens to be Black, and so wasn't naive enough to believe that race,
ethnicity, gender, class and other social markers were of no consequence to how Americans live or to their opportunities to partake in
the "American Dream." He was speaking of American culture: our
movies and music, the stories we tell and the language and slang we
use to tell them, the games we play, the ways we walk, dance, dress.
Our mutt culture, bless its shaggy, unruly heart. A culture in which
Whites, Blacks and all manner of Others have been influencing, imitating, insulting, irritating, mocking, mimicking and ripping one
another off from the very start.

Knowing our history, maybe we really shouldn't be so startled to
see White comedians in blackface and Black comedians in whiteface
in the twenty-first century. The problem, of course, is that so few of
us know our history. It begins well before the first blackface minstrel
ever appeared, with the first organized contacts between Europeans
and Africans.

2

QUEER PEOPLE OF THE WORLD
Africans on Display

A Crew of Pyrates are driven by a Storm they know not whither, at length a boy discovers Land from the Top-mast, they go on Shore to Rob and Plunder; they see an harmless People, are entertained with Kindness, they give the Country a new Name, they take formal Possession of it for their King, they set up a rotten Plank or a Stone for a Memorial, they murder two or three Dozen of the Natives, bring away a couple more by Force for a Sample, return Home, and get their Pardon. Here commences a new Dominion acquired with a Title by Divine Right. Ships are sent with the first Opportunity, the Natives driven out or destroyed, their Princes tortured to discover their Gold; a free Licence given to all Acts of Inhumanity and Lust, the Earth reeking with the Blood of its Inhabitants: And this execrable Crew of Butchers employed in so pious an Expedition, is a modern Colony sent to convert and civilize an idolatrous and barbarous People.

—JONATHAN SWIFT, *Gulliver's Travels*

In 1441, a Portuguese trading ship returned from probing the Guinea Coast of West Africa, bringing back ten Africans for Prince Henry the Navigator. They had not been captured for sale, historian James Pope-Hennessy notes, "but simply to be shown to Prince Henry in the same way that rare plants, exotic butterflies or tropical birds might have been shown." In 1444, another Portuguese ship returned with what Pope-Hennessy wryly calls "a bumper harvest of two hundred and thirty-five African men, women and children," who became property of the court.

So, within three years, the Portuguese inaugurated two long-lasting institutions with far-reaching impact: the Atlantic slave trade, and the practice of displaying Blackness for the enjoyment and edification of White viewers. The slave trade would operate for roughly four centuries. Displaying Blackness for White audiences, of course, continues to this day, and sets a context within which to view blackface.

It is a sad fact of human nature that when people of different cultures meet, they are usually less impressed by the qualities they share—sum it up as their common humanity—than they are fascinated and repulsed by what's different about them. From their first encounters, the West Africans and the Europeans who showed up on their coast impressed each other as exceedingly strange. Each side noted everything that was different about the other: the color of their skin and eyes, the texture of their hair, how they spoke and sang, how they smelled (a matter of particular revulsion on both sides), the food they ate, the tools they fashioned, the deities they worshipped.

One thing the two sides had in common was a misperception. The Western notion that Africans were "headhunters" and cannibals is well known, and remained in circulation at least through the Tarzan movies and cartoons of the 1930s. It's less well known that many Africans believed Europeans to be cannibals, too. They were convinced it was the reason the slavers were rounding up so many Africans and stuffing them into their sailing ships: They were taking them away to eat them. The Europeans' "red" faces, signaling their habit of feasting on bloody red meat, confirmed the belief. This terror of being eaten by the White cannibals instigated the famous rebellion aboard the *Amistad* in 1839.

The two sides had something else in common: They struck each other funny. We are all well schooled in the centuries-long tradition of Whites' laughing at Blacks, from early Sambo tales and cartoon caricatures through blackface minstrelsy up to the spate of Ebonics jokes and Shirley Q. Liquor's routines today. This is all commonly classified under the rubric of "racist humor."

There doesn't seem to be a similarly handy term for the jokes Africans made at the Europeans' expense. Evidently the winners write not only the history, but the jokes as well.

Africans made pitiless fun of their visitors, often to their faces. Following a long tradition of public satire, used as a way of both shaming bad behavior within the social group and taunting rival tribes, they made up songs and dances in which they parodied the way Whites looked, dressed and especially the way they moved. "Almost everything the white man did was funny to his African observers," historian William D. Piersen notes,

> as Captain Hugh Clapperton discovered while visiting the Yoruba in 1826 when a special series of plays was given in honor of his arrival. The third act featured a "white devil" which, Clapperton reports, "went through the motions of taking snuff, and rubbing its hands; when it walked, it was with the most awkward gait, treading as the most tender-footed white man would do in walking barefoot, for the first time over new frozen ground."

When the explorer René Caillie was among the Mandingo, the women "ridiculed my gestures and my words, and went about the village mimicking me and repeating what I had said." White travelers in Africa from Mungo Park to Richard Burton recorded the sarcastic hilarity their looks and behavior occasioned everywhere they went.

When they were brought to the Americas, Africans brought this tradition of mockery with them. In the John Canoe or Junkanoo festival that spread throughout the Caribbean and the South, and in the related Pinkster celebrations up North, slaves whitened their faces with flour, dressed in outrageous costumes and wigs that mimicked their masters' and mistresses' finest outfits, and marched around in open parody of Whites' stiffest, most formal behavior. Some clueless observers were amused and touched by what they took to be the Blacks' innocent imitations; others caught on that they were being mocked, and the festivities were gradually banned.

In Jamaica in the early 1800s, slaves at the docks in Port Royal greeted newly arrived British colonists—known as "buckra"—with a happy, smiling song of welcome:

New-come buckra,
He get sick,
He take fever,
He be die.

And in fact many buckra, unable to adapt to the Caribbean climate, promptly obliged.

Whitefaced Blacks have continued the mimicry and parody to this day, from Eddie Murphy and Chris Rock to Dave Chappelle and the Wayans brothers. Whiteface made it to the legitimate theater with the 1965 off-Broadway production of *Day of Absence,* by Black playwright Douglas Turner Ward. A one-act satire about a town of Southern Whites totally discomfited by the sudden disappearance of all the "Nigras" who did all the work, it was performed by an all-Black cast in whiteface.

By 1965, of course, a White cast in blackface satirizing Blacks would have been unthinkable. In 1981, even a very high-concept and well-intentioned use of blackface landed the experimental Wooster Group in trouble. *Route 1 & 9,* a multimedia deconstruction of Thornton Wilder's *Our Town* by Elizabeth LeCompte, involved White actors and actresses in blackface and references to Dewey "Pigmeat" Markham's vaudeville routines. The idea was to comment on Wilder's lily-white portrait of a "typical" American town, not to make fun of Black people, but some critics and audience members missed the point entirely. The New York State Council on the Arts cut the group's funding for 1982 almost in half, citing the "harsh and caricatured portrayals of a racial minority."

From the start, Africans and Europeans viewed each other not only with distaste and sarcasm, but with greed and envy as well. The Europeans were duly impressed with African kings' apparently boundless stores of ivory, minerals and gold, and set about scheming how to take it all from them. One imprudent king greeted them wearing a ceremonial outfit so heavy with gold he required several assistants to help him stand, and a few more to move his arms when he spoke.

For their part, the Africans were only too aware of the huge technological advantages the Europeans had over them. They saw the Whites' apparently magical (or demonic) sailing ships, their cannon and flintlocks, their compasses and writing tools, their calico and lace, and felt a mixture of awe, envy—and self-reproach. Why did the Whites have the knowledge of these things, and the Blacks not? A widespread lore developed in which the Africans blamed themselves. According to one common variant, in the beginning of the world God took the Black man and the White man to a clearing, where he showed them two items, a large box and a slip of paper, and told them to choose. The Black man went first and, thinking he was getting over on the White man, chose the box. In it he found some gold and some iron, but had no idea what to do with them. The White man read the slip of paper, which gave him the knowledge of many things. Thus Africans condemned themselves to a life of ignorance and toil, while the Europeans developed the arts, sciences and technology they used to conquer them and take their gold away.

This lore also survived in the Americas. As late as the 1920s and 1930s, the great folklorist Zora Neale Hurston heard Black Americans in the South telling versions of this tale, ending with the moral "So ever since then de nigger been out in de hot sun, usin' his tools, and de white man been sittin' up figgerin'. Ought's a ought, figger's a figger; all for de white man, none for de nigger." Today, we may still be hearing echoes of this sentiment in the accusations of Uncle Tomism and Eurocentrism leveled against Black Americans who succeed in business, science, politics or other manifestations of "the White man's knowledge."

The Europeans came away from their encounters with Africans harboring their own feelings of inadequacy, which have also survived into the present. To this day, Whites admire, envy and seek to emulate such supposed innate qualities of Blackness as inherent musicality, natural athleticism, the composure known as "cool" and superior sexual endowment.

THOSE FIRST AFRICANS KIDNAPPED TO PORTUGAL IN THE 1440s were not destined for slavery or the foul cruelties meted out to those who followed. They were either pampered as exotic pets, or received with a missionary zeal as ignorant heathens to be educated and saved. Some were taken into Portuguese homes and baptized; some went on to become priests and nuns. In what would be a familiar pattern, their "natural" musical abilities were recognized early, and many a Lisbon nobleman prided himself on providing African musicians as entertainment for his guests.

The Atlantic slave trade started in earnest fifty years later, when Columbus discovered the Americas, and the race for colonization was on. The colonies soon displayed a ravenous appetite for labor, which could not be satisfied even when Europe emptied itself of its dissidents, malcontents, visionaries, criminals, indigents, Irish and Scots. Besides, the bulk of the labor to be done was in hot, steamy Southern climes, to which cold-blooded European workers were ill suited. So the Europeans returned to hot, steamy West Africa, where an apparently infinite supply of cheap labor seemed ready for the taking.

The Portuguese would dominate the slave trade for two centuries, before yielding preeminence to the Dutch. It would be Dutch slavers who sold the first Africans to English colonists in North America in 1619. The French, the Spanish, the Germans—every Western European culture but the chronically disorganized Italians (with the exception of Genoese merchants)—would participate lustily. The British perfected what became known as the Triangular Trade, bringing goods from Europe (textiles, guns, brandy) to West Africa to trade for slaves, then carrying the slaves to the Americas (the infamous Middle Passage), and finally returning to Europe with the cotton, sugar, tobacco and rum they'd picked up in Brazil, Jamaica, the Carolinas. American slavers, especially from New England seaports, established their own version of the triangle. They sailed their "rum boats" to West Africa, where they traded the rum for slaves; they then carried the slaves to the Americas, usually to the West Indies, where they loaded up on molasses to bring to New England for the making of more rum. The slave ship that carries Kunta Kinte to America in *Roots* is one of these rum boats.

In four busy centuries, somewhere between 12 and 15 million Africans would be abducted to North America, South America and the Caribbean. Fewer than five percent were brought to North America; the vast majority went to Brazil, the Spanish empire and the West Indies.

The Europeans did not introduce slavery to Africa. Islam had been looting sub-Saharan Africa for slaves for some six centuries when the Portuguese arrived. The expansion of Islam was built on armies of Black as well as White slaves, the latter mostly from the Caucasus. Caucasian women were highly prized as concubines, the men as warriors, the fierce Mamelukes. In their heyday, Barbary pirates are said to have carried off as many as a million Europeans (and a few Americans) to be enslaved within the Islamic empire. While the West abolished slavery in the nineteenth century, it continued to be practiced legally in Arabic Islam until the 1960s.

Slavery had also been practiced within West Africa for centuries before the 1400s. A person, and his family, could be enslaved for unpaid debt, or for certain crimes like adultery or theft, or by being on the losing side of an intertribal war. The idea of buying and selling slaves like any other goods or chattel, however, seems to have been an alien one before the Arabs and Europeans arrived. It is said that slaves within Africa, if they were enslaved within their own tribe, were generally treated far less harshly than they could be in the Americas. They were valued for their labor, and as concubines both male and female; also, a king or queen gained prestige from maintaining a large, handsome retinue of slaves. Still, a great man's funeral was "a signal for wild and almost indiscriminate slaughter" of his slaves and wives; some number of his slaves' throats would be cut, his wives strangled to death, his loyal retainers walled up with him in his tomb. Slave children were used for ritual sacrifice on various occasions. Slaves acquired from other tribes through wars of conquest could expect to be treated much more harshly than slaves held within their own tribe. When slaver William Snelgrave visited with the warrior king of Dahomey in 1727, the king's first act was to show the Englishman some 1,800 recently captured prisoners of war, a large number of whom he then had slaughtered to impress the White foreigner with his fearsome power. Those survivors the king did not take for domestic slaves he sold to Snelgrave for a quantity of cowrie shells.

It has become politically correct for American schoolbooks and educational institutions, including the Smithsonian in Washington and the American Museum of Natural History in Manhattan, to contrast the kinder, gentler form of African slavery with the savage treatment of slaves in the Americas. No mention is made of wholesale slaughter of African slaves by African rulers. The message, which is sometimes just shy of explicitly stated, is: African slave-owners good, White slave-owners very, very bad. This is a bizarre lesson to be teaching our youth; isn't all slavery bad? It is at best disingenuous, at worst dishonest, and either way it says more about contemporary politics in this country than about African history. Commenting on this, Stanley Crouch has observed that "nothing inside the 'pure' African vision of life . . . would have ever led to the end of the slave trade, primarily because tribalism—which is the father of racism, by the way—was in full and bloody swing." Noting that American culture, for all its flaws, encompassed both slavery and the democratic ideals that abolished slavery, he adds that as for the African kings, "from beneath the tribal dress that identified these bigots . . . no inspiring pearls of social philosophy ascended. None. Absolutely."

While the idea of buying and selling slaves was new to Africans, many of them took to it with gusto. The early Portuguese expeditions had simply raided settlements along the coast for slaves, and it was bloody for both sides. They soon found African tribal leaders who were happy to round up members of other tribes for them. The aforementioned king of Dahomey used it as a pretext for his wars of expansion against his neighbors. When the Europeans abolished the slave trade, many a West African king complained bitterly that it was an act of hypocrisy and a personal affront after so many years of friendly and profitable relations.

The first Africans brought to English colonies in North America arrived in the small settlement of Jamestown in 1619. Eleven Africans were brought to New Amsterdam in 1626. Technically they were indentured servants, not slaves, and were manumitted (freed from their bondage) in 1644. But between the 1660s and 1700, slavery was legalized in the colonies. It concentrated in the South, where the agrarian economy needed large populations of laborers. In the North, where slaves were often domestic servants, they tended to be treated less harshly than on the plantations. Northern states gradually ended slavery between 1780 and 1830, making them havens for fugitives from the South. Although Congress forbade the importation of new slaves in 1807, the trade continued illegally for years.

IN PARALLEL WITH THIS INDUSTRY CREATED FOR PUTTING Africans to work grew the business of putting Africans on display. When those Portuguese first arrived off the Guinea Coast, the Europeans were just entering a prolonged epoch of exploration and expansion, during which they would exploit their technological advantages to extend their power and influence around the globe. But only a minority of Europeans actually ever saw the lands and peoples they were conquering; the vast majority of them, excepting sailors and those who shipped out or were packed off to the colonies, lived and died very close to the place where they were born.

So the explorers, sailors and adventurers brought the world to them. On the one hand, this took the form of a vast literature of travelogues, seafarers' journals, and treatises on botany, geography, biology and ethnology, at all levels of competence and credibility. These works stretch from Marco Polo's tales of the thirteenth century through the sea journals collected in Richard Hakluyt's *Voyages* of 1598 to James Cook's massive journals of his Pacific voyages in the 1770s and Mungo Park's African travels of the 1790s—followed by an absolute torrent of books by explorers and adventurers of the empire-mad 1800s, such as Richard Burton, Henry Stanley and David Livingstone.

These works in turn inspired many libraries' worth of fictional accounts of exotic lands and peoples. Much of it was hack work and "boys' adventure" tales, for which "deepest, darkest Africa" provided a virtually inexhaustible setting. The genre thrived through the novels of H. Rider Haggard (*King Solomon's Mines*) and Edgar Rice Burroughs (the Tarzan books) to survive into the middle of the twentieth century, when no boy's bookshelf was without a tome like Thomas A. Lahey's *King of the Pygmies* of 1944, in which the young hero, Joe Holland of Brooklyn, "makes the trip that most boys dream of: a trip through the African jungle." Along the way, a few fictional travelogues turned out to be great literature, like Defoe's *Robinson Crusoe*, published in 1719, and Swift's brilliant *Gulliver's Travels*, published in 1726. Swift was unique among all of this voluminous writing in using his exotic fictional lands and cultures to satirize his own people, and to offer some distinctly unfavorable commentary on the entire empire-building epoch. (As an Irishman, Swift knew a few things about the expansionist British.)

Along with their stories, explorers and travelers also hauled back actual specimens of exotic plants, animals and cultures by the trunk-, boat- and caravan-load. Much of this nimble-fingered acquisitiveness was in the service of genuine scientific discovery; but much was purely in aid of showbiz. Humans have an insatiable curiosity for the rare, the exotic, the freak and the new. The reality TV and Jerry Springers of the early twenty-first century can trace a direct lineage back through the freak shows and circuses of the early twentieth, to Barnum's American Museum in the nineteenth, to the seventeenth-century cabinet of curiosities—right back to those Africans brought to Lisbon to amuse and edify Prince Henry. In the era of global European expansionism, it mattered little to the audience if the rarity on display was a Saharan camel, a two-headed goat, a Hottentot or a Navajo. It was all curious and fascinating, sometimes frightening, sometimes sexy. Most important, it was *out of the ordinary*, appearing in places and at a time when the ordinary could be very ordinary indeed.

"One reads of live Eskimos being exhibited in Bristol as early as 1501," Africanologist Bernth Lindfors writes, "of Brazilian Indians building their own village in Rouen in the 1550s, of 'Virginians' canoeing on the Thames in 1603, and of numerous other native specimens from the New World, Africa, Asia, Australia, and the Pacific Islands being conveyed to European cities and towns as biological curiosities." In the 1850s, a pair of diminutive Bushmen entertained the patrons of an inn outside London, singing English songs and playing the piano. In the same decade, a troupe of Zulus performed in front of a painted "African" backdrop; they pretended to be unaware of the audience as they went about what was supposedly their daily routine. This conceit, that audience members were unobtrusive observers, like anthropologists in the field, would be continued in the "native village" displays that were de rigueur for every Victorian and Edwardian world's fair. Exotic performers regularly appeared on the bill at lecture halls and music halls, county fairs and amusement parks. They worked the vaudeville circuit throughout its span. Barnum's circuses and his American Museum were never without rare and strange human displays, from Chang and Eng to Madagascar albinos to Zip the pinhead.

Of all the "primitive" and "savage" humans who appeared in these settings, none provided such consistent fascination as Africans. They were Black, therefore the least White of all peoples on the earth. In the Great Chain of Being, with European Man at the apex, they occupied the lowest rung of humanity, closest to the beasts. When Darwin's theories of evolution were being debated from 1859 on, Africans—especially Pygmies, who had been captivating the imaginations of Europeans since the time of Homer and Herodotus—were widely seen as representing an early stage of evolutionary development, far from Civilized Man, much nearer to the primates they supposedly resembled. Thus Bronx Zoo director William Temple Hornaday had no misgivings about exhibiting the Pygmy Ota Benga in a cage next to that of an orangutan in 1906. Forty thousand people a day flocked to see the "wild man."

As the enduring interest in Pygmies indicates, most fascinating of all were Africans who combined their inherent exoticism with some aspect of freakishness. An "African hermaphrodite," born in Angola, was popularly exhibited in London and elsewhere in the 1740s. Ubangi women wearing their lip-stretching disks were never-fail attractions at world's fairs and expositions well into the twentieth century (and were caricatured in innumerable comics and animated cartoons).

The most famous example of this eroticized freakishness is Sarah

Baartman, who first appeared in London in 1810, billed as the "Hottentot Venus." "Hottentot" is an invented European name for a South African nomadic people who call themselves the Khoikhoi. They probably got the nickname, derived from Dutch dialect for "stutterer," because of their clicking language. The Khoikhoi had repeated and usually violent encounters with Europeans from as early as the 1480s, as the Cape of Good Hope became a busy midway stop for trade voyages to and from Portugal, Holland, England and the Orient. No less an adventurer than Vasco da Gama battled with the herdsmen, and was wounded by them. As the Dutch settled the Cape and spread outward, the Khoikhoi were pushed off their ancestral lands, with many murdered, and others taken as laborers or, like Baartman, as domestic servants.

Baartman caught the Europeans' attention because of her striking symptoms of steatopygia, an extreme enlargement of the buttocks. In European eyes this made her an anatomical oddity and yet "a most correct and perfect Specimen of [her] race," as she would be advertised. In other words, she wasn't a freak within her own people—they were all freaks. Baartman went to London voluntarily as a paid performer, but it's clear that she was never happy or comfortable being gawked at. Like Jayne Mansfield's huge hooters, her giant booty became the talismanic focus of much sleazy eroticism—early London audiences, who were mostly male, were even allowed to touch it. This ended after a legal challenge from an abolitionist group. Baartman moved to Paris in 1814, where her display was less sideshow, more serious ethnology, but it doesn't seem to have been much less degrading. By the time of her death in 1816 she had sunk into drug addiction and part-time prostitution.

As the final indignity, her body was carved up in autopsy, and her skeleton, brain and genitals were put on display at Paris' Musée de l'Homme—where they remained until 2002, when Thabo Mbeki's South African government finally persuaded the French to send her home. Speaking at her grave site, the characteristically outspoken

President Mbeki said, "It was not the lonely African woman in Europe, alienated from her identity and her motherland, who was the barbarian, but those who treated her with barbaric brutality."

"Authentic" Pygmy villages and troupes of actual Zulu warriors remained in such high demand into the first few decades of the twentieth century that showmen sometimes ran out of real Africans to exhibit. They turned to African-American ringers, some of whom made excellent livings impersonating their wild and savage cousins. One of the most successful impostors was Bata Kindai Amgoza ibn LoBagola, celebrated vaudeville performer, university lecturer, soldier of fortune, friend to the crowned heads of Europe, and author of the memoir *An African Savage's Own Story*, published by Knopf in 1929. LoBagola claimed to be a Black Jew from the "African Bush," but he was really from Baltimore, where he was born Joseph Howard Lee. Despite his impoverished start and lack of education, despite skeptics continually questioning his authenticity, despite a series of scandalous arrests and prison time related to homosexual activities, Lee/LoBagola maintained a long and colorful career as a faux African. His homosexuality, rather than his false identity, was his undoing; he spent his last thirteen years in Attica prison, convicted of sodomy, and died in 1947.

Often it wasn't just the faux-exotic performers but the impresarios presenting them who adopted invented personas. The Victorian showman Guillermo Antonio Farini, aka the Great Farini, began his career as a tightrope walker in the late 1850s, went on to found the famous trapeze artists the Flying Farinis (including the stupefyingly agile Mademoiselle Lulu, who was actually his adopted son in drag), and invented the human cannonball act. Starting in the 1870s, Farini presented widely celebrated African-themed variety show/freak show/circus extravaganzas featuring performers ranging from Zulu warriors to Pongo the gorilla. Farini's real name was William Leonard Hunt; he was born in Lockport, New York, and raised in Ontario. He later claimed that when he ran away to join the circus, he

Representing the Boer War at the St. Louis World's Fair, 1904.
(Courtesy Library of Congress)

changed his identity so as not to bring shame and embarrassment to his straitlaced family. But no doubt the nice sound of "the Flying Farinis," as opposed to, say, "the Highwire Hunts," had something to do with it as well.

The midways of turn-of-the-century world's fairs—like those of Chicago in 1893 (the Columbian Exposition), San Francisco in 1894, Buffalo in 1901, and St. Louis in 1904—were lined with ethnological displays of foreign and exotic cultures. The Chicago exposition's displays were organized in part by the anthropologist Franz Boas, mentor of Zora Neale Hurston. Strolling fairgoers could take in re-created Eskimo and Dahomeyan villages, "living exhibits of Turks and Arabs, a 'Singhalese Lady,' 'Javanese sweethearts,' Penobscot Indians and their dwellings, and various other 'tribes' of people including Germans and Irish." Note that exhibiting European "foreigners" side by side with more "exotic" peoples was quite common at the time. Their skins may have been lighter than most Africans', but the Irish, Scots, Germans, Poles, Jews, Italians et al. were not yet considered as White as the purest, Whitest of White folks, the Anglos. An evolutionary progress was implied by how the cultures were lined up along the midway, starting with the most "savage" of them, the Dahomeyans and Native Americans, and culminating with the Irish and Germans, who most closely resembled—without quite achieving—the glory of American civilization. In fact, before 1900 anthropologists rarely if ever used the word "cultures" in the plural; there was only Culture, which was more or less synonymous with Civilization, which of course was White. One of the goals of Victorian anthropology was to figure out how all those other cultures stacked up below the White folks.

Americans, at least those who wrote for the papers, got the message that the Africans were as far as humans could possibly be from White civilization. The *Buffalo Express* noted that the African villagers were "as black as the ace of spades, black as ebony, black as dulled tar, black as charcoal, black as cinders, black as crows, black as anything that will convey to the mind absolute undiluted sunless, moonless, starless blackness." A writer in *The New York Times* declared, "Nothing else I have seen conveys such an impression of wild savagery. . . . The Indians are conventional citizens beside them." Nonetheless, the writer went on, "they did not impress one as wicked or vicious *any more than an animal is wicked or vicious*" (my emphasis).

White Americans were amused to see how Black American fairgoers reacted to the Africans on display, and had much sport comparing their clothing and deportment with those of the "savages." The humor magazine *Puck* celebrated the Chicago exposition with a two-page cartoon by Frederick Burr Opper, "Darkies' Day at the Fair." It shows Africans and African-Americans parading together, eating watermelon together and so on, indistinguishable but for their clothes, with an accompanying poem made up of verses like:

> *But a Georgia coon, named Major Moon,*
> *Resolved to mar the day,*

"Darkies' Day at the Fair," from *Puck* magazine, 1893.
(Courtesy Library of Congress)

Because to lead the whole affair
He had not had his way.
Five hundred water-melons ripe,
(The Darky's theme and dream,)
He laid on ice so cool and nice
To aid him in his scheme.

As to how the savages felt about being gawked at, the women of the Dahomeyan exhibit in Chicago provide a humorous clue. Fairgoers who saw them joyfully singing and chanting assumed that they were expressing how delighted they were to be in America and how amazed they were by the technological wonders at the fair. In fact, when their songs were translated, they were more along the lines of, "We have come from a far country to a land where all men are White. If you will come to our country we will take pleasure in cutting your White throats."

Along with the savages and foreigners, the Columbian Exposition put another subset of humanity on display: women. In a nod to the suffrage movement, which was by then half a century old (and still a quarter-century away from achieving its goal), the Exposition featured a Women's Building. The activities there, organized by a board of respected society ladies, included the expected displays of "feminine" arts and crafts like embroidery and jewelry-making. But there was also a lecture hall for a series of addresses including "The Evolution of the Business Woman" and "The Progress of Society Dependent on the Emancipation of Woman." There was one titled "The Organized Efforts of Colored Women in the South to Improve Their Condition," and three accomplished Black women—Fannie Barrier Williams, Anna Julia Cooper and Frances Jackson Coppin—spoke on "The Intellectual Progress and Present Status of the Colored Women of the United States Since the Emancipation Proclamation."

Williams had studied at the New England Conservatory of Music and the School of Fine Arts in Washington, D.C., and was married to a prominent Black lawyer in Chicago. Cooper, who had been born a slave, was an Oberlin graduate and the principal of a Black high school in Washington. Coppin was also an Oberlin grad, and the principal of what would later be known as Cheyney University. After hearing their remarks, Frederick Douglass declared his joy at witnessing "refined, educated colored ladies addressing—and addressing successfully—one of the most intelligent white audiences" he'd ever seen. It gave him hope that one day "this great country of ours will be possessed by a composite nation of the grandest possible character, made up of all races, kindreds, tongues, and peoples."

These three speakers hardly fit the common stereotypes of Black Americans, as seen in the *Puck* cartoon—and were not presented as typical representatives of either their race or their gender. They were, rather, exemplars of the levels of civilization Blacks (and women) might achieve, given proper guidance and support. So the Exposition could truly claim to present the entire Darwinian ladder of civilization, from savages who were little more than animals to Irish and Germans and even Black women who seemed not so many rungs below Whites.

Another Black woman, Nancy Green, was appearing at the Exposition at the same time. Born a slave in 1834, she was performing as a real, live Aunt Jemima.

As soon as the Columbian Exposition ended, the Barnum & Bailey Circus hired a number of the exotic peoples who'd been on view there and put them on the road as the Great Ethnological Congress—continuing the genius for wedding science and showbiz that had marked Barnum's career (he'd died in 1891), and that took museum curators a century to understand and imitate.

AS THE TWENTIETH CENTURY PROGRESSED, MAINSTREAM anthropology gradually stepped away from the Victorian mania for classifying and ranking all human groups by the shaky concept of race. What developed was a relativist focus on cultures rather than races, with the understanding that ranking cultures on some arbitrary scale of civilization or placing value judgments on cultural differences must be resisted. This value-neutral approach was not universally followed. The Nazis took nineteenth-century racialist thinking to vicious extremes, as did racist and nativist Americans, while in their own way multiculturalists at the end of the century promoted racialist theories as heavily value-laden as anything the Victorians had obsessed over.

In encyclopedias and world books at least through the 1930s, you can see the well-intentioned authors struggling, with varying levels of success, to shed the worst excesses of Victorian cultural smugness while still pandering to readers' curiosity about exotic peoples. An eleven-volume encyclopedia for young readers called *Our Wonder World* was first published in 1914, and as late as the 1927 edition I'm looking at included a lengthy section of ethnology called "The Queer People of the World." A century later, such a title would probably signal a positivist argument for the universality of gayness, but this volume uses "queer" in the old sense of "odd" or "curious." The section subhead is unequivocal about which of the world's cultures may strike the young reader as queer: "The Black, Brown, Red, and Yellow Races and Their Ways." Interesting that a book published in the United States in the twentieth century presumed that all of its young readers would be White.

As repulsively racist as this all might sound today, the authors actually open the section with a brief session of diversity training that gently challenges the preconceptions that young readers might bring to it:

What makes a people queer? Perhaps the best answer is found in the story of the old Quaker who said to his wife one day, "Everybody in the world is queer but thee and me, and sometimes I think thou art a bit queer!" To be queer is to be different from what is ordinary and normal. Each one of us decides from his own experience and surroundings what is natural and reasonable. Then we feel that everybody who departs from these ways of ours is a bit queer.

So "queer peoples" are no more strange and odd to us than we are to them.

That was not a terrible idea to be placing in young White heads in the 1920s—even if what follows is a Great Ethnological Congress in print. "The true black people are the Negroes, whose home is in the middle part of Africa," the reader learned. "They are the people with the black skins, the woolly heads, the thick lips, the flat noses, and the beautiful white teeth."

This is a description of Blackness that could come straight out of any blackface minstrel show—and any kid reading this book in the 1910s or 1920s might well have made that connection. Many White Americans up to that time—and, it could be successfully argued, a good many of them up to this day—had very limited personal experience of Black Americans. What they knew of Blackness was what was displayed to them—on the midway, in ethnology texts and Tarzan books, in the stereotyped images of cartoons and comics and advertising panels, in the artificial Blackness of the minstrel stage, the coon show, vaudeville and Hollywood.

Although many Black Americans participated in creating this wealth of imagery, the control of the images of Blackness was almost always in the hands of Whites. Sometimes Whites displayed this imagery with the best of intentions. In the years building up to the Civil War, for instance, the antislavery abolitionist movement in the North used strategic displays of Blackness in its battle to win the hearts and minds of White Americans. No abolitionist rally was complete unless a runaway slave or two could be brought up on stage, sometimes to address the crowd, sometimes just to stand as mute and pitiful witness to the horrors of the plantation. If this was just another example of pandering to Whites' prurient fascination with Blackness, it was also a powerful tool for engaging their sympathies and galvanizing their political will to end slavery.

In the fine arts, a long list of American masters—including John Singleton Copley (1738–1815), Charles Zechel (dates unknown), William Sidney Mount (1807–1868), Nathaniel Jocelyn (1796–1881), Theodor Kaufmann (1814–1896), Winslow Homer (1836–1910) and Thomas Eakins (1844–1916)—presented serious portraits of Black Americans that, given the era and context of their creation, are marvels of realism, sensitivity and psychological insight.

Still, it cannot be doubted that the images of Blackness that were most familiar to many White Americans into the twentieth century were not Blackness at all, but some version of blackface. Blackness as interpreted and re-created by White people, often in mockery, but sometimes in genuine and sincere imitation. Blackface is best known from the minstrel stage, yet it can be seen as a recurring meme in many genres of American popular culture: in literature and film, in advertising and fashion, in rock and hiphop. In its various manifestations, it has been integral to American popular culture for a very long time.

3

BLACK LIKE YOU

Blackface Minstrelsy, the Rock & Roll Years

When American life is most American it is apt to be most theatrical.... We wear the mask for purposes of aggression as well as for defense; when we are projecting the future and preserving the past. In short, the motives hidden behind the mask are as numerous as the ambiguities the mask conceals. —RALPH ELLISON

Unfurl a white man in blackface if you want to see some bloodshed and tears. —GREG TATE

In 1832, a young man named Thomas Dartmouth Rice shuffles across the stage of the Bowery Theatre, a rather low-class establishment that caters to the young rowdies from the surrounding slums and tenements of lower Manhattan. At his appearance, the crowd of boys and young men (the only females in the house are some whores trolling the balcony) bursts into thunderous applause, shouts, laughter and foot-stomping. T. D. Rice is a local lad, born and raised among them, who escaped the slum to seek fame and fortune in showbiz. While touring "out West" in places like Cincinnati and Louisville—frontier towns in those days—he has developed a new act. For the last several months he's been touring it to great acclaim back from the frontier and up the East Coast. Tonight is his triumphal homecoming, debuting this routine for his homeboys.

Rice claims to have been inspired by watching an old Black slave mucking out some stables in Louisville. Though his back was bent and he was lame, this old man, as every good old darky was expected to, went about his sweeping and hay-raking with a light heart, singing an oddly catchy little ditty and dancing an eccentric little dance. Rice says he so enjoyed the old man's unself-conscious song-and-dance routine that he just had to adapt it for the stage. The old man's name, he says, was Jim Crow.

So now here's T. D. Rice, a ghetto White boy from New York, shuffling across the Bowery stage in the character of a Southern Negro. His costume is threadbare, like a slave's humble rags. His face is grotesquely shiny with a tar-black makeup that's a paste of burnt-cork ashes mixed with a little water. Contrasting red lips are painted clownishly wide. There's nothing remotely "Negroid" about this "Negro" masquerade—Rice's features and his mussed-up hair are distinctly Caucasian—but that's part of the joke, the wink to his delighted audience. He's hardly the first performer they've seen in blackface. In fact, many of them have worn an amateur version of it themselves. They're all in on the joke.

His back crooked, his knees comically splayed, one hand on hip, the other saluting the roaring crowd, Rice goes into his song. It's an utterly simple little ditty, like something a country fiddler might idly scratch out. In fact, it's almost idiotic in its simplicity; yet, as with any good pop tune, there's a quirkiness to the melody, a curious lurch in the rhythm, that makes it stick in your mind, whether you want it there or not. And there's something about the rustic lack of ornament or pretension that appeals directly to the rough street gangs in the audience. At a time when popular songs are mostly treacly sentimental ballads or fussily ornate imitations of highbrow concert music, this artless, silly song is like a blast of fresh air in a stuffy parlor. It's got a pulse and a sense of humor. It's new and exciting.

By way of structure it's just an endless repetition of two-line verses and a two-line chorus, verse-chorus-verse, over and over. Rice sings it in a broad, theatrical "Negro" drawl:

Come, listen, all you gals and boys, I'm just from Tuckyhoe;
I'm gwine to sing a little song, my name's Jim Crow.

CHORUS
Wheel about, an' turn about, an' do jis so;
Eb'ry time I wheel about, I jump Jim Crow.

Jim Crow.
(Courtesy Library of Congress)

I went down to de river, I didn't mean to stay,
But there I see so many gals, I couldn't get away.

CHORUS

I'm for union to a gal, an' dis a stubborn fact,
But if I marry an' don't like it, I'll nullify de act.

CHORUS

I'm a rorer on de fiddle, an' down in ole Virginny,
Dey say I play de skientific, like massa Pagganninny.

CHORUS

I cut so many munky shines, I dance de galloppade;
An' w'en I done, I res' my head, on shubble, hoe or spade.

CHORUS

I met Miss Dina Scrub one day, I gib her sich a buss;
An' den she turn an' slap my face, an' make a mighty fuss.

CHORUS

De udder gals dey 'gin to fight, I tel'd dem wait a bit;
I'd hab dem all, jis one by one, as I tourt fit.

CHORUS

I wip de lion ob de west, I eat de alligator;
I put more water in my mouf, den boil ten load ob 'tator.

Wheel about, an' turn about, an' do jis so;
Eb'ry time I wheel about, I jump Jim Crow.

As he sings, Rice does his dance. An old man's shuffle for the verses, something like what would later be called the soft-shoe; then, illustrating each chorus, he does a slow heel-and-toe spin, a kind of voguing with one hand on bent hip and the other in the air. Finally, at the words "jump Jim Crow," he winds up with a little crow-like hop.

It ain't grand ballet, but the boys in the crowd eat it up. As Rice does his last little hop, bringing the song to an end, they explode in clapping, stomping, whistling. Rice bows and bows, grinning and grinning, his teeth flashing inside those red lips. A shower of pennies rains on the stage—the ultimate sign of approval from this crowd. Clapping and stomping in unison now until it feels like they could shake the building down, they demand an encore. And Rice, grinning, grinning, obliges.

Come, listen, all you gals and boys, I'm just from Tuckyhoe;
I'm gwine to sing a little song, my name's Jim Crow.

Wheel about, an' turn about, an' do jis so;
Eb'ry time I wheel about, I jump Jim Crow. . . .

A star is born. A new figure, Jim Crow, is launched into American popular mythology. His song, "Jump Jim Crow," rockets to the top of the pops throughout the English-speaking world. It is soon heard everywhere, as maddeningly ubiquitous as a Muzak Beatles tune. Shopgirls hum it in Boston; slaves sing it in fields of Virginia tobacco; noblemen on their country estates in England set their scullery maids into fits of giggles imitating the funny little shuffle and hop. According to one account, the U.S. ambassador to Ecuador, on arriving in the Mexican city of Mérida, is greeted by a brass band playing the song, who think it's our national anthem. One traveler claims to hear Hindu street performers singing it in Delhi.

Thomas Dartmouth Rice was not the first blackface minstrel, and he was very far from the last. But he was the genre's first international superstar—its Elvis, if you will. And "Jump Jim Crow," as long as we're stretching a metaphor, was its "Hound Dog."

For the next half-century, blackface minstrelsy would be the dominant form of popular music in America. The huge minstrel-show spectacles that roamed throughout cities, towns and provinces after the Civil War were the first truly American form of mass entertainment. Charles Dickens was a fan, as were Mark Twain and Abe Lincoln. Minstrel music was played and enjoyed by both Whites and Blacks. It was also despised by both Whites and Blacks. It was enormous in England, where it remained popular long after it petered out in the States.

What was it about blackface minstrelsy that made it so extraordinarily popular? Where did the minstrel man come from? In what kind of social context did he thrive? What did he mean?

CENTURIES BEFORE THE FIRST AMERICAN MINSTREL PUT on "the burnt-cork mask," blackface was a familiar theatrical device in Europe. The most famous blackface performance in the legitimate theater is Shakespeare's *Othello,* first produced in 1604 and almost always with a White actor in blackface in the title role until nearly the end of the twentieth century. Verdi's operatic version will no doubt continue to be sung by blackfaced Whites until opera develops enough strong Black tenors to take over the role. As theater historian Robert Hornback explains, Shakespeare did not invent theatrical blackface, but was consciously using a convention with a very long tradition and some very specific implications for his audience. From the folk rituals of pagan Europe through medieval religious pageants to the theater of Shakespeare's day, a black face and black skin were used to denote both evil and folly. The symbolism was basic: white/light/day equaled good, black/dark/night equaled evil. Europeans simply carried the symbolism over to "light" and "dark" skin. A blackened, sooty or begrimed face was the sign of the scapegoat in pagan rituals. From the early Middle Ages, blackface, black masks, black gloves and leggings, frizzy-haired wigs and other devices made up the costumes of Satan, his fallen angels and the souls of the damned. Dark skin was also associated with the biblical "mark of Cain" (an association of which American minstrel men were well aware). Feast of Fools festivities were often led by black-faced or black-masked figures, the Lords of Misrule. The evil trickster Harlequin was routinely played in a black mask in the sixteenth and seventeenth centuries. The morris dance in rural England was led by a black-masked fool, known variously as King Coffee, Old Sooty-Face or Dirty Bet. As late as 2005, every winter in the fishing village of Padstow, in Cornwall, England, townsfolk were still blackening their faces and parading through the streets in festivities clearly descended from the Feast of Fools. Unfortunately, they called the event "Darkie Day"—leading to charges of racism and attempts to outlaw the centuries-old practice.

The blackfaced Moor is a figure found in dozens of London plays from at least twenty years before *Othello* and for decades afterward. In court masques and other costume affairs of the period, blacking up as Moors was quite popular; the queen consort Anne and a dozen of her ladies-in-waiting blackened their faces and arms, and apparently wore frizzy-haired wigs, at a masque the year after *Othello* premiered, causing one noble gentleman in attendance to shudder and remark, "You cannot imagine a more ugly Sight."

So in his character of Othello, Shakespeare was both drawing on a rich tradition of symbols and allegory, and toying with his audience's expectations that a blackface figure would represent evil (which he assigns to the real villain of the play, the White Iago), as well as folly and ritual scapegoating (both of which Othello plays to the hilt).

The English colonists brought all those blackface traditions with them to America. Blackface characters were appearing on the stages of America's earliest legitimate theaters well before the first blackface minstrel strutted his stuff. Historian Dale Cockrell offers the astounding estimate that between 1751 and the appearance of the first full-fledged minstrel-show troupes in 1843, around 20,000 blackface performances were given in American theaters. Topping his list is *Othello* itself, first performed in America in 1751 and by far the most popular "blackface" play in early America. Why? Cockrell believes that it played directly to one of the greatest fears of the White elite who founded the nation: race-mixing, which the Founding Fathers and city fathers were convinced would dilute the American stock. John Quincy Adams read *Othello* as a morality tale about the dangers of miscegenation, and saw in Desdemona's destruction a lesson to be learned by all White women who might be tempted to mate with Black men.

Other early plays featuring blackface characters, some imported from England and some written in America, include Isaac Bickerstaffe's *The Padlock* (first performed in America in 1769), *The Irishman in London* (1793) and Frederick Reynolds' *Laugh When You Can* (1799). Quite often the performer in the blackface role would be called upon at some point in the action to sing a "Negro" song. As titles like "Negro Philosophy," "The Desponding Negro" and "The Negro's Humanity" suggest, these would generally portray "the black man sympathetically as either a tragic or pitiful figure." Negroes were almost invariably servants in these plays—often wise servants, following a tradition that stretches at least from Molière to Hattie McDaniel. In the romantic comedy *Laugh When You Can*, Sambo is a freed slave who's clearly smarter and more moral than his upper-class twit of a master. When Cubba, the Black female servant in *The Irishman*, becomes the object of a White man's affections, she tells him, "Me love a you dearly—but me no want you love me—dat be very wrong—your face white, me poor negro. . . ." Adams doubtlessly approved.

In the indigenous American theater of the 1830s, blackface figures shared the stage with rough-hewn frontiersman types (*The Kentuckian*, 1833) and sharp-witted Yankees (*The Yankee Pedlar*, 1834), forming Constance Rourke's triumvirate of archetypes. The meeting of these types was usually played for comic frisson. In *The Kentuckian*, when the young rustic Jedediah meets Bill the Black slave, he ogles and earns a humorous upbraiding:

JEDEDIAH. Are you a nigger? I never seen a real one, but I guess you be. Ar'nt ye—you?

BILL. Who's you call nigger?

JEDEDIAH. Well, I only ask'd you. Why he's mad as a hen a'ready. Did your mother have any more on you?

BILL. Dere child, you better keep quiet, and mind what you say to me, you little bushwacker; if you am saucy I'll spile your profile, you mind dat now. . . . You only just trying to breed a scab on your nose, you up country looking ball face.

Meanwhile, the appearance of actual Black actors on an American stage was exceedingly rare. The most famous was Ira Aldridge, born in New York City in 1807, who began his professional career playing Romeo at the African Grove, the country's only Black theater, in lower Manhattan. William Alexander Brown, a free Black from the West Indies, opened the Grove in 1821. It hosted operas, plays, comic farces and musical variety shows, all performed by Blacks. Because it catered to mixed Black and White audiences, Brown's theater was mercilessly hounded by New York's disapproving city fathers on the one side, and subjected to hooliganism from gangs of Bowery boys on the other. It's not clear whether the boys objected to it because it was Black-run, or because it was a highfalutin theater like the nearby Park, which they also attacked. Probably both. At any rate, it was forced to close after a brief and troubled existence. Aldridge fled this hostile environment for England in 1824 and remained overseas; he died in Poland in 1867. He became a renowned Shakespearean actor; in addition to being one of the few Blacks to play Othello before the twentieth century, he did Hamlet, Richard III, Macbeth, Lear, Shylock—all in whiteface. He also took up formerly blackface comic roles.

But in England, too, Aldridge's blackness made him an exotic target; one British comedian, Charles Matthews, developed a blackface sketch in which he pretended to be Aldridge playing Hamlet at the

African Grove when he suddenly loses control and bursts into the minstrel song "Opossum Up a Gum Tree," then spouts lines like, "To be or not to be, dat is him question, whether him nobler in de mind to suffer . . ." Remarkably, Aldridge would later incorporate the song into his own one-man variety show—which can be seen as either a tragic capitulation to the racism of his surroundings or a canny way of turning the tables on his tormentor, mocking the man who mocked him.

There's something else we should know about early American theater. Beyond the small circles of educated elite audiences who patronized such palaces of thespian artistry as Manhattan's Park Theatre, most Americans, then as now, did not have very high-flown tastes. Like today's Broadway audiences, they wanted to be entertained, not edified. Constance Rourke writes hilariously of the touring theater troupes who ventured, brandy flasks tight in hand, out of the Eastern cities into the hinterlands and boondocks, crossing the Alleghenies, sailing down the Ohio, bringing theater to the buckskinned yahoos in every small town, Indian-fighting fort and stranded little frontier settlement along the way. These folks had simple tastes. In drama, they liked real blood-and-thunder melodrama, tales of brigands and villains and distressed damsels, bursting with high romance, stage-pistol shots and swordplay. An actor playing the villain had to take care not to be too convincing as he threatened the damsel, lest the menfolk in the audience rush to her defense and give him a good thrashing. In Shakespeare, they preferred the ones with the best special effects: the ghost in *Hamlet,* the witches in *Macbeth* and of course the blackfaced *Othello.* And all Americans, back East as well as in the boondocks, loved comedies—very broad comedy, farces, burlesques. A lot of early American theater entailed poking fun and parody: parodies of Shakespeare's plays and popular operas; lampoons and satires of famous singers, dancers, actors, lecturers, political figures; and plenty of insulting jokes lobbed at whole groups of people—Yankees, Negroes, females, the Irish, the Jews, the wealthy.

BLACKFACE FOLK RITUALS ALSO CROSSED THE ATLANTIC with the settlers. When young men went wilding, which they did a lot, it could involve all sorts of outlandish costumes, disguises, cross-dressing and "ethnic drag." Some festivities were seasonal, like the pre-Lenten Carnival, which spread throughout the Americas. The most famous is Mardi Gras in New Orleans, which included Whites in blackface and Blacks in whiteface. Mumming plays, which went door-to-door demanding food and drink, survive today as Philadelphia's Mummers Parade, which allowed blackface among its outrageous costumes into the 1960s. Around New Year's, mobs of young men would roam the streets in "callithumpian" bands, making a horrendous din banging on pots and pans and blatting horns. Their faces were often blackened with soot, and their costumes could be anything from women's clothing to their own clothes worn inside out.

Mobs of disguised young males took to the streets at nonseasonal times to express social or political discontent. The "Indians" of the Boston Tea Party are only the most famous instance. In the practice of "charivari," they'd descend in the middle of the night on the house of someone in the community whom they accused of some transgression—adultery, philandering, wife-beating, or in Cajun country, when an older man married a much younger bride. Their raucous behavior was intended to shame the person in front of neighbors. Charivari could often boil over into mob violence. Tarring and feathering, making someone "ride the rail" (to be run out of town straddling a rail or pole), the lynch mob and even the costumed vigilantism of the Ku Klux Klan can all be seen as extreme versions of charivari. Even stranger are the race riots that periodically broke out in the tenements and slums of lower Manhattan, when mobs of poor and discontent White youths ran wild in the streets. Their faces often blackened, they not only ransacked establishments symbolic of upper-class Whites, like the Park Theatre, but also targeted the homes, businesses and persons of their Black neighbors, producing the bizarre image of blackface-on-Black violence. Some members of T. D. Rice's audience at the Bowery in 1832 had undoubtedly blackened their own faces and participated in this kind of street violence.

There was a third and very important source for minstrelsy: the circus. While not the lavish affairs we think of today, some early, rougher form of traveling circus was popular in America from Revolutionary times—George Washington was a fan. Blackface clowns performed in them from at least the 1810s and maybe before; they were a staple by the 1820s. The wide red or white mouth painted on by modern clowns is a remnant of the blackface mask. Many of the first stars of the minstrel stage apparently toured as or with blackface circus clowns in their early years, doing brief song-and-dance routines between the other acts. In many respects minstrelsy was born when these performers moved their acts from the tent to the stage of American variety theaters.

Certainly there was a strong element of clowning in minstrelsy. The blackface mask was a clown's disguise, exaggerating the facial features into a cartoon, a caricature. The blackface clown may be the precursor of today's anodyne circus clown, but otherwise the two are as opposite as blackface and whiteface. The blackface clown is more in line with older traditions, from Native American to African to medieval European to ancient Egyptian—the social function of the clown as an Outsider, an Other, a creature of difference. Who in nineteenth-century America was more of an Other than the Negro? What better mask than blackface? In many traditions the clown would show some physical deformity, like a hunchback, dwarfism—or like Jim Crow, lameness. And because he was different, an Other, the clown was allowed to say and do things no one else could. As the court jester, he could satirize and make political comments, telling the king rude truths no one else dared utter. Satire and parody were central to minstrelsy. It's interesting that in the West African cultures from which most slaves came, the poet-singer griot served the same satirical jester function when the occasion arose. That may have something to do with the curious (to us, looking back) case with which Southern Blacks accepted not just the music but even the demeaning humor of minstrelsy.

But none of this—blackface in theaters, blackface on the streets, blackface clowning—would have come together as minstrelsy without the crucial elements of music and dance. The origins of minstrel music have been the source of debate and argument since, well, the origins of minstrelsy. The minstrels themselves are of no help, and often history has simply shrugged and backed the guy who boasted loudest. In an era before media could pry so intently into celebrities' business (not to say that they lacked the will), minstrels, being showbiz types, tended to tell whatever story they thought would sound best. Sometimes they'd claim to have learned a song or dance firsthand from an authentic Black slave of their personal acquaintance. Then again, sometimes they'd spin the PR in the other direction, and claim sole authorship of a song. Either way, they were often . . . exaggerating. Show business was a rough-and-tumble game. Borrowing or outright theft of another performer's work was considered fair, as long as you got away with it. You might see an act you liked in Buffalo, and next week copy it in Philadelphia—adding, of course, that your version was "the original." In the post–Civil War years, there were dozens of traveling minstrel shows whose names began with the words "The Original." Or, in that era before copyright protection, you might hear a song you liked in Ohio, write it down, bring it to New York and sell it to a publisher, pocketing the dough as sole author and composer. A "hit" might be performed by numerous minstrels, and songsheets of different versions were issued by multiple publishers, sometimes with completely different melodies and lyrics—making life tough on future musicologists.

Well into the twentieth century, scholars naively took the minstrels' word for it that they were faithfully re-creating the authentic songs and dances, even the lives and very characters, of plantation Negroes, which they had researched on their travels in the South. Then, beginning in the civil rights era, historians abruptly turned about-face and condemned all blackface performance as vile racist mockery, created out of whole cloth by the overheated imaginations of Northern Whites who'd never been anywhere near a plantation, or met a Southern Black.

Very recently, a third wave of scholars has gone back to the origins of blackface minstrelsy and turned up a lot of very compelling evidence that things were not, let's say, so black-and-white. Eileen Southern tells us in *The Music of Black Americans* that Blacks and Whites admired and picked up each other's music and dances from the earliest colonial days. Though they'd come from numerous lands—they were Wolof, Yoruban, Igbo, Ashanti, Ewe, Fons—the West Africans brought to America a shared culture suffused with music and dance as ritual, celebration and recreation. In the colonial British settlers, and in the Irish and Scots workers, they met people for whom music and dance were equally important—both the sacred songs and hymns they sang in church, and the secular playing and dancing that was their chief form of entertainment for decades. No tavern was complete without music, sometimes a bit bawdy by the day's standards, and dances were frequently organized in any hall or barn large enough to hold them. Christmas, New Year's and Easter were celebrated with days of music and dance. Music was important in colonial homes as well; someone in every family could play the violin/fiddle, the flute or fife, maybe the harpsichord or piano. The favorite old ballads colonists brought over with them—"Lord Randall," "Barbara Allen"—were joined by new, indigenous hits, "Yankee Doodle" among the earliest.

The Africans instantly proved themselves willing and adept students of the Europeans' music and instruments. There are innumerable records from the early 1700s onward of slaves who were accomplished not just in singing, drumming and playing the violin/ fiddle, as we might expect, but also on the French horn, the trumpet, the flute and other, more arcane instruments. Black fiddlers were soon ubiquitous, and their playing highly praised. American troops in the Revolutionary War often marched to the music of black fifers, drummers and trumpeters. The brass bands at the head of parades and in park bandshells throughout the 1800s frequently included Black musicians, and some of the very finest were all-Black.

In New England, slaves went to church with the Whites and sang—from their segregated pews—their choral hymns with them. When they began to form their own Black churches in the late 1700s, they blended the White church music with their own African-rooted vocal styles and traditions. Blacks also had an obvious impact on the shout-out, spontaneous call-and-response singing that characterized the large camp meetings of the Second Great Awakening, the grassroots revivalist movement that swept up both White and Black Protestants in the early 1800s. These "spirituals" were incorporated into Black church music, and gospel music was the result.

The exchange went both ways. Whites loved learning the banjo, which the Blacks had brought with them from Africa. Blacks loved the piano, and learned to play it with Promethean genius. When, after the Civil War, mass-produced guitars could be bought cheaply from any Sears catalogue, everybody learned to play them. Blacks loved to dance to Celtic jigs and reels, Whites learned to imitate Black field hollers, and both sides shared a love for plaintive airs and ballads. There was affinity between the sung poetics of the Gaelic bard and those of the African griot. Other influences accompanied other waves of immigrants—German polka rhythms, Latin rhythms, soulful rabbinical voices—or were simply enjoyed and appropriated, like the Viennese waltz and the Italian aria.

And on and on. T. D. Rice's story of having learned his routine from an actual Jim Crow strikes one as just too pat to be entirely true. But it is quite possible that he heard slaves' music and observed their dancing while "out West." Although most minstrels, like Rice, were Northerners, it seems that many of them did travel west and south with circuses and theater troupes, and based at least some of their songs and routines on their observations. Still, it was very rare for them to have had any long or intimate association with the "plantation life" they claimed to be representing; some of the most popular writers of "plantation" songs, including Stephen Foster, never set foot near one. As a general rule, it seems that minstrels' presentations were one part "authentic" to three parts comic caricature and sentimental fantasy.

But even that makes it sound less muddled than it really was. Some minstrel songs started as Negro folk songs, were adapted by White minstrels, became widely popular, and were readopted by Blacks. Others, like Stephen Foster's, were the work of White composers trying to evoke a plantation life with which they were wholly unfamiliar, but nevertheless became as popular in the slave shacks of Southern Blacks as they did in the parlors of Northern Whites. There were also Black performers and composers involved in minstrelsy from early on, and after the Civil War, Black minstrel troupes eventually came to dominate the form. While they conformed to what had become the minstrel show's set conventions by then, they were also intent on making the images and music more authentic to Southern Black culture. Certainly by that point the question of whether minstrelsy was White or Black music was moot. It was a mix, a mutt—that is, it was *American* music.

IN MINSTRELSY'S EARLY, BREAKOUT YEARS, FROM THE LATE 1820s into the early 1840s, its very Americanness was a big part of its appeal. In his remarkable book *Raising Cain,* historian W. T. Lhamon, Jr., has proposed that one useful way to think of early minstrelsy is as an outbreak of rebellious youth culture, not unlike the early years of rock & roll or rap in the next century. In the 1820s, there wasn't a lot of music in America that a hot-blooded youth could embrace as his own. A lot of it was awfully stodgy. The music approved by the middle and upper classes came in three basic, equally stuffy forms: church music; classical or pseudoclassical music imported from Europe; and wan, sickly-sweet parlor-room ballads. (Think of Foster's "(I Dream of) Jeanie with the Light Brown Hair," though he didn't actually publish it until 1854.) About the only fun stuff around—and the only really American music—was dance music, the rustic, up-tempo jigs and reels being sawed out by (often Negro) fiddlers everywhere from New Orleans ballrooms to Manhattan dance halls. It's no coincidence that the music for many early minstrel songs came straight from these jigs and reels. For instance, "Ole Zip Coon," a song that rivaled "Jump Jim Crow" for popularity in the mid-1830s, was sung to a fiddle dance tune that every American knows to this day—"Turkey in the Straw." The very instruments on which the music was played—the fiddle, the banjo, the jangling tambourine, the bone castanets and the downright spooky jawbone (the dried jawbone of an ass or horse, the loose teeth of which rattled when it was enthusiastically shaken)—were considered rude, "callithumpian" noisemakers highly offensive to the refined ear. That all these instruments were originated by or associated with Southern Blacks lent them immense cool with the Northern White boys who learned to play them, and scandalized the White mainstream. Think the teenage Rolling Stones learning to play the blues, or White rappers.

With that context in mind, let's go back to the Bowery Theatre, but let's make it 1828, four years before T. D. Rice introduced Jim Crow there. Rice is probably in the house. He was born and grew up a few blocks away, in the notorious Five Points slum later made famous by Herbert Asbury's *The Gangs of New York*. As a lad, like most of his peers, he was apprenticed to learn a trade, carpentry. But he abandoned working with his hands and decided to make a run at showbiz. In 1828 he's working in the theaters of the neighborhood, doing mostly stagehand jobs, but also getting his first small acting parts—no doubt to both cheering and razzing from his rowdy pals in the pit.

Pretty soon he's going to join a traveling troupe and head out West, but for tonight let's have Rice, a twenty-year-old wannabe, somewhere backstage, maybe watching from the wings, as George Washington Dixon struts the stage and introduces his new blackface hit, "The Coal Black Rose." It's a number he's been doing to great success in Buffalo for several months, but this is the first time the Bowery boys have heard it.

And they're loving it. They laugh and whistle and clap as Dixon, in shiny blackface, acts out the story of Rose and Sambo, star-crossed darky lovers, singing the simple, repetitive ditty in a broad "Negro" dialect with liberal applications of pure gibberish:

Lubly Rosa, Sambo cum
Don't you hear de Banjo tum, tum, tum.
   Oh Rose der coal black Rose
I wish I may be cotch'd if I don't lub Rose
   Oh Rose der real coal black Rose.

Tay a little Sambo, I cum soon,
As I make a fire in de Backa Room.
   Oh Rose Bress dat Rose
I wish I may be burnt if I don't lub Rose
   Oh Rose der coal black Rose.

Make base Rose lubly dear,
I almose tiff as poker tandin here.
   Oh Rose I almose froze
I wish I may be burnt if I don't lub Rose,
   Make base Rose, I almose froze.

The sexual innuendo of Sambo 'tiff as a poker is not lost on the boys, who hoot and cheer. As the song rattles on, Sambo comes inside, and Rose has him sit by the fire.

I laff to tink if you was mine lubly Rose
I'd gib you plenty de Lord shure knows
Of Possum fed a Hommany, sometime Rice,
Cow heel and Sugar cane ebry ting dats nice . . .

Suddenly, things take a bad turn:

What is de corner dar Rose dat I py,
I know dat nigger Cuffee by de white ub de Eye.
Dat not Cuffee tis a tick of wood I sure.
A tick of wood wid turkey en you tell me dat shure?
    Oh Rose take care Rose
I wish I may be burnt if I don't lub Rose
    Oh Rose you black Snake Rose.

Let go my arm Rose, let me at him Rush,
I swells his two lips like a black a ball a brush
Let go my arm Rose, let me at him Rush,
I swells his two lips like a black a ball a brush
    Oh Rose take care Rose
Take care Rose, take care Rose
    I wish I may be beat if I don't hate Rose.

He clar himself for Sattin,
He cut a dirt and run,
Now Sambo follow arter,
Wid his tum, tum, tum,
    Oh Rose farewell Rose
I wish I may be burnt if I don't hate Rose
    Oh Rose you black snake Rose.

Sambo chases his rival offstage and the music ends with a flourish. The boys cheer, Dixon goes back out to take his bows, and Rice, in the wings, thinks, *Hmmm* . . .

To us, "The Coal Black Rose" looks like pure racist mockery, poking cruel fun at the silly darkies. But to the boys at the Bowery, there was a lot more going on. Here was music they could really get into. It was simple and rough, with a tune that was easy to remember and a good beat. It was funny, and perhaps more important, it was rude and in bad taste. It not only made fun of Negroes, but through them also lampooned the sighing, moonfaced young lovers who populated so much of the treacly parlor music of the day. It was low-class, vulgar and coarse. It was loud and noisy. It was everything they weren't supposed to like. Of course they loved it. It was *bad*.

Should we condemn these young men as racists? Sure, if you like. But that's about as useful as declaring all gangsta rappers racists, or proclaiming that Shirley Q. Liquor is not a cabaret act. Clearly there was more to a song like "The Coal Black Rose" than simply cracking vile jokes at the expense of Negroes. From behind the strange yet to them familiar blackface mask, these young men were broadcasting tremendous emotional complexity—or probably more accurately, confusion. Onto the hapless figures of Rose and Sambo, they projected both romantic longing and sexual panic. The lyrics are drenched with desire and fear. The female is a Rose, a classic romantic cliché, but she's also coal-black and a black snake. Sambo, 'tiff as a poker with lust, is allowed in—she lets him stand next to her fire, as Jimi would sing a century and a half later—and Sambo dreams a kind of parody of comfy, middle-class domesticity, with an absurd meal of possum and cow heel. It's a cynical and streetwise retort to the then popular "Home, Sweet Home," written several years earlier. In "Rose," domestic bliss is revealed as a cruel illusion, a dream indeed, as Sambo discovers that Rose is already two-timing him with Cuffee, hiding in the corner with his half-eaten turkey leg in his fist. The song descends into a burlesque of betrayal, sexual jealousy, violence and revenge.

In Rose and Sambo, the Bowery boys found dark, chthonic anti-heroes to put up against the (equally ridiculous) young lovers of the nostalgic parlor ballads so popular at the time in middle- and upper-class homes. They may have been laughing at Rose and Sambo, but they also knew that as poor 'tiffs from the slums themselves, their domestic lives would probably look a lot more like "The Coal Black Rose" than "Home, Sweet Home," or atrociously mawkish fluff like "I'll Pull a Bunch of Buds and Flowers," which was also making the rounds. Sambo ain't pulling no poesies. He's busting lip.

Let's look again at Jim Crow, shuffling across the same stage a few years later. With his blackface mask, his bent back and his gimp leg, Jim is the very figure of the jester, the lame Other who can speak the truths and crack the jokes no one else can. But he's also a larger-than-life frontiersman, a blackface Davy Crockett, a roarer and a rambler who's the very opposite of urbane East Coast gentility. He's a braggart and a swaggerer, a coxman who can satisfy "many gals" and "hab dem all, jis one by one." He's a two-fisted American who can "wip de lion ob de west" and "eat de alligator" with "ten load ob 'tator," then whip out his fiddle and speed-riff "like massa Pagganninny." In other versions of the song—there were many, many versions—his "munky shines" get him tossed in jail, and

> When I got out I hit a man, his name I now forgot,
> But dere was nothing left 'sept a little grease spot.
>
> So I knocked down dis Sambo, and shut up his light,
> For I'm just about as sassy, as if I was half white.
>
> But he soon jumped up again, an 'gan for me to feel,
> Says I go away you niggar, or I'll skin you like an eel.

Rice even had Jim issue the startling challenge:

An I caution all white dandies, not to come in my way,
For if dey insult me, dey'll in de gutter lay.

Jim's an outrageous figure, and a comic one, but this is not simple racist trash. Like Jim, who's "half white," it seems more complicated than that. The boys were laughing at Jim, but they were also
singing and dancing along. Like Davy Crockett, he was a two-fisted,
dick-swinging comic hero they could identify with.

To complicate things even further, there's Jim's rival Zip Coon,
whom George Washington Dixon brought to the lower-Manhattan
stages in 1834. Zip was a big talker like Jim, but where Jim was all
country, Zip Coon was a Black urban dandy, putting on airs, dressed
to the nines in top hat and bright blue tails, his famous "long-tail'd
blue." He's a "negar" who "acts White." (Historian David Roediger
notes in *The Wages of Whiteness* that "coon" in those days seems to
have been slang for a rural White man, perhaps derived from the
frontiersman's iconic coonskin cap. It was probably Zip's popularity
that caused the word to slide over into a slur on Blacks. "Zip" was
short for Scipio, a common slave name.)

Dixon probably modeled Zip on free Black dandies he'd seen in
Northern cities, who were the topic of much sarcastic comment in
editorial cartoons, broadsheets and comic theater. Unlike Jim Crow,
Zip seems more an empty braggart, a Black who doesn't know his
place, who prances around the stage and spouts fancy-sounding
gibberish (to the tune, remember, of "Turkey in the Straw," showing
his country background):

O ole Zip Coon he is a larned skoler,
Sings posom up a gum tree an cooney in a holler,
posom up a gum tree, cooney on a stump,
Den over dubble trubble, Zip Coon will jump.

George Washington Dixon as Zip Coon, 1834.

(Courtesy Library of Congress)

CHORUS

O Zip a duden duden duden zip a duden day.

O its old Suky blue skin, she is in lub wid me
I went the udder arter noon to take a dish ob tea;
What do you tink now, Suky hab for supper,
Why chicken foot an posum heel, without any butter.

CHORUS

Did you eber see the wild goose, sailing on de ocean,
O de wild goose motion is a berry pretty notion;
Ebry time de wild goose, beckons to de swaller,
You hear him google google google google gollar.

CHORUS

I went down to Sandy Hollar tother arternoon
And the first man I chanced to meet war ole Zip Coon;
Ole Zip Coon he is a natty scholar,
For he plays upon de Banjo "Cooney in de hollar."

CHORUS

My old Missus she's mad wid me,
Kase I wouldn't go wid her into Tennessee
Massa build him barn and put in de fodder
Twas dis ting and dat ting one ting or odder.

CHORUS

I pose you heard ob de battle ob New Orleans,
Whar ole Gineral Jackson gib de British beans;
Dare de Yankee boys ob de job so slick,
For dey cotch old Packenham an rowed him up de creek.

CHORUS

I hab many tings to tork about but just don't know wich come first,
So here de toast to ole Zip Coon before he gin to rust;
May he hab de pretty girls, like de King ob ole,
To sing dis song so many times, 'fore he turn to mole.

What a mess these lyrics are. They sound like they're patched together from several unrelated sources—which they may have been. It was a not uncommon practice. One minute Zip addresses us directly, the next he's speaking of himself in the third person. He's a city slicker in one verse, but in the next he's back in the country, shirking the massa's work. He gives himself the airs of a "skoler," but his song is full of barnyard crudities—the turkey goes "duden duden duden," the goose goes "google google gollar"—that make hash of his urbane pretensions. Zip's long-tail'd blue, apart from its obvious phallic symbolism, also seems to mark him as a blue jay. Like the crow, the jaybird's a common figure in minstrel lyrics and folklore of the time. Jays were notorious for their loud and raucous behavior. And "jay" was also slang for a country rube who comes to the big city—it's the source of the word "jaywalking." Perfectly apt for ole Zip.

Frankly, these young men sound hopelessly confused. They're obviously fascinated with Blackness, admire Black music and dance, but they're simultaneously dismissive and insulting. Are they sincerely imitating Blacks, or just poking fun? Are they attracted or repulsed? Do they admire Blacks or despise them? Love them or fear them?

In a word: Yes.

IT'S NO COINCIDENCE THAT THE MINSTRELS ROSE IN POPularity just as Andrew Jackson rose to power. In the democratic upheaval that swept the country and swept Jackson into the White House in 1828, working-class Whites were pulled in several directions at once. They underwent what we could call a group identity crisis. Clinging to the bottom rungs of the social ladder, they had long associated with, and to an extent identified with, Blacks, and seen middle- and upper-class Whites as their enemy and oppressors. Now they were seeing opportunities to climb that ladder, and as they did they left Blacks behind. Now Blacks in fact became the enemy. Minstrelsy becomes popular just as these Whites begin their upward move.

Before this time, lower-class Whites and Blacks had mixed fairly freely. It may have been no Ebony and Ivory paradise of mutual respect and admiration, but still, tossed together at the bottom of society, they had shared a lot.

The American colonies had a voracious hunger for laborers. Early attempts to "civilize" Indians by enslaving them proved fruitless, but West Africa was an apparently bottomless resource of manpower. Some half a million Africans were brought here in chains during the Atlantic slave trade, the beginnings of a Black American population that neared five million in the 1860 census, of whom nine in ten were slaves.

Some hundreds of thousands of White workers were imported as well, both for brute labor and as skilled artisans and craftsmen. Many of these came under conditions little different from that of African slaves. In the years leading up to the Revolutionary War, as many as four-fifths of the skilled artisans who came from England came as indentured servants. They had contracted out their labor for a period of time—some for as little as five years, but many longer—after which they would be freed to pursue their craft. "By most accounts the indenture's unfreedom and hardship, though of short duration, were in some respects worse than any institutionalized form of labor exploitation," David Roediger writes in *The Wages of Whiteness*. "Transported in abysmal conditions alongside convicts, often sick and always filthy on arrival, indentured servants were sold at auction, sometimes after being stripped naked. If not sold retail on the coast, they were wholesaled to 'soul drivers' who marched the white servants, sometimes in coffles, through the countryside, selling them individually or in small lots. Not surprisingly, British contemporaries likened this 'infamous traffic' to chattel slavery. A letter in a Yorkshire newspaper, for example, found the indentures to be 'sold for slaves at public sale' and 'subject nearly to the same laws as the Negroes [with] the same coarse food and clothing.' Unfree whites often worked alongside slaves in cities like Philadelphia and New York City and sometimes ran away with slaves. The indentured servant was legally 'chattel of the master,' though with greater protection—through custom, terms of indenture and recourse to magistrates—than slaves had and, of course, with an end to bondage in sight."

In short, they were White slaves. And those were skilled English workers. England was also in the habit of shipping off criminals and lowlifes, much as it would do in Australia, to serve out their terms in America as virtual slaves. Irish and Scots brought to America could be treated even more straightforwardly like slaves. In Scotland in the mid-1600s, vagrants, beggars and other unruly types were rounded up, transported in shackles to the colonies, and sold at auction as slaves. Oliver Cromwell, like a West African warrior king, was in the habit of sending Scots and Irish prisoners of war to be sold at auction in the colonies. He shipped off as many as 300,000 Irish men, women and children to North and South America in a program of ethnic cleansing that spanned the 1640s and 1650s. These folks were sold to English planters in places like Barbados, where to this day people of Afro-Celtic descent speak a creolized Gaelic. Because so many of them had been peasant farmers with no marketable crafts or skills, the Irish were thought good for only the lowest brute labor—aka "nigger work." In the North, they worked alongside Blacks on dangerous, exhausting jobs such as digging the Erie Canal. In the South, slave owners often hired the Irish to do work like building levees, where they didn't want to risk their costly slaves.

An injured or dead nigger was money down the drain, but who cared if a Paddy or two were lost? There were more Paddies coming every day, and they came cheap.

It's said that the derogatory terms "hillbilly," "redneck" and "cracker" all have Gaelic roots. It was plantation Southerners who dubbed lower-class Scots and Irish immigrants "white trash," and who described them in terms indistinguishable from those used for Blacks. The well-known actress and diarist Frances Kemble, to cite one example, described poor Southern Whites as "filthy, lazy, ignorant, brutal, proud, penniless savages," utterly lacking "the nobler attributes." Stanley Crouch has declared the Civil War "the biggest con job in the history of the nation. . . . These crackers who were never considered as valuable as slaves . . . were whipped up into believing that they were somehow defending themselves, *their* culture, *their* way of life, *their* liberties and all the rest of it . . . [and] found themselves dying or maimed as a result of having defended a system that looked upon them with limitless contempt."

White laborers—especially the Irish and Scots—worked alongside African slaves throughout the Americas from early colonial times into the nineteenth century. They were auctioned off together, suffered together, died together, and more often than many people would want to admit later (although everyone knows it's true), slept together. Their shared songs, dances and stories became the foundation of indigenous American music and folklore. They ran away together, lighting out over the mountains or into the marshland, where they sometimes joined up with Indians. (There were, and are, numerous mixed-race tribes all up and down the East, variously identified as Seminoles, Melungeons, Moors, Maroons and Mestees and by other monikers.) They also rebelled together; many of the slave revolts, from the Caribbean sugar plantations to the streets of New York and Boston, included Whites as well as Blacks in their planning and execution. They formed a large mongrel underclass, and into the 1830s, their shared class conditions, and their common mistreatment at the hands of their Anglo-American overlords, could easily outweigh their racial differences. "The proximity of unfree whites and Black chattel slaves on a continuum of oppression helped create sympathies," David Roediger writes. "One hates to say it," Dale Cockrell agrees, "because it sounds today so naive and openly controversial, but the inescapable conclusion is this: White working people saw an ally in the black laborer against their common superiors, not simply an inevitable enemy."

Nowhere is this mongrel underclass more evident than in lower Manhattan in the early 1800s. From its very inception as the tiny Dutch outpost New Amsterdam, the city had been a uniquely polyglot, "multicultural" place. Whites and Blacks were equal under many sections of Dutch law, and slaves could own property and pass it along to their children. Sexual relations between Whites and Blacks were common enough that White-looking slaves shared the streets with ostensibly Black freemen. Conditions hardened for Blacks and slaves under English law after 1685, but by then the city's creolizing social customs were already well established.

Manhattan was growing at a breathless rate by 1800; its population virtually doubled in only ten years, from 1790 to 1800. Blacks—enslaved, freed and fugitive—made up an unusually large percentage of that population. New York State abolished slavery in two steps. First, all children of slaves born after July 4, 1799, were born free. Then slavery was abolished altogether in 1827. Meanwhile, many freed or runaway slaves from the South and as far away as the French West Indies fled there. In the early 1800s, the Black population of Manhattan swelled to a tenth of the total. It became the largest urban Black population outside Charleston.

Many of the city's poor and working-class inhabitants, Black and White, were indiscriminately stuffed into squalid, boisterous slums like those of the East River waterfront and the infamous Five Points neighborhood, what Herbert Asbury called "the cradle of the gangs," where the literally slumming Charles Dickens found "all that is loathsome, drooping and decayed." "Thousands eked out a wretched existence in the garrets and damp cellars with which the district abounded," Asbury writes in his lurid way, "and the bulk of the population was in the most abject poverty, devoting itself almost exclusively to vice and crime." The area abounded with "thieves, murderers, pickpockets, beggars, harlots and degenerates of every type," he says, to which we can add sailors, dockworkers, fishmongers and greengrocers, publicans and washerwomen, various artisans and their young apprentices, and a huge cadre of the under- or unemployed young men who composed the rank and file of Asbury's gangs. The area was three-to-one White, those Whites being mostly what Asbury calls "low-class Irish."

It is well documented that in these slums of the eighteenth and early nineteenth centuries, not just in New York but in other cities, such as Boston, Philadelphia, Buffalo and Albany—all early centers of blackface minstrelsy—poor Blacks and Whites mingled more freely and intimately than they ever would again in this country. Cockrell writes of "a common world in which blacks and whites lived by, worked with, drank among, fought with (to be sure and not to be understated), and loved each other." Free Blacks held small businesses in the Five Points—Almack's dance hall, Thomas Mooney's barbershop, John Rolloson's saloon—and established churches of their own, like St. Philip's African Episcopal and the African Baptist Church. Asbury declares that miscegenation was "rife," and the vigorous exertions of the ruling classes to ban and suppress it bear him out. Cockrell notes that "court reports are filled with mixed-race couples being brought into the halls of justice for the 'unnatural' sin." They'd go to prison, then get back together on release. At a time when President John Quincy Adams, the quintessential New England prig, thought that *Othello* was a morality play about the evils of race-mixing, lower-class Whites and Blacks seem to have been mixing it up with abandon.

Then, as always, the lower classes loved their rough entertainments. Asbury reports that the area in and around the Five Points was home to a few hundred bars, saloons, taverns, blind tigers (speakeasies) and "greengrocers," where the vegetables rotted in the front room while rotgut was consumed in the back. There was also a plentiful supply of whorehouses, and low-lit dance halls where the dancing was free as long as you regularly stopped to buy a drink. We can be certain that Black fiddlers provided the music. Almack's popular dance hall was owned and operated by a Black man, Peter Williams. Its swinging musicians, singing waiters and dancing wait-resses drew not only locals but slumming swells, including Dickens. (Nearby, in the next century, a young Ira Gershwin would begin his music career as a singing waiter at a joint called the Pelham Café, nicknamed Nigger Mike's. Owner Mike Salter was not in fact a "nig-ger," but a Russian Jew with a dark complexion.)

For staged entertainment, there were the rowdy variety theaters like the Chatham and the Bowery. There were a few high-tone the-aters nearby, like the Park, which drew the city's elite with opera and serious drama. But the Bowery and the Chatham were more like the chaotic precursors of burlesque and vaudeville theaters. Better yet, as W. T. Lhamon suggests, think of the setting for a rock & roll show or rap concert. Except for the whores in the balconies, the audience would be almost entirely young males—Asbury's gangs, the Bowery boys, unruly louts from the streets of the Five Points with lots of pent-up energy and little adult supervision. There would be very few females on the stage, either, until later in the century. Female roles, as they had been since time immemorial, were played by men or boys in drag. This mostly male environment would lead some late-twentieth-century scholars to read an awful lot of homosexual and "homosocial" desire into minstrelsy—but then, the late twenti-eth century was a period when many scholars seemed convinced that everyone was gay.

Into the 1830s some Black youths seem to have freely mixed with Whites in these raucous audiences, whose antics were part of the evening's entertainment as much as anything happening on the stage, which they would frequently bumrush. Indeed, audiences controlled the stage action more than the beleaguered performers did. If they enjoyed a song, they would roar for encore after encore after encore, until the poor singer was too hoarse to go on. If a dramatic scene engaged them, they'd jump up onstage and get into the action. Unloved performers were shouted down, pelted with garbage, manhandled. Fights, riots and pitched attacks on the hopelessly outmanned constabulary regularly spilled out to the streets, the coppers' clubs cracking young heads as expertly aimed paving stones bounced off theirs. The city fathers, the uptown elite, newspaper editors and preachers constantly decried the vulgarity and violence; laws were passed, countless editorials written, theaters shut down and replaced with venues for more refined activities—the Chatham, most aggravatingly to the boys, would be converted into an abolitionist chapel. It was all part of a decades-long war between the city's elite and its roiling underclass for control of the area.

The entertainments continued out on the streets, where street singers, sword swallowers, acrobats and Punch & Judy shows competed for strollers' coins. Negro children sold strawberries, yams and other goodies, but Asbury says they were no competition for the Hot Corn Girls, pretty lasses strolling in the evenings, selling roasted ears of corn out of cedar buckets. The young toughs would fight bloody duels over these girls, prized for both their beauty and their ready income; one bravo beat out dozens of rivals to marry his Hot Corn Girl, only to kill her soon afterward because she wasn't bringing home enough money. He then had the honor of being the first convicted murderer hanged in the brand-new Tombs in 1839.

Lhamon identifies the area's waterfront as a key breeding ground for future minstrels and their fans. T. D. Rice, who grew up just a few blocks away, surely spent time as a boy hanging around Catherine Slip and the Catherine Market, at a spot between what are now the Manhattan ends of the Brooklyn and Manhattan bridges. There,

Black slaves who'd come over from farms in Brooklyn or the Jersey waterfront, after selling their wares, would entertain the butchers, fishmongers, shoppers and loitering Irish youth by demonstrating their dancing skills. The slaves would compete for tips, with the day's winner earning a dish of eels. (Remember Jim Crow's line, "Says I go away you niggar, or I'll skin you like an eel.") They placed a board or "shingle" on the ground as their makeshift dance stage. A contemporary observer, Thomas De Voe, thought that the small stage was a way for the owner to confine the slave to a place where he could keep an eye on him. That may have been an ancillary benefit, but the shingle was an innovation the slaves themselves brought. It was a way of declaring and delimiting an impromptu performance space. It was also, very important, a percussion instrument, resounding with and amplifying the rhythms of dancing feet. Break dancers on Manhattan streets would use flattened cardboard boxes in a similar way some two hundred years later.

I saw a similar dance competition in a very different setting— County Clare, in the West of Ireland, where, in the 1980s, I was helping produce a TV documentary on traditional Irish music and dance. There, they take a door off its hinges and lay it on the ground as a stage for solo dancers. Dancers told us this "door dancing" originated centuries ago, when homes had uneven dirt floors that made for poor dance surfaces. The door, like the slaves' shingle, provided a flat dance surface and amplified the rhythmic knocking of the dancers' heels. By the 1980s, door dancing had become a competitive event, with dancers male and female, young and old, happily vying with one another. The Irish had added a characteristic twist, placing full pints of Guinness at the four corners of the door; the best dancer, who spilled the least stout, won, and got to drink the spoils. It makes me wonder—did Irish slaves teach door dancing to Africans in the Indies in the 1600s?

It is no coincidence that the first blackface minstrels shot to superstardom in precisely this neighborhood at exactly the moment they did. In 1828, the year the rabble swept Andrew Jackson into the White House and Davy Crockett again into Congress, the rabble of the Five Points was first cheering Dixon's "The Coal Black Rose."

Radical political change always comes at a price. The same democratic movement that was extending political and social power to the White commoners began to drive a rift between those Whites and Blacks, a rift that in some ways has still not been repaired. Poor and working-class Whites in the Northern cities came to see Blacks less and less as allies and increasingly as competitors or even enemies.

Roediger describes how from the moment the colonies declared their independence, White workers in America were struggling to declare and define their independence as well. British visitors in the 1780s learned that familiar terms like "master" and "servant" were now considered insulting to American domestic workers. Those words smacked of slavery. White workers preferred to be called "hired help," a term they innovated, and by the 1820s they had replaced "master" with the Dutch-derived "boss." Nondomestic workers, meanwhile, confronted a new species of slavery: wage slavery. As the Northern mills, factories and shipyards became increasingly mechanized and regulated in the early 1800s, workers found their skills devalued, their ability to earn a living regulated by the clock and production quotas, their humanity reduced to cogs in the machine. A worker was valued no longer for his craftsmanship, but only for showing up on time and cranking out x units of whatever it was his workplace was producing. Before the term "wage slave" was adopted, these workers were complaining bitterly that they had been reduced to "White slaves."

The abolition of slavery in the Northern states heated up White workers' fears into something close to panic. Once Blacks were free men, White workers saw them as free to compete with them for limited jobs. They were terrified that Blacks would become their equals or even their betters. Ironically, then, it's the *end* of slavery in the

North that most exacerbates working Whites' fears of slavery. Which they equate with Blackness. Which accelerates their efforts to distinguish themselves in any way possible as free White workingmen. As White workers organized, they explicitly excluded Blacks from their ranks.

The same process of exclusion was evident in that most sacred of all rights to the Jacksonian White rabble, the one that most marked them as citizens and "freemen"—the right to vote. The Revolution had shaken off the yoke of the British despot, but had left the new republic in the hands of an oligarchic elite—you had to have land and wealth to vote. By 1820, the generation of the Founding Fathers had pretty much all passed on, and the next generation of Americans demanded more of a say in the running of the new nation. Universal suffrage for White males swept the states in the 1820s. The rabble flexed its political muscle, and rough-hewn frontiersmen like Andrew Jackson and Davy Crockett came to Washington—much to the horror and chagrin of the old East Coast elitists like President Adams, whom Jackson replaced.

While the vote was extended to White males, it was specifically denied to women, most Blacks—and the poor Irish. In New York City in the mid-1820s, only about one free Black male in two hundred was allowed to vote. Whites justified this racism with the notion that since Blacks had been slaves for so long, they were unused to and incapable of making up their own minds as voters, and thus were easy fodder for political demagogues who might lead the young nation to ruin.

A similar fear that the Catholic Irish were subject to a "foreign power"—the pope—was the excuse to try to bar them from voting as well. So-called "native" Americans in fact equated Blacks and the Irish. "*Low-browed* and *savage, groveling* and *bestial, lazy* and *wild, simian* and *sensual*—such were the adjectives used by many native-born Americans to describe the Catholic Irish 'race' in the years before the Civil War," Roediger writes. "The striking similarity of this litany of insults to the list of traits ascribed to antebellum Blacks hardly requires comment." Early census data counted three types of non-Black people: native-born, foreign-born—and Irish.

As citizenship and the ability to work were restricted along racial lines, the Irish had to decide which side of that line they were on. Would they continue their long association with Blacks, or fight for their right to be accepted as White? Understandably, they chose the latter. Tragically, in their determination to be considered White, they became rabidly anti-Black. Some of the worst racist violence of the 1830s into the 1860s was perpetrated by rioting gangs of Irish youth. While they fought nativist gangs on one side, they brutally attacked Blacks on the other. Irish street violence against Blacks became so regular that Blacks nicknamed flying brickbats, one of the hooligans' weapons of choice, "Irish confetti."

In a lot of ways, early minstrelsy was like a sound track for this period of turmoil and transition. It's a mess of entertainment and politics, love and hate, attraction and repulsion, class and race consciousness, sincere imitation and cruel mockery. It is telling that for decades blackface minstrelsy was an entertainment dominated by young men of Irish descent. (Later in the century, German-Americans (aka "Dutch"), who were similarly derided as stupid and lazy by the natives, would provide some of minstrelsy's brightest stars. In the early 1900s, the baton would be passed to yet another group of poor new immigrants, Eastern European Jews.)

In their roles as jesters, Jim Crow and Zip Coon often commented on the social issues and politics of the day. Rice and Dixon freely added verses to keep up with the headlines. One published version of "Jump Jim Crow" runs to sixty-six verses. In 1832, Rice had Jim Crow wholeheartedly stumping for Andrew Jackson:

> *But Jackson he's de President,*
> *As ebry body knows;*

He always goes de hole Hog,
An puts on de wee-toes [vetoes].
Old hick'ry, never mind de boys,
But hold up your head;
For people never turn to clay
'Till arter dey be dead.

The "clay" referred to is Henry Clay, Jackson's despised rival and Whig (i.e., old Eastern elite) opponent in the 1832 presidential election. The Bowery boys no doubt cheered; in the Five Points, a vote for Jackson was a vote against the local aristocracy, whom the boys saw as their oppressors. Rice's blackface adds a layer of ambiguity. After all, Jim Crow, supposedly a Southern Black, would not have been allowed to vote for Jackson or anyone else. And if he had been allowed, would he have gone for Jackson, who, for all that he was a two-fisted man of the people, was also a Southerner and slave owner?

In the same year, Rice had Jim Crow make this rather astonishing declaration:

Should dey get to fighting,
Perhaps de blacks will rise,
For deir wish for freedom,
Is shining in deir eyes.

And if de blacks should get free,
I guess dey'll see some bigger,
An I shall consider it,
A bold stroke for de nigger.

I'm for freedom,
An for Union altogether,
Although I'm a black man,
De white is call'd my broder.

It's hard to know who's speaking here, T. D. Rice or Jim Crow. Maybe both. That's the importance of the blackface mask: Rice, as a White man, probably would not have stood up before an audience of Five Points rowdies and openly advocated a violent revolt by "de nigger." But as Jim Crow he could. And the same Bowery boys who put on blackface themselves to hurl brickbats at their Black neighbors cheered the idea of Blacks (in the South anyway) rising up.

Zip Coon's political utterances were characteristically grandiose and uppity:

And de bery nex President, will be Zip Coon.
An wen Zip Coon our President shall be,
He make all de little Coons sing posum up a tree;
O how de little Coons will dance and sing,
When he tie dare tails togedder, cross de lim dey swing.

Now mind wat you arter, you tarnel kritter Crockett,
You shant go head without old Zip,
He is de boy to block it.
Zip shall be President, Crockett shall be vice,
And den dey two together, will hab de tings nice.

What a strange concatenation of images, working the jokes on several levels. The Bowery boys would have guffawed at the idea of President Coon. Zip was thinking way above his station, as the vulgar coon jokes sandwiched into the middle of the verse remind us—those poor little coons literally bound to their place by their tails. He's dreaming of becoming the president at a time when most free Blacks aren't even allowed to vote. Then again, as Cockrell observes, how much more outrageous was the notion of President Coon than the idea of Ol' Hickory in the White House, or of Crockett's serving two terms as a congressman for Tennessee? Still, what chutzpah for

Zip to brag that the only way Crockett would succeed was to ride the coattails of Zip's long-tail'd blue.

A tremendous amount of political and class tension is compressed in the figure of Zip. He's a symbol of upwardly mobile Jacksonian democracy, of the rabble who were then contesting with the oligarchs for power everywhere from the halls of Congress to the Bowery and Chatham theaters. But he also signifies the growing rift within the rabble, along racial lines, that was festering and hardening. He symbolized the terror that lower-class Whites had of being left at the bottom if "niggars" like Zip got too uppity. When Zip Coon was onstage acting fancy-pantsed, they roared with laughter. When they thought they saw him on the streets of the Five Points, they roared with rage.

"Settin' on a Rail," believed to be from the 1840s, proceeds for its first four verses as a typical minstrel tale, beginning with:

> As I walk'd out by de light ob de moon,
> So merrily singing dis same tune,
> I cum across a big raccoon,
>   A sittin' on a rail, sittin' on a rail,
>   sittin' on a rail, sittin' on a rail,
> Sleepin werry sound.

But note this verse (the fifth), a seditious little digression that seems dropped in from an entirely different song, or universe:

> My ole Massa dead an gone,
> A dose ob poisin help him on,
> De Debil say he funeral song,
>   Oh bress him, let him go, bress him, let him go,
>   bress him, let him go, bress him, let him go,
> An joy go wid him too.

Who poisoned ole Massa? The fact that the narrator doesn't say is a fair indication. Historians who argue that minstrelsy was un-relievedly racist believe this verse is a remnant of an original Negro song from which this one was adapted, and the minstrels simply didn't notice its sardonically witty antislavery sentiment. That would make minstrels both racist and stupid. Maybe so. Or maybe they knew exactly what they were singing, and slipped it in with a wink and a nod. How else to explain a song like "Walk, Jaw Bone," popularized by a minstrel with the fabulous stage name Cool White in the 1840s:

In Caroline, whar I was born,
I hust de wood, an' I chop de corn,
A roasted ear to de house I bring,
But de driver cotch me and he sing:

CHORUS
Walk, jaw bone, Jenny come along,
In come Sally wid de bootees on,
Walk, jaw bone, Jenny, come along,
In come Sally wid de bootees on.

De [corn] de driver from me rob,
An' he make me eat de cob;
I chaw de cob until my gums
Stick out like Carolina plums.

Dey fasten me up under de barn,
Dey feed me dar on leaves ob corn;
It tickled my digestion so,
Dat I cotch de cholerophoby, oh.

Dey mad me a scar-crow in de field.
And a buzzard come to get his meal,

But in his face I blowed my bref,
An' he was a case for ole Jim Death.

Next come a hungry eagle down,
Oh! gosh thinks I, dis nig's done drown;
But he winked an' cried "I'se de bird ob de free
And won't eat de meat ob slabery."

Next come a weasel for my juice,
An' he gnawed till he untied me loose,
An' den I mad off wid a quick salarm,
An' lef' him be widout a dram.

Den down de bank I see'd de ship,
I slide down dar on de bone ob my hip;
I crossed de drink an' yare I am,
If I go back dar, I'll be damn!

Beneath the shiny blackface surface, could this song be any clearer in its sympathy for the escaped slave who narrates it?

Rice would go on performing songs like "Jump Jim Crow" and the sprightly jig "Clare de Kitchen" ("In old Kentuck in de arternoon, / We sweep de floor wid a bran new broom, / And arter dat we form a ring, / And dis de song dat we do sing") until his death in 1860. He would also star in staged productions of *Uncle Tom's Cabin*, blackface burlesques of *Othello* and other material, and write and produce his own "Negro farces." He was minstrelsy's first international superstar, and like a pop star of the future, he enjoyed living large. The boy who'd grown up in the ghetto and become rich and famous adopted the macking moniker "Daddy Rice," and took to wearing vests and coats with gold coins for buttons—obvious precursors of bling—which he'd tear off and toss into his adoring crowds.

Dixon, as Cockrell describes in detail, fared less well. He abandoned his blackface act for more direct social intervention, becoming a mediocre muckraking journalist and failed politician. He died in obscure poverty.

Jim and Zip lived on as independent characters long after their originators stopped performing them. They were adopted by many performers, and became popular figures in satirical broadsheets and pamphlets. When the blackfaced White gangs went wilding, they often used "Jump Jim Crow" as their fight song. In the 1870s, Jim Crow's name was appropriated as slang for the brutal system of apartheid that Southern Whites instituted to put Blacks back in their place after the Reconstruction period sputtered to an end.

Even when they weren't specifically named and their signature songs weren't sung, elements of Jim and Zip became fixtures in later minstrel shows, usually teamed up to comic effect—the ragged country coon and the big-talking city slicker. It's a tradition that endured long past the era of the minstrel show itself, when *Amos 'N' Andy* and *Sanford and Son* carried into the TV age.

4

"YOU MAY BE A HAWAIIAN ON BROADWAY . . ."

The Minstrel Show, Coon Songs & Vaudeville

Coon! Coon! Coon!
I wish my color would fade.
Coon! Coon! Coon!
I'd like a different shade.
Coon! Coon! Coon!
Morning, night and noon.
I wish I was a white man
'Stead of a Coon! Coon! Coon!
—GENE JEFFERSON, *"Coon, Coon, Coon"*

Blackface minstrelsy's emergent years, its rock & roll decade, ended in the early 1840s. In a pattern that would be repeated a few times in the twentieth century, what began as rebellious, noisy youth music grew up, grew tame, and was embraced by the mainstream. It abandoned the streets and the low-class dives for the concert hall and the parlor room. Business managers and impresarios took over, groomed it, and turned it into mass entertainment. As such, its form became as repetitive and familiar as the circus or the TV sitcom.

Nonetheless, for mass entertainment, it's remarkable how slippery

(Courtesy Library of Congress)

the minstrel show could still be in its meanings and messages. Simply condemning it all as an entertainment that pandered to White racism does not begin to account for its complexities, its confusion, its neuroses. It simultaneously laughed at and wept for Southern Blacks. In the years leading up to the Civil War, minstrel songs proposed both pro- and antislavery positions. After the war, minstrel performers were as likely to be actual Blacks as blackfaced Whites. At the end of the nineteenth century, the most vilely racist form of stereotyping yet—the infamous "coon song"—was pioneered by a Black entertainer.

The transition to the full-bore minstrel show begins in 1842–1843, when Edwin P. Christy in Buffalo and Daniel Decatur Emmett in lower

Minstrel show poster, 1899.
(Courtesy Library of Congress)

Manhattan first expanded the form from a solo act to a four-piece band. They also transformed it from a brief novelty routine performed between plays in the variety theater to a stand-alone evening of song and dance in a concert setting—thus inventing the first true "minstrel show." Who had the idea first, Christy or Emmett, has been a matter of controversy ever since. But because Emmett had the good sense to form his band in Manhattan, not out in Buffalo, he earned the loudest bragging rights.

Dan Emmett is the undisputed superstar of this second phase of minstrelsy. He was born in 1815 in the frontier town of Mount Vernon, Ohio, where he learned to play the fiddle as a boy, probably from Black fiddlers. According to legend—and Emmett was a Barnum at promoting his legend—he debuted one of his most famous songs there when he was just fifteen. It was "Old Dan Tucker," the hoedown fiddle-scraper with an infectious sing-along chorus that's still taught to kids today, though usually as "Old Man Tucker," and with the original "offensive" lyrics cleaned up.

Emmett claimed that it was in his room at a boardinghouse on Catherine Street, a spit from the Catherine Market, where the slaves had danced for eels, that he got the idea to form a minstrel band with three other local fellows, all with backgrounds doing blackface in touring circuses or theater troupes. That group, the Virginia Minstrels, debuted at the Bowery Amphitheatre on February 6, 1843. It was Emmett on fiddle, Billy Whitlock on banjo, Frank Brower on bones and Dick Pelham on tambourine. They advertised themselves as a "novel, grotesque, original and surpassingly melodious Ethiopian Band," and promised that their act was "entirely exempt from the vulgarities and other objectionable features which have hitherto characterized negro extravaganzas." W. T. Lhamon argues that this puffery, along with the formal concert setting, was clearly an attempt to get respectable folks to come hear what had in the previous decade been considered low-class entertainment for ghetto youth. But it's also hard not to believe the boys' tongues were firmly in their cheeks

with this highfalutin ballyhoo, which so closely parodies the snob-
bish advertisements for "refined" musical concerts of the day. And
in fact their performances sound more like rock concerts than piano
recitals. Dressed in outlandish "Negro" costumes, their blackface
masks grotesquely cartoonish, the quartet banged and sawed and
rattled through an exuberant and loosely organized set of upbeat
dance tunes and ditties like "Jim Along Josey" and "Old Dan Tucker,"
"De Boatman Dance" and "Miss Lucy Long," punctuated by frequent
outbursts of apparently spontaneous hoofing, with lots of impromptu joking around in broad Negro dialect.

It caught on like wildfire. The Virginia Minstrels were an instant
smash hit. In two short months they were touring England and
Ireland (unsuccessfully, it turned out, but evidently more because
of lousy tour management than a lack of interest on the part of
audiences there). If Rice had been minstrelsy's Elvis, the Virginia
Minstrels were its Beatles, and their success spawned instant imitation. Within a year, minstrel shows were being performed all
across the United States. Over the next fifty years, minstrel troupes
absolutely dominated the American stage. A very partial list of
troupes gleaned from Edward Rice's 1911 *Monarchs of Minstrelsy* includes Wood's Minstrels, Sanford's Minstrels, Campbell's Minstrels,
Peel's Minstrels, Hooley's Minstrels, Pettengill's Minstrels, Kelley &
Leon's Minstrels, Cotton & Murphy's Minstrels, Newcomb & Arling-
ton's Minstrels, Moran & Dixey's Minstrels, Simmons & Slocum's
Minstrels, the Original San Francisco Minstrels (who were from
New York), the Original New Orleans Minstrels, the Kitchen Minstrels, countless groups calling themselves Christy's Minstrels or
Georgia Minstrels, Richards' & Pringle's Colored Minstrels, Buck-
ley's Serenaders, the Nightingale Serenaders, the Ethiopian Sere-
naders, the Sable Melodists, the Ironclads, Ordway's Aeolians, Pike's
Harmoneons . . .

Dan Emmett rode the wave from one success to another. In 1859,
performing with Bryant's Minstrels in New York, he introduced

what would be one of the most famous and enduring of all minstrel songs, "(I Wish I Was in) Dixie." He claimed to have written it in his damp and chilly New York City apartment, pining away for sunnier Southern climes. Though accepted as gospel for a very long time, his account was contested by a pair of Black musicians, Ben and Lew Snowden, who'd been Emmett's neighbors back in Ohio and who claimed to have taught him the song.

What we think of as the full-blown minstrel-show format developed in the 1850s. The original four-man band expanded into orchestras of a dozen or more players behind full choruses. Star singers, dancers and comedians were added, as were lavish costumes and sets. For a long time, the cast continued to be exclusively male, which afforded opportunities for a lot of comic cross-dressing. Over the decades, impresarios competed to outdo one another with sheer size and spectacle, until giant minstrel troupes of a hundred or more entertainers roved the landscape by rail. As with traveling circuses, a minstrel troupe's engagement in a city often began with a grand parade from the train station to the performance space. In the 1930s, A. J. Liebling would sit around New York bars, jawing with the last of the old-time minstrel men, who fondly remembered these parades. "No band ever sounded like a minstrel band," one told Liebling. "The boys doubling in brass were performers, and each wanted the center of the stage. Real window-breakers." "On the coldest mornings we had to turn out," another reminisced with a wink. "Sometimes it was so cold the horns'd freeze and we'd all have to step into a beer saloon to thaw them out."

By the mid-1850s, the Virginia Minstrels' loose concert format had been elaborated into a full evening of variety-show extravaganza—"set," Constance Rourke writes, "within a ritual which grew more and more fixed, like some rude ceremonial." The show was presented in three acts. The first was devoted to song and dance, and came closest to the original concert idea. The musicians would be seated in a wide semicircle, with the host, Mr. Interlocutor, in the center. The "endmen" at either end of the line played the Negro characters Tambo and Bones. After a big, boisterous opening number, the Interlocutor would seek to establish order with the famous command "Gentlemen, be seated!" But Tambo and Bones would be comically unruly, interrupting him with jokes, breaking into song, going into "impromptu" Negro dances. This first act would proceed with various songs, solos, dance numbers, liberally seeded with jokes and tomfoolery, and end with a big, rousing production number, such as a full-orchestra medley of favorite songs.

In later years this first-act finale would often include a "walkaround," when Black or blackfaced couples in fine outfits—the men with Zip Coonish top hats and canes, the ladies in flowing ball gowns—promenaded across the stage, usually dancing the cakewalk. The cakewalk is one of those intriguing confluences of Black and White American cultures. Blacks on the plantation had developed it as a satire of their White masters. Their backs stiffly arched, their butts held tight, their elbows out and their knees kicking high, they strutted, bowed, and twirled their canes in a blatant parody of the way tight-assed, stiff-necked White folks moved. White folks loved to see Black dancers execute a fine cakewalk, and demanded to be taught how to do it, apparently unaware that they were being mocked. (The Library of Congress archives preserve a very brief film strip from 1903 showing a Black dance troupe, the Americus Quartet, demonstrating the cakewalk. No wonder they're smiling so broadly. The joke was on the audience.)

After an intermission came the "olio" (said to be derived from the Spanish *olla podrida,* or stew). A direct precursor to vaudeville, not to mention *The Ed Sullivan Show,* the olio was a hodgepodge of songs, dances and, as the years went by, whatever else the impresarios could come up with—jugglers, animal imitators, magicians, comic duos. The "stump speech," described below, became a popular fixture of the olio.

The second intermission was often followed by a short one-act burlesque, or "burletta," also called an afterpiece, spoofing a popular novel, opera or play. Parodies of Shakespeare's plays abounded: *Othello* was of course a popular source, yielding farces with titles like *Desdemonum,* but there was also *Hamlet the Dainty,* and one called *Shylock* that seems more intent on working Jewish stereotypes than Black ones. Shylock's opening lines give the flavor of the piece: "Aha! my frients; how's pishness dis cold day? / I've brought you vun pair pants, and lettle veskit, eh!"

The *Hop of Fashion* mixes up characters from *Macbeth* with contemporary comic stereotypes—a couple of blackfaced Negro figures, a couple of brawling Irishmen—into a nonsensical folderol of bad one-liners and clownish sight-gags, which ends in a free-for-all with stage directions worthy of Alfred Jarry: "A general row—all fight at random. Gong strikes. LADY MACBETH flying to and fro all over the stage. CURTAIN."

Zip Coon got a one-act of his own, *Old Zip Coon,* in which the high-stepping, big-talking dandy ("I'd hab you know dere aint no niggahs now. I belongs to de upper crust") shows his true color(s) when a fiddle sounds and he can't resist doing a little shuckin' and jivin'.

One of the best-known and best of these farces was written by T. D. Rice in the early 1830s and revived by various minstrel troupes for decades. The humor in *Oh, Hush!* would be familiar to anyone who remembers *The Amos 'N' Andy Show* or *Sanford and Son.* Sambo Johnson is another Zip Coonish figure; having "drawed a high prize in de lottery and retired," he talks like the Kingfish and acts like Fred Sanford. Updated a little, much of the dialogue would fit any episode of *Amos 'N' Andy*:

JOHNSON (looking through his eyeglass). Gemblem, is you distressing your conversation to me?
CUFF. Yes, sar, I is distressing my observation to you inderwidually, collectively, skientifically and alone.

Minstrel show poster, 1899.
(Courtesy Library of Congress)

JOHNSON. Well, sar, den I would hab you to know dat my name,
    sar, is Mr. Samuel Johnson, Exquire, an' I don't wish to be address
    by such—(pointing to crowd)—low, common, vulgar trash!

As the overall architecture of the minstrel show became fixed,
other aspects grew more formulaic as well. Dale Cockrell describes
how the rough and eccentric edges of the early music were smoothed
down and glossed over to appeal to a mass audience—like, say, the
taming of early rock & roll into Pat Boone pop. Minstrel songs eventually came in three basic flavors—catchy, straightforward dance
tunes; novelty numbers, performed by whistlers or basses or "male

sopranos"; and nostalgic tearjerkers that were effectively indistinguishable from the parlor ballads the original minstrels had
spoofed.

The characterizations also flattened into stock types. The minstrel show birthed few figures with the mythic stature of a Jim Crow
or Zip Coon; the few it did present, like Uncle Tom and Topsy, or the
blackfaced Shylock and Hamlet, were borrowed from elsewhere.
Like the songs, minstrel-show characters came in basic flavors:
shuffling country coons, voguing Black dandies, large choruses of
"plantation darkies," gibberish-spouting "preachers," the virtually anonymous Tambo and Bones, plus a few drunken Irishmen, wheedling
Jews, funny-talking Germans and so on. It's at this point, when the
characterizations are reduced to familiar stereotypes and stock images, that the racism becomes thoughtless reflex—that is, truly
racist. At least the boys on the Bowery had long and intimate contact with the Black folks onto whom they projected their confusion
of love and hate. In the last few decades of the 1800s, as America became increasingly segregated, and Blacks and Whites became more
and more strangers to each other, the only "Black people" many
Whites ever "met" were the blackfaced performers in the minstrel
shows. It's this point when even Mark Twain, a real human soul with
great appreciation and knowledge of actual Black culture, could
rhapsodize about "the genuine nigger show, the extravagant nigger
show . . . the show which to me had no peer . . . a thoroughly de-
lightful thing."

And so a lot of minstrel show antics are reduced to horrid racist
doggerel. Here are partial lyrics to "Root, Hog, or Die," popularized
in the mid-1850s by Ordway's Aeolians of Boston:

I'm right from old Virginny wid my pocket full ob news
I'm worth twenty shillings right square in my shoes
It doesn't make a dif of bitternance to nieder you nor I
Big pig or little pig Root, hog, or die.

I'm chief cook and bottlewasher, cap'n ob de waiters;
I stand upon my head,
When I peel de Apple dumplins.

I'se happiest darkee on de top ob de earth
I get fat as possom in de time ob de dearth
Like a pig in a tate patch dar let me be
Way down in old Virginny whar its Root, hog, or die . . .

These lines are from "De History ob de World," published in 1847:

Oh, dis world was made in six days,
    And den dey made de sky,
And den dey hung it ober head
    And left it dar to dry;
And den dey made de stars
    Out ob nigger wenches eyes,
For to gib a little light
    When de moon didn't rise . . .

O, lightning is a yellow gal,
    She libs up in de clouds,
And thunder he's a black man,
    For he can hollow loud;
When he kisses lightning,
    She dodges off in wonder,
Den he jumps and tares his trowsers,
    And dat's what makes de thunder.

O, de wind begin to blow,
    And de rain begin to fall,
And de water came so high,
    But it drown'd de niggers all. . . .

Minstrel show poster, 1900.
(Courtesy Library of Congress)

And the opening lines from the 1872 hit "Oh! Sam":

Oh, Sammy, put dat banjo down,
O Sam! You good for nuffen lazy houn',
O Sam!
Drive de dog in, out de rain,
Milk de cows for Liza Jane;
Liza's got de hoopin' cough,
De ole man's drunk in de stable loff.

Oh! Sammy, just you put dat banjo down,
De hog's in de garden rootin' up de groun',
De mule am dead, an' de hoss am sick,
Come here, Sam, I want you quick—you hear me, O Sam!

And how about these lovely sentiments:

My Susy looms it bery tall
Wid udder like a cow
She'd give nine quarts easy
But white gals don't know how.

Yet even at this loathsome stage, the minstrel show was not quite the purely racist juggernaut it's often portrayed as. For instance, in the years leading up to and during the Civil War, minstrel songs simultaneously expressed pro- and antislavery views, and could be both Unionist battle hymns and antidraft race-baiting. Sentiments in the North were never monolithically behind "Mr. Lincoln's war to free the slaves." When Lincoln instituted a draft in 1863, poor and working-class Whites in Northern cities resisted having to go fight and maybe die for "Uncle Sambo," especially when rich men's sons were allowed to buy their way out of service. The worst draft riot, not coincidentally, was conducted by mobs of mostly Irish youth in lower Manhattan, in four days of looting that targeted Black homes, businesses and churches, and culminated in a dozen Blacks' being beaten to death or lynched.

Many minstrels fell squarely on the antiabolitionist, antiwar side. In 1852, the instant Harriet Beecher Stowe's antislavery novel *Uncle Tom's Cabin* came out, minstrels were parodying it, for both its weepy sentimentality and its abolitionist politics. The association of minstrelsy and antiabolitionist sentiments was strong enough that one editorial cartoon of the era spoofed Lincoln as a blackfaced Othello. Minstrels stooped to new lows as they propagandized for the antiwar side. One song japed:

Abram Linkum said to me
Send de sojers down!
He's gwine to make de niggers free
Send de sojers down!

Another punned on Lincoln's name:

> *I wish I was a blinkin', a blinkin', a blinkin'*
> *I wish I was a blinkin'*
> *I'll tell you what I'd do . . .*
> *Oh, if I was much bigger—some bigger—great bigger,*
> *Oh, if I was some bigger I tell you what I'd do:*
> *I'd buy up all de niggers—de niggers—de colored African*
>   *American citizens,*
> *I'd buy up all de niggers, and—sell 'em, wouldn't you?*

But abolitionists and Union patriots also used, or maybe the word is "appropriated," the minstrel form. The best-known at the time to do so was Henry Clay Work, a Connecticut abolitionist and abolitionist's son (his father, Alanson Work, was said to have helped some four thousand slaves to freedom). In addition to popular battle hymns like "Marching Through Georgia," Work composed a number of pro-emancipation songs like the 1863 "Babylon Is Fallen!"

> *Don't you see de black clouds*
> *Risin' ober yonder,*
> *Whar de Massa's old plantation am?*
> *Neber you be frightened,*
> *Dem is only darkies,*
> *Come to jine an' fight for Uncle Sam,*

> *Look out dar, now!*
> *We's agwine to shoot!*
> *Look out dar, don't you understand?*
> *(Oh, don't you know dat)*
> *Babylon is fallen!*
> *Babylon is fallen!*
> *An' we's agwine to occupy the land. . . .*

Mass was de Kernel
In de Rebel army,
Eber sence he went an' run away;
But his lubly darkies,
Dey has been a-watchin',
An' dey take him pris'ner tudder day.

We will be the Massa,
He will be the sarvant,
Try him how he like it for a spell;
So we crack de Butt'nuts,
So we take the Kernel,
So the cannon carry back de shell.

Another abolitionist, Benjamin Russell Hanby, predicted in the 1861 "Ole Shady" the day when (two years later) emancipation would be declared:

Oh! yay! yah! darkies laugh wid me,
For de white folks say Ole Shady's free,
So don't you see dat de jubilee
Is a coming, coming,
Hail mighty day. . . .

Good bye Mass' Jeff, good by Mis'r Stephens,
'Scuse dis niggah for takin his leavins,
'Spect pretty soon you'll hear Uncle Abram's
coming, coming,
Hail mighty day.

Probably inspired by *Uncle Tom's Cabin*, Hanby penned the tragic tale "Darling Nelly Gray" in 1856:

There's a low green valley on the old Kentucky shore,
   There I've whiled many happy hours away,
A sitting and a singing by the little cottage door,
   Where lived my darling Nelly Gray.

Oh! my poor Nelly Gray, they have taken you away,
   And I'll never see my darling any more,
I'm sitting by the river and I'm weeping all the day,
   For you've gone from the old Kentucky shore . . .

One night I went to see her, but "she's gone!" the neighbors say,
   The white man bound her with a chain;
They have taken her to Georgia for to wear her life away,
   As she toils in the cotton and the cane. . . .

Minstrels addressed a broad array of other social issues through the comic vehicle of the stump speech. In the years before electronic media, the stump speech was the chief way politicians put their opinions and their faces before the masses. Enormous crowds would turn out to hear a great speechmaker on the stump; a crowd of 200,000 once greeted Teddy Roosevelt, one of the greatest. Stump speeches tended to be long and grandiloquent—which made them excellent targets for parody. The parody stump speech was a regular feature of the minstrel show from early on—the Virginia Minstrels used it to great hilarity. Stump speeches made hash of the important topics of the day, demonstrating that minstrels and their audiences had more on their minds than simply laughing at Negroes—though that was always the conduit for their commentary. Historian Robert Toll writes:

Before the Civil War, minstrels ranged widely in their social commentary. They lampooned other entertainments, from Barnum to
Jennie "Leather-lungs" Lind, and joked about the telegraphic cable to

England, the world's fair in London, and the country rubes falling in love with Hiram Powers' nude sculpture "The Greek Slave." Through their ignorant black characters, they "explained" natural phenomena like gravity and electricity. They sympathetically conveyed both the high hopes and the bitter disappointments produced by the California gold rush; and they made light of some of the cults and fads of the day—Millerites, spirit-rapping, "free-knowledgery" (Phrenology), and the Shakers.

Seeking in 1842 to explain the Millerites' prediction that the world would end the following year, the blackface "Reverend Snowball" preached a sermon to his Five Points "bruddren" that was as thick with indecipherable gobbledygook as a Professor Irwin Corey lecture. (The world did not end in 1843, and the Millerites became Seventh-day Adventists.) When "Professor Julius Caesar Hannibal" lectured on "freenology" in the mid-1850s, he used a sheep's skull for his demonstration, figuring it was as good as a human head "'kase it hab got de wool on." Minstrels spoofed the burgeoning women's suffrage movement in terms that would change little over the next century:

When woman's rights is stirred a bit
De first reform she bitches on
Is how she can wid least delay
Just draw a pair ob britches on.

In the decades after the Civil War, stump-speech topics ranged from the corruption and delinquency of the nation's youth to the greed of the upper classes. Some of the greatest minstrel-show comics made the stump speech their signature routine, and the best could weave ripped-from-the-headlines commentary into a prepared script with dazzling wit.

In the Library of Congress there's a late example of the form, a marvelous thirty-seven-page typewritten manuscript, dated 1914, of a Dockstader's Minstrels stump speech titled "Back from the Land of the Nut." It was performed by the potbellied Lew Dockstader, considered one of the premier monologuists in showbiz. In this routine he played a blackface Teddy Roosevelt, just back from a trip in the Amazon rain forest, addressing the "Ananais Club" with proto-Kingfish eloquence:

"While I am not a member of this club, it was founded, confounded and dumbfounded by me. Every member on its long rolls was proposed, seconded and unanimously elected by an overwhelming majority of myself.

"The Ananais Club is an organization of political dead ones. Its purpose, to provide an institution where distinguished stiffs—after I have laid them out—can LIE in state."

Ananais (actually Ananias) is a man in the New Testament who lies to Peter and immediately dies for it. "The Ananias Club" was popular slang for a long list of political enemies Roosevelt had accused of being liars. Roosevelt had decided to vacate the White House in 1908, turning it over to his friend and handpicked successor, William Taft. But Taft was a disappointment (a "stiff"), and Teddy missed the presidency, so in 1912 he made a brilliant but unsuccessful run for it as the Bull Moose candidate. He came in second to Woodrow Wilson, with Taft finishing a distant third. In late 1913, with nothing better to do, Roosevelt went on one of his famous big-game expeditions, this time in the Amazon rain forest. It was a disaster, and nearly killed him.

Dockstader's routine draws on all of this, plus Roosevelt's infamous tendencies to bloviate, for merciless satire. Of his Amazon trip, Dockstader's Teddy recalls: "They admire me more than any other American since Abraham Lincoln. There is no doubt about it. I told them so myself." (In fact, the Brazilians did love him, and named a tributary of the Amazon River after him, Rio Roosevelt.) There is wordplay about how, attacked by giant mosquitoes in the

Lew Dockstader delivering a stump speech, 1898.
(*Courtesy Library of Congress*)

Amazon jungle, he "declined to run" (a dig at his decision not to run
for reelection in 1908), jokes about his meeting an Amazonian chief
who had at his side "a great big stick, all spiked, knotted and lumpy"
(a reference to Teddy's famous dictum about talking softly but carrying a big stick), and so on. The speech eventually turns to Wilson,
whom Teddy despised, and who comes in for several pages of lam-
basting himself.

Though many of the jokes and puns are obscure to us now, they
would have been easily recognized by Dockstader's audience. Obviously, there's a lot going on in this routine that has nothing to do

with simple racist mockery. It's political commentary, savaging the current president and a beloved but faded former one, and making rich sport of their personalities and their policies. It's the 1914 equivalent of a bravura-length skit on *The Daily Show*. Though it was done in blackface, there's not one word about Black people in it. The blackface added another, unspoken layer of satire, linking Teddy Roosevelt's inflated posturing with that of a Zip Coon.

ONE OF THE ODDITIES OF THE MINSTREL SHOW WAS THE way it balanced its cruel, dehumanizing jokes at the expense of Black people with a fond, often tearjerking nostalgia for the South—a South few of the performers, and fewer of their audience members, knew anything about. The minstrel South was another fantasy onto which White folks could project their desires—a lost preindustrial paradise where "the sun shines bright" and "the darkies are gay" and "de time is neber dreary." A mythic Eden filled with ripe watermelon and stacks of steaming hoecakes, smiling mammies, kindly massas, wily catfish and ringing banjos. Small wonder that folks in the cold, hard Northern cities dreamed about it and so enjoyed seeing it portrayed on the stage. Their jobs increasingly mechanized and regimented, their tenement flats cramped and chill, their fun circumscribed by rigid Victorian morals and chastising temperance societies, they fantasized about the South the way folks today dream of a trip to Cancún or Club Med.

The nostalgia intensified after the Civil War, when the North was seized by paroxysms of guilt over the very plantation culture it had destroyed and then tried to supplant with its Reconstruction programs. The worse the situation got in the South, as Jim Crow laws were promulgated from the 1870s on, the more people fantasized about the good old plantation days.

"While it contains a certain irony, the North's postwar embrace of the Old South seems easily understandable," writes historian

Matthew Martin. "No longer a political or economic threat, after the war the dreams of the plantation South could be indulged as pure fantasy. . . . Nostalgia is most appealing to a society encountering tumultuous change. In America's Gilded Age, nostalgia for the Old South fed anxiety about the present and future by proclaiming that things were better in a lost past, and, at the same time, assuaged those fears by giving assurance that the past can be relived through memory. Perhaps even more importantly, in a nation tired of war and the strife of Reconstruction, images of a glorious South served the double purpose of giving meaning to the war by creating a heroic foe, and of welcoming the prodigal siblings back into the fold by acknowledging the virtues of their society and the tragedy of its loss. Evocation of the plantation myth also allowed northerners to ignore the issue of racial justice in America, allowing the problems of incorporating freed African Americans into society to disappear, if only temporarily, beneath the smile of the happy darky."

No one promoted the fantasy better than Stephen Foster. He was born outside Pittsburgh in 1826, lived his last days, most appropriately, on the Bowery, and died wretchedly in Bellevue Hospital in 1864. In between, his only trip to the South was by steamship, for a delayed honeymoon in New Orleans, so the plantation life he evoked in his songs was as much a fantasy for him as for any listener. Foster seems to have been most fond of his parlor songs, treacly stuff frankly imitative of Irish and Scottish ballads, like "Beautiful Dreamer" and "(I Dream of) Jeanie with the Light Brown Hair." But as well liked as those songs were, it's his minstrel music that was and remains most popular. "Oh! Susannah," "Camptown Races," "My Old Kentucky Home, Good-Night!" and "The Old Folks at Home" ("Way Down Upon the Swanee River"); "Old Uncle Ned," "Old Black Joe" and "Nelly Was a Lady"; "Nelly Bly," "Ring, Ring de Banjo!" and "Massa's in de Cold Ground" were all huge hits. In these songs, Foster is often credited with inventing the formula for American pop music. He mixed bits of African-American musicality with elements of that Scots-Irish balladry, and German polkas, and Italian opera arias, and so forth, then laid on some sentimental, romantic or nostalgic lyrics, to create hits that were indisputably American and of widest possible appeal.

Foster's a good example of what a complex of White neuroses the minstrel show could be. He liked minstrel music, but not the vulgarities of the minstrel show, and he was conflicted about his participation in it throughout his brief but stellar career. From his first minstrel hits in 1848, he introduced an uncommon gentility and humanity to the genre. Coming from Pittsburgh, a center of abolitionism, he had a close friend who was an abolitionist, and who seems to have ridden his conscience about it. "My Old Kentucky Home" grew out of an earlier effort, "Poor Uncle Tom, Good Night," written after Foster had been deeply moved by *Uncle Tom's Cabin.* His melodies were always pretty, whether upbeat thigh-slappers or lachrymose ballads, and the stories he told in his lyrics were unusually sweet and kind, even though he employed standard minstrel-show language and imagery. Compare "Old Uncle Ned," an early song, with some of the other minstrel lyrics we've been reading:

> *There was an old Nigger, his name was Uncle Ned,*
> *He's dead long ago, long ago,*
> *He had no wool on de top ob his head,*
> *De place whar de wool ought to grow . . .*

> *When Old Ned die, Massa take it mighty bad,*
> *De tears run down like de rain,*
> *Old Missus turn pale and she look'd berry sad,*
> *Kase she nebber see Old Ned again.*

Compare the lovers in "Nelly Was a Lady" with Rose and Sambo:

Nelly was a lady,
Last night she died,
Toll de bell for lubly Nell,
My dark Virginny bride.

Now I'm unhappy and I'm weeping,
*   Can't tote de cotton-wood no more;*
Last night, while Nelly was a sleeping,
*   Death came a knockin' at de door . . .*

Down in de meadow 'mong de clober,
*   Walk wid my Nelly by my side;*
Now all dem happy days am ober,
*   Farewell, my dark Virginny bride.*

Still, while sympathetic and humane, Foster's fantasies of the plantation could also be awfully naive and patronizing, as in one of the songs his fans rarely mention today, "Massa's in de Cold Ground":

Round de meadows am a ringing
De darkeys' mournful song,
While de mocking-bird am singing,
Happy as de day am long.
Where de ivy am a creeping
O'er de grassy mound,
Dare old massa am a sleeping,
Sleeping in de cold, cold ground.

Down in de corn-field
Hear dat mournful sound:
All de darkeys am a weeping —
Massa's in de cold, cold ground. . . .

The strains of weepiness and morbid sentimentality that run through Foster's work reflect the hardships of his own life. Though he was far and away the most popular songwriter of his day, that was no way to make a living in the mid-1800s. There were no provisions for "intellectual property rights" or songwriter's royalties, and the faster he cranked them out, the broker he got. Demoralized and alcoholic, he died with thirty-eight cents in his pocket, possibly from complications after a drunken fall, at the age of only thirty-seven.

Foster never consciously worked the plantation fantasy for the pernicious effect many other minstrels did. Images of happy darkies serenading their kindly massa and missus encoded the political message that Blacks were better off as slaves than free. Implicitly anti-emancipation in the years before the war, this imagery was also an excuse for supporting the apartheid system of Jim Crow from the 1870s on. At a time when many Blacks were fleeing the economic hardships and increasing brutality of the South, songs like "I'se Gwine Back to Dixie" ("I miss de ole plantation, / My home and my relation") and "I Want to See the Old Home" were basically telling them to go back where they came from:

> I've wandered very far away
> From the clime where I was born,
> And my poor heart has been so sad,
> Dejected and forlorn;
> No master kind, to treat me well,
> To cheer me when in pain,
> I want to see the cotton fields,
> And the dear old home again.

BLACK PERFORMERS PARTICIPATED IN MINSTRELSY FROM its earliest days. According to one legend (remembering that minstrel history is full of competing and conflicting legends, not to mention PR puffery), "Jump Jim Crow" was an authentic Negro folk song sung by Black banjoist John "Picayune" Butler on the streets of New Orleans, where it was heard by George Nichols, a blackface circus clown, who later taught it to T. D. Rice. Butler came to lower Manhattan in the 1840s, where he played in many competitions and taught many White minstrel banjoists. Fittingly, he himself became the hero of a hit minstrel song of the 1850s, "Picayune Butler's Come to Town." Another Black New Orleans street performer, known as Old Corn Meal, was said to have taught Nichols several tunes, including the one that became internationally known as "Ole Zip Coon."

By far the most famous Black performer associated with antebellum minstrelsy was the reel and jig dancer William Henry Lane, who went down in history as Master Juba. The juba was a West African step-dance the slaves brought with them and spread throughout the Caribbean and the Southern plantations, where it became known as "patting juba," because the slaves, denied drums by Massa—who feared they were using their "jungle drums" to communicate and plot rebellion—kept time by patting or slapping their bodies. The ban on drums also prompted the development of the bones and jawbone. Much like Jim Crow, Juba became a character as well as a dance, as in this song:

> *Juba dis and Juba dat,*
> *Juba kill a yaller cat.*
> *Juba up and Juba down,*
> *Juba runnin' all around.*

The juba was eminently adaptable to the White folks' jigs and reels, and Lane was its preeminent performer. He seems to have been born a free Black in New England. By the early 1840s he was in the Five Points, dancing at places like Almack's, where he apparently impressed Dickens. Soon he was touring America and England with

White minstrel troupes, probably performing in blackface. He was tremendously popular and even earned top billing at some venues, a first for a Black minstrel performer. Other Black dancers who toured with minstrel groups included "Japanese Tommy," a dwarf, who also sang and played the fiddle. Of course, their moves were studied and imitated by scores of blackfaced White dancers.

After the Civil War, Black performers by the hundreds flooded into minstrelsy. This would be viewed disdainfully later, with the idea that Blacks who participated in the demeaning institution of minstrelsy were race traitors. This is a very simplistic point of view, and anyway it's always easy to assume the moral high ground with the benefit of hindsight. Actually it makes total sense that Black performers would want to join the minstrel tradition. They'd been enjoying and variously helping create the genre for half a century. Now they could perform it professionally, make a living at it, travel the world doing it—who wouldn't? Professional opportunities for Black performers and composers were rare otherwise. There were a few famous Black opera singers and classical musicians in the latter 1800s, but only a few, and they were treated as exotic novelties. The minstrel stage, for all that it was "low" culture, proved to be quite open to Black talent. In one sense, we can almost say that the blackfaced White performers of the antebellum period were paving the way for the actual Black ones who came along after the war.

Stage adaptations of *Uncle Tom's Cabin* integrated large groups of Blacks with blackfaced Whites; Black stars eventually assumed the leading roles of Uncle Tom and Topsy. The Georgia Minstrels, a company of former slaves formed in 1865 by White impresario W. H. Lee, is believed to be the first Black minstrel troupe; a rival group of the same name was formed shortly thereafter by minstrelsy's first Black entrepreneur, Charles "Barney" Hicks. He was a light-skinned man who could pass for White, which probably explains how he could successfully negotiate in the White world of show business. Even so, he was ultimately squeezed out, and his troupe taken over by White managers. But a number of other Black managers founded troupes and successfully toured them throughout the remainder of the minstrel show's history. They often performed in blackface, though some groups forsook the burnt cork from early on. The presence of real Black performers on minstrel stages across the country, many of them ex-slaves, helped somewhat to alleviate the more fantastical and stereotypical excesses of their White colleagues.

The work of Black songwriter James A. Bland (1854–1911) rivaled Stephen Foster's for popularity and ubiquity. "At the height of his fame," Eileen Southern writes, he was "advertised as 'The World's Greatest Minstrel Man' and 'The Idol of the Music Halls.' His songs were sung by all the minstrels—black and white—by college students, and by the American people in their homes and on the streets. Most of them did not even know that they were singing songs written by a black man. The big white stars of minstrelsy for whom he wrote often published the songs under their own names." Southern adds that the same can be said of Foster, and many other minstrel songwriters.

Like them, Bland had little firsthand knowledge of the plantation life he evoked in his most famous songs, like "Carry Me Back to Old Virginny" and "Oh! Dem Golden Slippers." Born in Flushing, New York, he was raised in Washington, D.C., where his college-educated father worked at the U.S. Patent Office. Bland studied liberal arts at Howard University, but threw it over for a life on the stage. He toured with several Black minstrel shows, and wrote something like seven hundred songs. But like Foster, he died penniless, to be buried in an unmarked grave. In the twentieth century, "Carry Me Back to Old Virginny" was made the state song of Virginia, with lines like "There's where the old darkey's heart am long'd to go, / There's where I labored so hard for old massa" amended to whitewash the song's blackface legacy. In the face of increasing controversy, the Commonwealth dropped the song in 1997.

Dan Lewis, another Black composer, wrote popular minstrel hits including "Way Over Yonder," "Moses Cart Dem Melon Down" and "The Coons Are on Parade." Singer-actor-songwriter Sam Lucas and the Hyers Sisters were among the most popular Black entertainers of the minstrel stage. Lucas earned international renown for portraying Uncle Tom, toured with the Hyers in all-Black musicals, and wrote such songs as "Oh, I'll Meet You Dar," "Every Day'll Be Sunday By and By" and "Carve Dat Possum." Billy Kersands, a dancer who toured with Bland in the all-Black Haverly's Genuine Colored Minstrels and also formed his own company, popularized a shuffling step known as the Virginia essence—the "soft-shoe." In addition to Black minstrel shows, there were several popular companies of Black "jubilee singers," whose repertoires of spirituals and church music, traditional and new, were popular with both White and Black audiences.

FROM 1865 THROUGH THE 1880S, THE MINSTREL SHOW dominated American entertainment, and was enormously popular in the British Isles and Europe as well. Giant minstrel troupes roamed the landscape the way the dinosaurs had ruled the Jurassic. All the big cities had their resident troupes; at one point New York City had ten.

Minstrel music also took over the middle-class parlor room. Sheet music for minstrel-show hits sold as many as 100,000 copies. In minstrelsy's final years, piano rolls and phonograph cylinders disseminated sentimental late-model minstrel ballads like "Bless My Swanee River Home," "The Pickaninnies' Paradise" and the iconic "My Mammy." What had begun as noisy youth music achieved, in its mature years, something very like Victorian respectability, suitable for the whole family.

As it did, the blackface mask became increasingly transparent. Posters and sheet music for minstrel shows often juxtaposed portraits of their star entertainers in blackface and without it, side by side. Peekaboo. Sometimes, just to make absolutely sure the audience got it, the blackface portraits would be labeled "As Plantation Darkeys," the whiteface ones "As Citizens." The point that this was theater, artifice, artistry, created for and by respectable White folks, couldn't have been made more graphic. Historian Stephanie Dunston argues that these images played a critical role in the acceptance of minstrel sheet music into the home, where the genteel lady of the house and her daughters played the piano in the parlor. "Representations of upstanding, well-groomed white performers began to appear along with the grotesque black characters they portrayed. . . . Cover illustrations seem to position the dapper entertainers as gentlemen callers, politely awaiting introduction into the refined space of the family parlor."

We can see how deeply minstrelsy had invaded polite society in an issue of the *Brooklyn Eagle* from 1893, reporting waggishly about an amateur minstrel show that a group of society ladies were planning to stage as a benefit for a children's hospital. The anonymous author imagined the typical boorish male telling the women, "Oh, well, there's one thing you women can't do. You can't run a nigger minstrel show." Which of course only made the ladies more determined to black up, grab the tambourine and bones, and prove him wrong.

Although it took its sweet time fading away (and never really disappeared altogether), the minstrel show's dominance was faltering by 1890. After half a century of ubiquity it had outlived its welcome, and gradually surrendered to two newer forms of entertainment, vaudeville and ragtime.

Vaudeville grew out of the same low-class variety theater that had sponsored minstrelsy, adapting the variety-show format into family-oriented entertainment in the 1880s. Writing in 1905, journalist Hartley Davis left us a wonderfully wry description of what "variety theater" had been like:

The stage performances that gave only a variety bill started on a pretty low plane, because managers sought to attract by them only those who had no respectable prejudices, to whom coarseness, evil jokes, and atrocious pantomime appealed most quickly. The variety theatres scattered through the country were dives for the most part, places frequented by men of the lowest order of intelligence. There was a stock company of a dozen or more poor painted women who appeared in the "First Part," like that of a minstrel show, but the strength of the show was in the olio, a variety performance given by traveling performers. There were "knockabout" teams, who drove home each joke by batting each other all over the stage, a form of fun that endures to this day, to the sad concern of optimistic philosophers, though the cynics have rejoiced in it. It merely exemplifies the painful fact that there is nothing which will provoke such immediate and spontaneous laughter as the physical mishap of another. And there was always a "seriocomic" singer, who usually warbled something about being "happy for to meet you" and "I'll not detain you long," with a reference to a "little shady dell." At least, it was nearly always "dell," and pretty sure to be shady. There were also musical acts and acrobatic acts—in fact, the general idea was practically the same as that which prevails today. But there is a vast difference in the character of the shows.

Three or four times a year a variety show would be presented in the first-class theatres by companies made up by the managers of the few really high-class variety theatres that were even then in existence, like Tony Pastor's in New York, Hyde & Behman's in Brooklyn, and the Howard Athenaeum in Boston, but these did not even try to combat popular prejudice. The existence of the average variety theatre was regarded as a reproach to a community, and with justice.

Davis, like other journalists of the period, credited a Boston impresario, B. F. Keith (the B. F. was for Benjamin Franklin), with creating vaudeville as we'd recognize it today. The term "vaudeville"—

supposedly derived from "Val de Vire," the name of an area of France long associated with lively songs—had been knocking around the United States since the opening of Boston's Vaudeville Saloon in 1840. A former circus and sideshow barker, Keith opened a dime museum (a kind of stationary sideshow) in Boston in 1883, where he hosted such acts as Baby Alice the Midget Wonder, along with performances of *Uncle Tom's Cabin* and other popular fare. It was not an entirely new idea; Barnum had profited from a similar mix of the freak show with more wholesome and uplifting fare at his American Museum well before the Civil War. Still, Davis quips, the scheme held special appeal in Keith's hometown, "where an honest belief in hypocrisy makes of that vice almost a virtue. Your true Bostonian is the sincerest individual that ever strove for light against fettering environment and tradition."

From the dime museum Keith went on to open the Bijou Theatre, where he claimed to have invented the "continuous performance" format—numerous variety acts performing in constant rotation throughout the day, with audiences free to drift in and out. Again, Barnum had done very similarly decades earlier. Keith may have been the first, at any rate, to put the idea into a theater and give it the classy-sounding name of vaudeville, also known as "polite vaudeville," to hammer home its distinction from vulgar entertainments. From Boston, Keith expanded his franchise into New York, Philadelphia and other cities; the idea was quickly copied by other impresarios and spread across the country—the Orpheum circuit in the West, the Palace chain, the Pantages and Paramount theaters.

By 1890 vaudeville was challenging the giant minstrel shows for supremacy, and by 1900 had replaced them as the dominant form of American mass entertainment. It's said that at its highest point, in the 1920s, there were something like 20,000 vaudeville acts crisscrossing the continent, playing to as many as two million paying customers a day. Clearly vaudeville had reached the oversaturation level, and it finally collapsed of its own weight in the early 1930s, helped to its grave by movies, which were cheaper, and radio, which was free, not to mention the sudden onslaught of the Depression. Many of the great vaudeville houses survived as movie theaters.

"For the benefit of those who have never enjoyed a vaudeville show of the continuous order," Keith wrote in 1898, "I might explain that it is designed to run twelve hours, during which period performers appear two or three times, as it would be manifestly impossible to secure enough different acts to fill out the dozen hours. The best class of artists appear twice, just as at a matinee and evening performance in a dramatic theatre, and the balance do three 'turns.'" As befitting the classy setting, Keith established "a fixed policy of cleanliness and order," and mandated that "the stage show must be free from vulgarisms and coarseness of any kind, so that the house and entertainment would directly appeal to the support of ladies and children." A bill featuring "light, frothy acts, with no particular plot, but abounding in songs, dances, bright dialogue and clean repartee" might also include pseudoeducational lectures, such as "'The Arctic Moon,' a relic of the Greeley expedition which was presented to me by Lieutenant Brainerd [sic]," along with acrobats and "equilibrists," jugglers, strongmen, magicians, mentalists, trained seals (or dogs or birds or other animals), horseback riders, regurgitators, ventriloquists, "the Living Picture production, the song-sheet novelty and the Biograph, the most improved of the motion-picture inventions." (The Greely expedition of 1881 was a harrowing attempt by the U.S. Army to establish a meteorological station in the Arctic. Of twenty-six participants, only six survived, including a Sergeant Brainard. Regurgitator acts were what the name suggests. The Living Picture and song-sheet novelty were some sort of tableau vivant or pantomime.)

As vaudeville and the minstrel shows intersected, minstrels White and Black performed on both stages. Blackface singers and comedians were featured on virtually every vaudeville bill through much of its reign. In the 1900s, when the touring minstrel shows had dwindled to a meager handful, vaudeville kept blackface minstrelsy alive, returning it to its roots as a novelty act on a variety stage. Just reading the titles of some of the comedy sketches tells you all you need to know about the quality of the humor: "Where's Mah Pants?" and "Chicken Lifters' Convention," "One Hambone for Two" and "Two Scared Coons."

It's important to remember that on the vaudeville stage these blackfaced "Ethiopians" rubbed elbows with various other brands of broadly played ethnic stereotypes and impersonations, for equally low laughs—the brawling Irish, wheedling Jews, oily Italians, thick-headed Germans, inscrutable Chinamen, gullible country rubes and so on. Maybe we should call these greenface, jewface, pasta-face, potatoface, yellowface and rubeface. "The Irish characters are drunk, belligerent, and dumb (dumb was the term commonly used in the comedy—it meant stupid or unintelligent, but it also meant culturally naive, 'green' or bewildered, 'unhip' as well). The Italians are happy rascals, promiscuous, profligate, and irresponsible, comically hyperemotional—and dumb; the Germans, usually called 'Dutch' in vaudeville from the same corruption of Deutsch which gave us the Pennsylvania Dutch, are lazy, stodgily conservative, and of course, also dumb. Blacks are lazy, dishonest, promiscuous, profligate, irresponsible and— guess what—dumb. Jews are usually 'canny' . . . that is, they are smart in the sense of too clever, manipulative, dishonest—but they are also portrayed, perhaps surprisingly, as dumb, especially as lacking in 'street smarts,' and potential suckers. Jewish men are also particularly weak, cowardly, the victims of bullies (including Jewish women). . . . Blacks are associated with an insatiable desire for watermelon, chicken, or pork chops; Italian immigrants are associated with crime and huge families; 'Dutchmen' with sauerkraut and beer, and so forth."

I think the blackface vaudevillian must be seen in the context of these greenface, jewface, pastaface, potato face, yellowface, rubeface and other faces. America is an experiment in offering the members of many disparate tribal groups the opportunity to get along, fight for their rights, and work for their rewards. Nobody can force us to like one another, but we are expected to tolerate one another, allow one another our equal rights and opportunities. Until the rise of multiculturalism and identity politics encouraged everybody to be "offended" by everything all the time, it was presumed that earning a spot for yourself was a rough-and-tumble procedure. It took a thick skin and a sense of humor. Other people were going to make fun of you—your accent, the way your cooking smelled, the way you dressed—and you made fun of them back. As mentioned before, the earliest European explorers to Africa and the Africans they met told jokes at each other's expense. So did the Indians and the earliest colonists to America.

In vaudeville, greenface cracked wise about jewface, jewface caricatured yellowface, rubeface guffawed at blackface, and everyone told Polack jokes. Everyone can be ignunt. You had to give as good as you got. Sometimes you duked it out on the streets. Sometimes you worked it out on the stage.

Vaudeville was America's most popular form of mass entertainment at a time when the melting pot was on high boil. The very term "melting pot," with the assimilation process it signifies, was coined in the theater of the era—it was the title of a very successful 1908 play by Israel Zangwill. Between the Great Migration of Blacks from the rural South into the Northern cities, and the influx of wave after wave of new "foreigners"—Jewish, Irish, Italian, Polish and so forth—issues of race and ethnicity were much on the minds and close to the hearts of all Americans. Especially in the cities, so many people were new, so many were rubes. People were openly, unabashedly curious about one another. People gawked at one another. Sometimes they snickered or sneered or laughed outright, too.

The vaudeville theater was a space where they could come together and stare at one another. In a primitive and limited way, vaudeville was as "multicultural" and "diverse" as any university campus is today. I'm not being facetious. Universities today routinely champion the notion that simply by being on a "diverse" campus, where you may encounter fellow students who do not come from the same tribe as you, your worldview will be enriched and you will become a better, more "sensitive" person. Easily affordable entertainment for the masses, vaudeville brought members of disparate tribes together both in the audience and on the stage. Audiences of workers and immigrants and families, of various descents and heritages, watched images of themselves and others onstage, sometimes in knockabout comic caricature, sometimes singing a familiar ballad or air from the Old Country (maybe your Old Country, maybe someone else's), sometimes overemoting in a tearjerking vignette. They laughed at themselves and at one another, bawled over one another's tragedies, went out humming scraps of one another's music. It didn't mean that they all loved one another, but it bred a certain familiarity, a starting point for tolerance.

For everyone except Black people. Black performers were sharing the stage with all those others, but that's about all they were allowed to share. Offstage, no matter how elegantly they dressed and danced onstage, they were still niggers. They couldn't stay in the same hotels as their colleagues. They couldn't go to a restaurant with them after the show for a mug of beer and a plate of chops. In general, if there were Black people in the vaudeville audience, they were segregated to the balcony—called "nigger heaven" by White theater managers. For newly arrived immigrants, mixing it up in vaudeville theaters was one part of the process of becoming assimilated and recognized as White, melting into the American pot. Blacks were still outcasts and beyond the pale, pun intended. A society of disparate member groups often seeks cohesion by organizing against an Other; it defines who belongs and is included by clearly specifying who does not belong and is excluded. America had designated Blacks as the Other long before the new great wave of immigrants at the turn of the twentieth century, and so they remained until they forced their way in through the civil rights movement.

So the vaudeville stage presented images of an integrated America that were a theatrical fantasy, a lie. But maybe it also was presenting an ideal, an image of possibility, of the future. Pop culture in America does have this way of offering images that are both unrealistic *and* idealistic—not true reflections of reality today, but sometimes hints of reality tomorrow.

Vaudeville certainly did not portray a UNICEF vision of impossible ethnic harmony; the various peoples represented on its stages were always knocking one another's hats off, making fun of one another, outfoxing and cheating one another. Much more like real life. America is an experiment in mutt culture. No one—at least no one before the present era of automatic tribal entitlements—said it would be easy. No one today has read Zangwill's *The Melting Pot,* so when we hear the term we think of the kitchen, a big pot where everybody's racial and ethnic differences dissolve into one big soup. Zangwill was more realistic than that. He wasn't evoking the kitchen, but something more like the steel mill. His melting pot was an industrial crucible, a *smelting* pot where the "metals" of various races and ethnicities would be hot-forged and hammered into a newer, stronger national identity, the American alloy. He didn't picture us all sitting down together for supper. He saw us rolling up our sleeves and working at it—working to create ourselves.

IN 1890, A MINSTREL AND VAUDEVILLIAN NAMED ERNEST Hogan sparked a national sensation with his song "All Coons Look Alike to Me." Set to the jaunty, newfangled rhythms of ragtime music—which in 1890 sounded as noisy and vulgar to refined listeners as "Jump Jim Crow" had in 1832, or "Hound Dog" would in 1956—this new craze, called "coon songs," took Negro stereotyping to levels of hateful, grinning crudity that even the worst minstrel shows had rarely achieved. By the end of the decade, when Lew Dockstader scored a hit singing "Coon! Coon! Coon!," an estimated six hundred coon songs had been published, and they continued to be popular until World War I.

Ernest Hogan, by the way, was Black.

Coon songs are relics of their time. Relations between Blacks and Whites had deteriorated to new lows by the 1890s. Jim Crow laws held the races more separate than they'd ever been, promoting hatred and fear; lynchings and other acts of racist violence were on the rise in the South; workers and new immigrants in Northern cities fretted that Blacks fleeing from the wasted rural South would take jobs away from them; resurgent White supremacists and nativists hated them all. Reflecting and exploiting these conditions, coon songs reduced Blacks to a small set of exaggeratedly iconic physical features—kinky hair, outrageously thick lips, bulging white eyes etc.— and comical activities—stealing chickens, smacking those lips over watermelons etc. You can hear it in the lyrics and see it in the shockingly vulgar sheet-music illustrations for songs with titles like "Little Alabama Coon," "Every Race Has a Flag But a Coon," "You Ain't the Kind ob Coon I's Lookin Fo,'" "If the Man in the Moon Were a Coon" and, most amazing of all, "You May Be a Hawaiian on Broadway, but You're Just Another Nigger to Me." That many coon songs were written and performed by Black entertainers would be a source of great shame and astonishment to later generations who didn't know what it was like to be Black and in showbiz in that era. But White songwriters joined in heartily, many of them unable to claim the slightest familiarity with the "coons" they were writing about. "If the Man in the Moon Were a Coon," for example, was written in 1906 by a German immigrant, Fred Fisher, who'd come from Cologne to Tin Pan Alley just six years earlier. He would go on to write the hits "Oh, You Beautiful Doll," "Peg o' My Heart" and "Your Feet's Too Big," and be the subject of of a 1949 Hollywood biopic.

The greatest Black minstrel of them all, Bert Williams, sang his share of coon songs, enjoying a long career in minstrelsy and vaudeville, on Broadway and in silent films. Like most other minstrels, he had no direct experience of the South. Born on the island of Antigua in 1875, he moved to New York and then California with his family as a boy. Forced to abandon his college study of civil engineering to earn a living, he turned his self-taught musical acumen and gift for comic mimicry into a lifelong career. As a foreigner, Williams observed the music, movements, voices and dialects of American Negroes with a sympathetic but detached curiosity not unlike that of Whites, which may explain why he seems never to have been ashamed to wear blackface: it was just clown makeup to him. In the 1890s he teamed up with song-and-dance man George Walker, and the duo became famous from the vaudeville circuit to Broadway. When illness broke up the act in 1909, Williams went on to be the highest-paid star—and only Black star—of the Ziegfeld Follies through the 1910s; he appeared in silent movies, and went out the way a showman should, collapsing onstage in mid-song in 1922.

Williams' trademark character was Mr. Nobody, whose magnificently sad-sack song would later be sung by everyone from Nina Simone to Johnny Cash:

> *When life seems full of clouds and rain,*
> *And I am filled with naught but pain,*
> *Who soothes my thumping, bumping brain?*
> *Nobody!*

> *When winter comes with snow and sleet,*
> *And me with hunger and cold feet,*
> *Who says, "Here's two bits, go and eat"?*
> *Nobody!*

> CHORUS
> *Ain't never done nothin' to nobody;*
> *I ain't never got nothin' from nobody, no time;*
> *And until I get somethin' from somebody, sometime,*
> *I don't intend to do nothin' for nobody no time.*

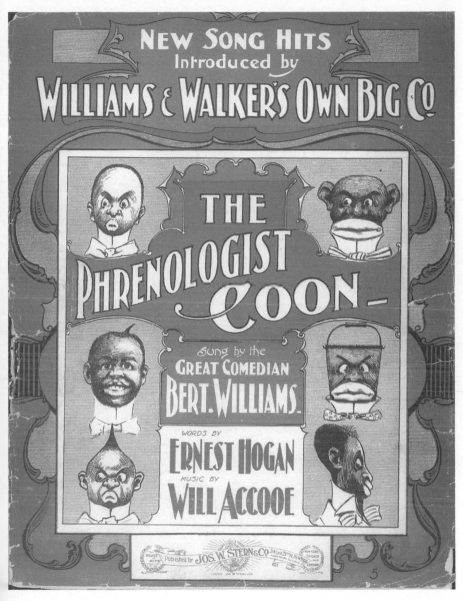

A Bert Williams hit of 1901.

(Courtesy Library of Congress)

For his adherence to blackface and the coon song tradition, Williams is often depicted as either a race traitor or a tragic Uncle Tom. It's true his partner was less sanguine about the blackface buffoonery: "Nothing seemed more absurd than to see a colored man making himself ridiculous in order to portray himself," George Walker said. But Williams was first and foremost a showman, and he accepted the conventions of the day, including the humiliations. One of the saddest stories told about him goes like this:

> On Aug. 23, 1919, Actors Equity declared a strike against New York stage productions, immediately darkening pretty much every theater in town.
>
> Bert Williams reported for work that night anyway.
>
> He didn't intend to cross the picket line. He just didn't know it existed.
>
> Despite 20-plus years as one of the most successful and respected stage performers in New York, Williams had never been invited to join Actors Equity.
>
> That was because he was, in the parlance of the day, colored.

When Williams' friend and admirer W. C. Fields heard the story, he pressured Equity into admitting Williams. Fields later would say that Williams "was the funniest man I ever saw. And the saddest man I ever knew."

Negro artists like Eubie Blake and Noble Sissle were performing on the vaudeville circuit without blackface from the late 1910s on. Blake and Sissle were billed as the Dixie Duo, even though, like so many others, they had only a glancing familiarity with the South: Blake was a Baltimorean, Sissle from Indianapolis. That did not stop them from writing ragtime coon songs like "Mammy's Lit'l Choc'late Cullud Chile" and "Gee, I'm Glad That I'm from Dixie."

In addition to Black artists appearing in vaudeville, a separate "chitlin circuit" developed for "Negro vaudeville," in which all-Black casts performed for Black audiences. In the rural Midwest and South, they played more often in churches and tents than in theaters or music halls. But they also toured Black-owned theaters, as on the twenty-six-city Dudley circuit maintained by the Black impresario Sherman H. Dudley, and the more grueling White-owned T.O.B.A. circuit. The initials stood for Theatre Owners Booking Association, but Black vaudevillians said it meant Tough on Black Asses. (The T.O.B.A. circuit is not to be confused with the so-called Toby shows, tent theaters that toured the countryside with simple melodramas and rustic comedies for usually all-White audiences of farm families from around 1900 into the 1930s.) The Apollo in Harlem opened in 1934 as a Negro vaudeville theater, which in some ways it has remained. Other famous stops on the chitlin circuit were the Regal in Chicago, the Royal in Baltimore and D.C.'s Howard. Josephine

George Walker, Ada Walker and Bert Williams.
In Dahomey, 1903.

Baker, Stepin Fetchit, Ma Rainey, Bessie Smith, Bill "Bojangles" Robinson, Ethel Waters and Jackie "Moms" Mabley, to name a few, started out in Negro vaudeville and "crossed over" to White audiences. During the Depression, the WPA in Philadelphia sponsored separate White and Black vaudeville troupes.

Not surprisingly, Black and White vaudevillians studied one another's routines and freely "borrowed" elements they admired. That's showbiz. This cross-pollination is sometimes presented as having been entirely one-sided: just another collection of White performers ripping off more innovative Black ones. (In his book *Hip: The History,* John Leland wittily refers to this as the myth of "the white boy who stole the blues.") It certainly happened a lot. Fred Astaire and Shirley Temple learned how to tap-dance from Bill Robinson; it's claimed in some quarters that Abbott and Costello stole their "Who's on first?" routine from Black vaudeville comedians; and so on. But as with minstrelsy, the influences worked both ways. The slim, elegant dance team Vernon and Irene Castle (Astaire's chief influence) were the model for popular, "high-class" and often high-yellow Black pairs like Norton and Margot, and Johnson and Dean, who incorporated into their acts such White-identified dances as the waltz and ballet. Singer Sissieretta Jones became renowned as "the Black Patti," a reference to her vocal resemblance to the hugely popular Italian soprano Adelina Patti. Jones sang her opera arias in vaudeville, where she led the Black Patti Troubadours from 1896 to 1915, and at Benjamin Harrison's White House. And obviously the whole field of Black vaudeville was a spin-off of something created by White impresarios and artists. When it comes to show business, who's on first is often a very good question indeed.

It fits our pattern of confusion and complexity that the same Black composers and performers who abetted the coon songs' vulgarities also invented a new kind of all-Black musical theater, in which they could gradually edge the portrayal of Negro life away from flat stereotypes toward something more humane and realistic.

The landmark *Creole Show* toured from 1890 to 1897, starring at various times the great Sam Lucas and the dance team of Charles Johnson and Dora Dean. While still within the minstrel-show format, it featured a shocking innovation—a female Interlocutor. The producer of *The Creole Show* experimented further with *The Octoroons* (1896), which packaged the minstrel-variety show within a framing story line. It produced a hit coon song with a reverse-coon message, "No Coon Can Come Too Black for Me."

In 1898 the team of Bob Cole and Billy Johnson began a highly successful tour of their musical comedy revue *A Trip to Coontown.* (The title played on that of a hit musical comedy from 1891, *A Trip to Chinatown,* which produced the hit song "After the Ball," borrowed by Oscar Hammerstein and Jerome Kern to give their 1927 *Show Boat* a Gay Nineties flavor.) That same year Oberlin-trained composer Will Marion Cook collaborated with Black poet Paul Laurence Dunbar (see the next chapter) on *Clorindy, or, The Origin of the Cake-Walk,* the first all-Black musical revue on Broadway, with Ernest Hogan in the lead. Both shows relied heavily on coon songs like "The Wedding of the Chinee and the Coon" and "Who Dat Say Chicken in Dis Crowd." Cook had studied in Europe with Dvořák; his mother was an Oberlin graduate. He later recalled that when she heard him working out the songs for *Clorindy,* she cried, "Oh Will! Will! I've sent you all over the world to study and become a great musician, and you return such a nigger!"

Over the next few years, Williams and Walker would score with several musical revues, including *Sons of Ham,* featuring the coon songs "My Little Zulu Babe" and "The Phrenologist Coon" (by Ernest Hogan). In 1902 they teamed up with Cook and Dunbar for *In Dahomey,* a return-to-Africa musical comedy that produced a number of hits, including "Evah Dahkey Is a King":

Evah dahkey is a king!
Royalty is jes' de ting

Ef yo' social life's a bungle
Jes' you' go back to yo jungle
An' remember dat a yo' daddy was a King!

That's probably not what Marcus Garvey would have in mind with his pan-African movement, but the idea that Blacks were as good as, or better than, White folks, even if it was delivered with a buck and a wing, was rather challenging. In fact, these Black musicals had been slipping subversive ideas like that in among the coon songs since *A Trip to Coontown*. This was the finale of that show, "No Coons Allowed!"

There's a dead swell gentleman of color
Saved up all the money he could find
He call'd one night and said to his baby
"My Lulu gal we'll go and cut a shine."

He put her in a cab and told the driver
"To drive us to the swellest place in town
I'm gwine to buy my gal a fine supper
So I want the finest place that can be found."

To a swell restaurant the driver took them
With his Lulu gal he started in so proud
But that coon almost went blind
When he saw a great big sign
Up o'er the door which read
"No coons allowed."

CHORUS
No coons allowed
No coons allowed
This place is meant for white folks that's all
We don't want no kinky-head kind

So move on darky down the line
No coons allow'd in here at all.

The gentleman hires a lawyer to take the restaurant to court.

So the lawyer took the coon to the courthouse
And they started in the courthouse with a crowd
But his head began to swim
When he saw that sign again
O'er the courthouse door which read
"No coons allowed!"

In 1903, the publication of W. E. B. Du Bois' *The Souls of Black Folk* heralded the era of "the New Negro," which came to full flower in the explosion of artistic and intellectual activity of the Harlem Renaissance. Widely read and discussed, Du Bois' call for a truly Black aesthetic pushed Black musicals to be bolder, within the limitations placed on them. Cole and Johnson's 1907 *The Shoo-Fly Regiment,* about Black soldiers in the Spanish-American War, and Williams and Walker's 1908 *Bandana Land,* their last show together, continued to play with subversive notions and subtly undermined old images, even as they seemed to perpetuate them. They were theatrical exercises in the "double-consciousness" that Du Bois identified as the Black American's necessary survival strategy, speaking truth through a grinning mask.

Whites' appetite for "authentic" Black music, dance, nightlife—anything Black, really—became ravenous during the Roaring Twenties. Broadway and what then amounted to off-Broadway were inundated with Black musicals such as Blake and Sissle's 1921 *Shuffle Along,* which launched the hit "I'm Just Wild About Harry." That show broke down a couple of long-standing Broadway color bars: It showed Blacks in romantic love relationships, which had been considered taboo, and Black patrons were allowed to sit among the

White audience, instead of being banished to the balcony. Black musicals always struggled to find backers, and were not always box-office successes, but they kept on flowing. After *Shuffle Along* came *The Chocolate Dandies* (featuring Josephine Baker); *Strut, Miss Lizzie; Plantation Revue, Africana, Rang Tang, Oh Joy!, Runnin' Wild, Messin' Around, Hot Chocolates* (with music by Fats Waller), *Deep Harlem, Bamboola* and the smash *Blackbirds of 1928*, which spun off several more or less annual sequels. Although the Depression and World War II diminished the flow, Broadway still hosted *Porgy and Bess* in 1935, Eubie Blake's *Swing It* in 1937, *Cabin in the Sky* in 1940 and *Carmen Jones* in 1943. Broadway wouldn't see as many Black musicals again until the mid-1970s, when, interestingly, a number of them nostalgically evoked the heyday of the genre, *Ain't Misbehavin', Eubie, Sophisticated Ladies* and *Jelly's Last Jam* among these.

THE AMERICAN MINSTREL SHOW AS POPULAR ENTERTAIN-ment was effectively dead by World War I. Yet some old-timers con-tinued to peddle blackface minstrel songs into the 1930s and 1940s, as solo acts or as novelty turns. Nick Tosches investigates the career of one of these late minstrels, the White man Emmett Miller, in *Where Dead Voices Gather.*

It's one of the curious and fascinating twists of history that in the early years of the twentieth century, the main purveyors of the old-fashioned blackface minstrel tradition were Black performers, who'd come up wearing the blackface mask and were reluctant to give it up. Touring rural venues and small towns with traveling medicine shows and carnivals, many blackfaced Blacks continued to entertain audi-ences of Whites and/or Blacks (Whites on one side of the aisle, Blacks on the other) with traditional minstrel routines. Lincoln Perry, who would later be Hollywood's first Black superstar, under the name Stepin Fetchit, began his career this way as a teen, performing in a comedy-and-dance duo billed as Step & Fetchit. Dewey "Pigmeat"

Markham, best known for his signature routine "Here Come da Judge," although he performed exclusively for Black audiences until very late in his career, refused to abandon the blackface mask until the 1950s. It was as integral to his performance as any costume.

In England, the lavish minstrel show as professional theater held on much longer than in American cities. There, a weekly BBC TV program called *The Black and White Minstrel Show,* complete with blackface, was a record-setting success from 1958 to 1978.

Though the large, professional minstrel show barely survived into the twentieth century, it left many traces. Minstrel music had a profound and lasting influence on both jazz and country music, and through them would later make itself felt in rock & roll. As we'll see, the blackface minstrel jumped from the stage to the movie screen and other media.

And long after it died as professional entertainment, putting on an amateur minstrel show remained a popular—if increasingly furtive and guilty—pastime for White Americans into the 1970s. During World War II, the USO sent materials to military bases and hospitals overseas to serve as guides for amateur theatricals and musicals; they included lots of minstrel songs and jokes. Glee clubs and civic groups, fraternal organizations and PTA fund-raisers, schoolkids and factory workers, prison inmates and volunteer firemen blacked up, banged the tambourine, and traded jokes. How-to guidebooks were popular from around 1900. Harry L. Newton's *Laughland: A Merry Minstrel Book* of 1909 is 106 pages of corny (but interestingly, almost never racially oriented) jokes and a few all-purpose stump speeches. From a Canadian dealer on eBay, I purchased a typed, staple-bound, hand-illustrated how-to entitled "Gentlemen, Be Seated." It's from Toronto, undated but apparently from the 1940s, and its audience includes, clearly, civic organizations and social clubs:

"To the older fellow, the Minstrel Show holds the greatest appeal of all amateur theatricals. It gives him a chance to show his ability as a vocalist and an entertainer.

"As negro entertainers have always been the most popular with the general public, the Minstrel Show ranks first as a revenue producer.

"As a means of promoting good fellowship among fellows, it is without equal. Everyone, at some time or other has felt the urge to 'blacken up'."

The pamphlet advises on organizing, writing and rehearsing the show. It offers tips for simple costumes and wigs. It suggests familiar songs that may be included: "Old Black Joe, Uncle Ned and Dixie Land have the desired effect. It is not essential that you use negro songs but they are really the best."

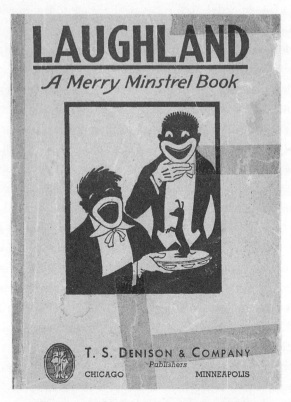

Do-it-yourself minstrel-show routines, 1909.

The notes and illustrations for blackening up indicate how simple the procedure is:

"If you follow the instructions as illustrated below, you will have no trouble in blackening up. First make a ring around your mouth as in figure 1. then blacken the whole face right into the hair. Do not forget the back of neck and ears. It is best to use cold cream before applying the black although you can get black that will come off easily without the use of cold cream. The best black that can be recommended is Lockwoods Burnt Cork."

The pamphlet handily offers a few dozen jokes your Interlocutor and endmen may choose from to build their banter. As in *Laughland*, few have anything to do with race, but those that do are doozies. In one, a character says he ate silver polish for breakfast because he heard that every dark cloud has a silver lining. In another, the Interlocutor asks the endman Henry what he was doing traveling around with the circus last summer. "Why, I was the lion tamer," Henry replies. Asked how he tamed the lion, Henry avers, "Why, I just walked right into the lion's cage and looked him square in the eye and he was tamed." The other endman, George, interjects, "Mr. Interlocutor, Henry ain't no lion tamer, *he's a lying nigger.*"

As late as September 1951 (a month before I was born), an American magazine called *Children's Playmate* ran a centerfold how-to for kids who wanted to stage their own minstrel shows. A Baltimore friend of mine recalls that into the 1960s his dad and his dad's friends would occasionally have a bit too much to drink on lazy weekend afternoons and would stage impromptu blackface revues in the backyards of their all-Italian neighborhood. Blacked up with shoe polish, the dads would sing X-rated lyrics to popular songs with some Southern feel to them. One example my friend remembers is the classic "Nothing could be finer than to be in her vagina in the morning, / Nothing could be sweeter than her lips around my peter in the morning."

In the journal *CounterPunch* in 2003, Michael D. Yates recorded uneasy memories of participating in a student minstrel show in 1959, when he was a high school freshman in the small industrial town of Ford City, Pennsylvania. The show was organized by an affable English teacher known to his students as Skinny.

"The minstrel show was a great success; not a single teacher or administrator criticized it," Yates writes. "We were all proud of our budding acting talents. We had enjoyed putting on black face and dressing in outlandish costumes. Best of all, we had relished being allowed to talk in front of a large audience the way the actors on 'Amos

Amateur minstrelsy continued well into
the twentieth century.

and Andy' talked. We were assured that what we had done was good when my friend, the 'expert,' told us that he had talked to a black girl in our grade, and she had told him that she had not been offended."

Yates goes on to write, "I can say now that I do not think that I have ever done something which has shamed me more than the minstrel show. I do not remember that it bothered me then, but it has bothered me a good deal since. The grossness of it, the inhumanity of it, the way in which it degraded not just my black classmates but all black people, the completely casual way in which Skinny assigned it and we did it, all of these things make me sick now."

Since the mid-1960s, White Americans have been assiduously schooled to associate such feelings of shame and guilt with blackface and minstrelsy. Black Americans have been schooled to associate similar feelings about the Black artists who historically participated in minstrelsy. The blackface mask became one of this society's few universally taboo symbols. In the twenty-first century, no White American who blacks up, from frat boys to Chuck Knipp, can credibly claim not to be cognizant of the guilty feelings Yates speaks of— they can claim only not to share them. And maybe to be exploring them, or flouting them, or exploiting them.

5

BLACK INK

Negro-Dialect Literature

"I'm gwine ter larn you how ter talk ter 'spectubble folks ef hit's de las' ack," sez Brer Rabbit, sezee.   —UNCLE REMUS

I t cannot be an accident of history that the early 1830s, the period when blackface minstrels like Rice and Dixon were shuffling and shucking their way to superstardom, also saw the rise of a kind of blackface literature. Or that in the 1870s and 1880s, when the minstrel shows were dominating the stages of America, this blackface literature became wildly popular as well. Throughout the second half of the 1800s, and well into the twentieth century, poems, stories and novels written in what various authors took to be a "Negro dialect" were devoured with great interest. As with minstrelsy, some of what would later be considered the most embarrassing and offensive examples of this literature came from Black writers. But the bulk of the authors were White, and in their fictional Negroes we can see all the emotional confusion of attraction and repulsion, love and hate that characterized minstrelsy. (The University of North Carolina at Chapel Hill hosts a fine selection of full-text works of Negro-dialect fiction online at docsouth.unc.edu.)

Well before the Civil War, White folks showed that they were as fascinated by how Black folks talked as they were by how they looked, sang and danced. African slaves arrived in the Americas speaking a variety of mother tongues, out of which gradually developed simplified pidgin languages, which served as linguae francae and allowed for basic communication among slaves and between slaves and their owners. The pidgin English of early slaves eventually grew into regional dialects of Black English. We'll look at the process more closely in a later chapter.

For now, what's of interest is how, from early on, White Americans tried to capture slaves' pidgin English and Negro dialects in writing. One of the earliest known written recordings is from the Salem witch trials of 1692, in the testimony of the Barbadian slave Tituba, who apparently spoke West Indian Creole English. Cotton Mather made note of slaves using pidgin in the 1720s, which seemed to amuse the dour man. By the Revolutionary era, written records of slave speech are common. In 1782, Benjamin Franklin wrote of a slave who told him how the White man "make de Black Man workee, make de Horse workee, make de Ox workee, make ebery thing workee; only de Hog, He, de Hog, no workee; he eat, he drink, he walk about, he got to sleep when he please, he libb like a gentleman."

By the nineteenth century, Negro characters speaking various authors' ideas of pidgin or dialect had become quite common in theatrical texts, as we saw earlier. They begin appearing all over American fiction around the 1830s, the decade when Constance Rourke's archetypes—the Yankee, the Frontiersman, the Minstrel Man—first found their voices in print. "Americans savored them in almanacs, newspapers and magazines; they read them to one another and quoted them from memory; they clipped them and carried them around or pasted them in scrapbooks for rereading; and they made books collecting them big sellers." It was the birth of a genuinely American literature, declaring its independence from its Anglo-European parents.

Among the Yankee wits were Jack Downing, a Maine rustic created by Seba Smith, and Thomas Chandler Halliburton's cunning peddler Sam Slick. Frontiersmen like Davy Crockett began spinning their tall tales in the same decade. Here's the start of a typical Crockett yarn from 1837:

It's most likely my readers has all heerd of Colonel Coon's wife Judy. She wore a bearskin petticoat, an alligator's hide for an overcoat, an eagle's nest for a hat, with a wildcat's tail for a feather. When she was fourteen years old, she wrung off a snappin turtle's neck, and made a comb of its shell, which she wears to this day. When she was sixteen years old, she run down a four-year-old colt and chased a bear three mile out through the snow, because she wanted his hair to make a toothbrush. She out-screamed a catamount, on a wager, and sucked forty rattlesnake eggs, just to give her a sweet breath, the night she was married.

During the Civil War, humorist Charles H. Smith, posing as a cantankerous Georgia Confederate named Bill Arp, wrote open letters to "Abe Linkhorn," while David Ross Locke, writing as the proudly disreputable Petroleum Vesuvius Nasby, dared to publish newspaper columns about why he refused to be drafted into Mr. Linkhorn's army and, scandalously, one lamenting Lincoln's assassination only because it hadn't come "in 1862, when it would have been some use to us." Alfred Henry Lewis perfected the art of the cowboy tale in his Arizona stories of the Old Cattleman and Jaybird Bob, told in a Southwest dialect that's a close cousin of the Negro.

It's been argued that the use of regional dialect in literature reached its highest achievement in Mark Twain's *The Adventures of Huckleberry Finn* (1884), written entirely in Huck's illiterate white-trash speech and Jim's Negro dialect. Toward the end of the century, new waves of European immigrants provided whole new types of characters speaking broken, heavily accented English, to comic effect—Irish, Italians, Germans, Jews.

A subgenre of this literature comprises White writers who passed themselves off as Blacks or Native Americans in bogus memoirs or novels, sometimes with noble intentions (abolitionist Richard Hildreth's 1836 *The Slave: or Memoirs of Archy Moore*). Hack writers simply exploited stock dialect to get a cheap laugh. But many writers of dialect sincerely wanted to record and celebrate the rich variety of ways American spoke. They often operated like amateur ethnographers, conducting serious "field research" to make their dialect use as informed and authentic as possible. Robert Burns' effective use of Scottish dialects inspired a few generations of American authors to work indigenous speech patterns into an all-American literature.

Viewing Negro-dialect literature in this broad context adds a level of perspective that lifts the best of it out of the knee-jerk presumption that it was all racist mockery or, at best, "condescending . . . literary slumming." The fact is, Negro-dialect writing was used by both White and Black authors in work that ranged across the spectrum from loathsome vulgarity to some of the greatest American literature of the era.

One of the best-known early examples is Edgar Allan Poe's short story "The Gold-Bug," published in 1843. It features "an old negro, called Jupiter, who had been manumitted before the reverses of the family, but who could be induced, neither by threats nor by promises, to abandon what he considered his right of attendance upon the footsteps of his young 'Massa Will.'" Somewhere between a coon and an Uncle Tom, "Jup" speaks a Carolinas Gullah dialect: "'Dey aint no tin in him, Massa Will, I keep a tellin on you,' here interrupted Jupiter; 'de bug is a goole bug, solid, ebery bit of him, inside and all, sep him wing—neber feel half so hebby a bug in my life.'"

William Gilmore Simms' *The Yemassee,* a novel first published in 1835, is a romantic adventure of life in the Carolinas in the early 1700s. A Black slave, Hector, plays a role that would become very familiar in American literature—the White hero's sidekick, who, "though a slave, was a favourite, and his offices were rather those of the humble companion than of the servant."

Simms also wrote his Negro's speech in a pretty fair literary version of Gullah:

"Hector," said his master, calling the slave, while he threw himself lazily along the knoll, and motioned the negro near him: "Hector."

"Sa—Mossa."

"You marked that sailor fellow, did you?"

"Yes, Mossa."

"What is he; what do you think of him?"

"Me tink noting about 'em, sa.—Nebber see 'em afore—no like he look."

"Nor I, Hector—nor I. He comes for no good, and we must see to him."

"I tink so, Mossa."

Hector is offered—and rejects—his freedom:

"Yes, Hector,—you are now free.—I give you your freedom, old fellow. Here is money too, and in Charlestown you shall have a house to live in for yourself."

"No, mossa.—I can't, sir—I can't be free," replied the negro, shaking his head, and endeavouring to resume possession of the strong cord which secured the dog, and which Harrison had taken into his own hand.

"Why can't you, Hector? What do you mean? Am I not your master? Can't I make you free, and don't I tell you that I do make you free? From this moment you are your own master."

"Wha'—for, mossa? Wha' Hector done, you guine turn um off dis time o' day?"

"Done! You have saved my life, old fellow—you have fought for me like a friend, and I am now your friend, and not any longer your master."

"Ki, mossa! enty you always been frien' to Hector? Enty you gib um physic when he sick, and come see and talk wid um, and do ebbery ting he want you for do? What more you guine do, now?"

"Yes, Hector, I have done for you all this—but I have done it because you were my slave, and because I was bound to do it."

"Ah, you no want to be boun' any longer. Da's it! I see. You want Hector for eat acorn wid de hog, and take de swamp wid de Injin, enty?"

"Not so, old fellow—but I cannot call you my slave when I would call you my friend. I shall get another slave to carry Dugdale, and you shall be free."

"I dam to hell, mossa, if I guine to be free!" roared the adhesive black, in a tone of unrestrainable determination.

The most important dialect novel of the pre–Civil War era—and arguably the most important American novel of the nineteenth century—was Harriet Beecher Stowe's *Uncle Tom's Cabin*. The book was a gigantic sensation from its first appearance in forty installments in the abolitionist weekly paper *The National Era* in 1851–1852. The first of many, many editions in book form was rushed out in the spring of 1852, and it became an international bestseller, translated into some thirty-seven languages. It was so familiar that its chief characters—faithful old Uncle Tom, the "tragic mulatto" Eliza, innocent Little Eva, the evil slave owner Simon Legree, the clownish pickaninny Topsy—all became indelible archetypes of the American imagination.

Stowe's message, meanwhile, raised a national furor. *Uncle Tom's Cabin* challenged White readers with the then startling notion that slavery was inherently evil because Blacks were human beings, endowed with all the faculties, desires, dreams and rights of any White person. Today, her Black characters such as the almost savage Topsy and the saintly Uncle Tom strike us as flat caricatures. But in light of much of the minstrel-show foolery that was happening onstage when the book first appeared, Stowe's insistence on their *humanity* was quite a progressive statement, and an explosively provocative one that went straight to the heart of the slavery debate. For its passionate condemnation of slavery, her novel was vilified in the South as well as in proslavery circles in the North. ("In one memorable instance, a free Black in the slave state of Maryland received ten years in jail as punishment for owning a copy of *Uncle Tom's Cabin* and a map of Canada.") Abolitionists, on the other hand, regarded it as something close to a sacred text, although some took issue with the book because there are hints in it that Stowe—like Thomas Jefferson, Abraham Lincoln and Marcus Garvey—was inclined to believe that the best course for freed Blacks was to form their own nation somewhere away from White America. At any rate, *Uncle Tom's Cabin* started so many arguments, and had such an impact on the national debate over slavery, that Lincoln is reputed to have said, tongue somewhere near his cheek, that it had caused the Civil War.

When a novel has such social influence, it's almost beside the point to talk about its literary worth. That's just as well, because *Uncle Tom's Cabin* is a lousy novel. Like much serialized fiction, it rattles and rambles on interminably, reaching a full five hundred pages in book form, with subplots dangling like dead fruit from its twisted narrative arc. There isn't a chapter or a scene that wouldn't benefit from vigorous pruning. The tone strays from the self-righteously preachy to the tear-jerkingly melodramatic, and is always overripe with sentimentality. And all of the characters, Black and White, are symbolic ciphers, either annoyingly goody-goody or Snidely Whiplash evil.

The preachiness came naturally to Stowe. She was raised in a family of straitlaced New England Puritans, daughter of a Congregationalist minister and sister to Henry Ward Beecher, the famous pastor of Plymouth Church in Brooklyn Heights. (A few blocks from where I live. I pass his statue every day.) She had no firsthand knowledge of slavery until the family moved for a few years to Cincinnati; there, and on short trips to Kentucky, she formed the impressions that went into her book. Then she moved back to New England and started to write.

On the plus side, maybe as a result of her limited contact with Southern Blacks, she exercised a rather light hand with Negro dialect, as in this famous scene:

"How old are you, Topsy?"

"Dun no, Missis," said the image, with a grin that showed all her teeth.

"Don't know how old you are? Didn't anybody ever tell you? Who was your mother?"

"Never had none!" said the child, with another grin.

"Never had any mother? What do you mean? Where were you born?"

"Never was born!" persisted Topsy, with another grin, that looked so goblin-like, that, if Miss Ophelia had been at all nervous, she might have fancied that she had got hold of some sooty gnome from the land of Diablerie; but Miss Ophelia was not nervous, but plain and business-like, and she said, with some sternness,

"You mustn't answer me in that way, child; I'm not playing with you. Tell me where you were born, and who your father and mother were."

"Never was born," reiterated the creature, more emphatically; "never had no father nor mother, nor nothin'. I was raised by a speculator, with lots of others. Old Aunt Sue used to take car on us."

The child was evidently sincere, and Jane, breaking into a short laugh, said,

"Laws, Missis, there's heaps of 'em. Speculators buys 'em up cheap, when they's little, and gets 'em raised for market."

"How long have you lived with your master and mistress?"

"Dun no, Missis."

"Is it a year, or more, or less?"

"Dun no, Missis."

"Laws, Missis, those low negroes,—they can't tell; they don't know anything about time," said Jane; "they don't know what a year is; they don't know their own ages."

"Have you ever heard anything about God, Topsy?"

The child looked bewildered, but grinned as usual.

"Do you know who made you?"

"Nobody, as I knows on," said the child, with a short laugh.

The idea appeared to amuse her considerably; for her eyes twinkled, and she added,

"I spect I grow'd. Don't think nobody never made me."

Uncle Tom's Cabin is one of those overlong novels that begs for somebody to wring a dramatic story out of it. And given its enormous, instant and enduring impact, it was inevitable that it would inspire all manner of spin-offs and what today would be called merchandising, from dolls to commemorative china. It was also adapted for the stage, in versions ranging from mawkish melodrama to parody. Typical of stage (and later screen) adaptations, they generally simplified the story and amplified its most tragic or heart-pounding elements. And many, especially after the Civil War, strayed very far off-message. (A phenomenal website, "Uncle Tom's Cabin & American Culture," curated by historian Stephen Railton, offers a wealth of materials on these shows, at www.iath.virginia.edu/utc.)

In New York City, competing productions hit the stage before the ink had dried on Stowe's pages. The National Theatre on Chatham Street staged a version in September 1852, followed by T. D. Rice appearing as "Otello." (The National had been founded as an opera house by none other than Lorenzo Da Ponte, Mozart's librettist on *Don Giovanni* and *Le Nozze di Figaro*, who moved to New York in 1805. When it failed as a venue for high art, it turned to more humble fare.) Barnum fired back with a five-act adaptation of the "in-

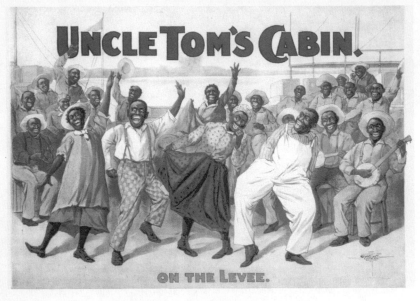

Poster for a touring production, circa 1899.
(Courtesy Library of Congress)

tensely interesting American Moral Drama" at his American Museum, pointedly advertised as "the only truly sensible version," complete with "original music, choruses, a moving panorama diorama, and other expensive and highly effective auxiliaries." A new version of the play, first staged in Troy, New York, and considered the first "serious" stage adaptation, set box-office records when it came to the National in 1853. Seeing how well it was doing there, the enterprising owner of a nearby dime museum offered a magic-lantern version in twenty-five projected slides. (Later slide versions produced for projection at home further trimmed Stowe's five-hundred-page epic to a mere twelve key scenes, such as "Tom Saves Eva from Drowning" and "Legree's Cruelty to Tom.")

T. D. Rice played Tom nightly "to admiration" at the Bowery in 1854. "Zounds!" a newspaper ad read. "Will't never stop? No, until every man, woman and child has seen UNCLE TOM'S CABIN at the

Bowery Theatre." That's typical of how canny producers promoted the show before and during the Civil War, suggesting it was a moral imperative for "every man, woman and child" to see it. A century later, *Roots* would be promoted in much the same way.

Touring "Tom Shows," as they came to be called, traveled throughout the North and West (skipping the South, naturally), as well as Canada, for decades, from midsized cities in the Midwest to one-horse outposts on the Great Plains to the loneliest reaches of Saskatchewan and Manitoba. As many as five hundred different productions were on tour in the 1890s.

Minstrel shows were also quick to incorporate familiar elements of the story into their revues. Minstrel men were especially fond of dressing up in pickaninny drag and gamboling about the stage as Topsy, which allowed them to show off their wildest and most ridiculous darky dance moves. As early as 1854, Christy & Wood's Minstrels were performing *Uncle Tom's Cabin* as an "operatic bur-letta," with George Christy himself as Topsy. In *Monarchs of Min-strelsy*, Edward Rice recalls that when his father took him to his first minstrel show in Philadelphia when he was "about six or eight years of age" (which would have been the mid-1880s), he was entranced by the "nigger singers," but especially by star performer Bobby New-comb's Topsy. "Oh! I'se So Wicked" is a Topsy song from 1854, sung and danced to a sprightly whirligig of a tune:

> *Oh! white-folks, I was never born,—*
> *Aunt Sue raise me on de corn,*
> *Send me errands night and morn,*
> *Ching a ring a ring a ricked.*

> *She used to knock me on de floor,*
> *Den hang my head agin de door,*
> *And tare my hair out by de core,*
> *Oh! I was so wicked.*

As productions of *Uncle Tom's Cabin* grow'd like Topsy, proliferating across the country, it inevitably generated parodies and burlesques, often reducing Tom to the cruelest coon-show caricature, shuffling across the stage and drooling doggerel. The 1874 *Uncle Tom: An Ethiopian Interlude* had Tom dragging a stuffed bag onto the stage:

UNCLE TOM. Buy a coot-coot-cooter, maussa?
PETE. A coot-coot-cooter? What's that? What you got in de bag?
UNCLE TOM. Cooter, maussa, snackin' turple.
PETE. Snackin' turple? What's dat?
UNCLE TOM. Swine in de water, git down in de mud.
PETE. Oh! I see, you mean a snappin' turtle?
UNCLE TOM. Yeth! Yeth!! Make bully stew, make your mouf smack. Buy a cooter, maussa?

Writing on the 150th anniversary of *Uncle Tom's Cabin* in 2002, Kendra Hamilton noted that an estimated "fifty people saw the stage show for every one person who bought or read a copy of the book. And the stage show took massive liberties with the book. For starters, most of the antislavery content dropped out of the stage shows as producers concentrated on elaborate set pieces that could entertain or enthrall audiences.

"For example, the episode in which the beautiful mulatto Eliza flees across the ice to freedom in Ohio takes all of three paragraphs in Stowe's novel. However, onstage it became a tour de force staged with live horses, bloodhounds and, in one memorable production . . . alligators."

One production boasted its "six parts and twenty-seven tableaux"; another that it presented "100 people on the stage," "Songs, Dances, Plantation Melodies and Banjo Solos," "the renowned Siberian Bloodhounds and the Trick Donkey, Bruno." A production from the mid-1880s, possibly covering for weaknesses in its actors, highlighted its "Wonderful Performing Dogs."

Post–Civil War productions of *Uncle Tom's Cabin* represented a mini-industry for Black performers, who began to crowd blackfaced Whites off the stage. By the mid-1870s it was common for a grand touring production to feature song-and-dance troupes of former slaves like the Alabama Jubilee Singers, in numbers like "Tell Us Where Miss Eva Gone" and "Massa's Gwine to Sell Us." A giant 1878 production in New York offered the Louisiana Troubadour Quartet, the Four Eccentric Coons and a chorus of no less than four hundred "freed men, women and children." A version of 1895 touted "75 people in the production," including the Oriole Pickaninnies, the Great Bird and Animal Imitator, and the Great Buck and Wing Dancers, and noted that the cast incorporated "40 colored people, nearly all of whom are natives of the South, who will appear and sing the Cabin Melodies of the Sunny South, vividly illustrating Slave Life Before the War."

In short, the more spectacular productions grew, and the further in time they got from the Civil War, the further they strayed from Stowe's antislavery message—until, as we can see in an ad from 1895, they were actually reversing it. For White audiences, *Uncle Tom's Cabin* went from being a condemnation of slavery and an abolitionist warning about the future of the nation to minstrel-show nostalgia for the good old days of the "Sunny South." For Blacks, Uncle Tom went from being a heroic figure of faith and perseverance to Massa's obedient pet slave, a figure of shame—which is how it became an insult to call a Black person an Uncle Tom. Historian Ernest Allen told Kendra Hamilton:

> "I don't recall seeing anyone in the 1920s using the term 'Uncle Tom' as an epithet. But what's amazing is how fast it caught on (in the 1930s). Black scholars picked (the term) up and just started throwing it at each other." . . .
>
> Allen says the militancy of the 1930s—with the Depression, the rise of the Communist Party, the organizing and marching, the out-

"TOPSY"

An American icon.
(Courtesy Library of Congress)

rage over the Scottsboro Boys—was crucial in tarnishing Uncle Tom's reputation among both the Black intelligentsia and the Black masses.

"People are struggling and fighting for social change, and those who seem prepared to accept the status quo are not looked upon kindly," Allen says. "The 1960s were very similar. There's a sharp political struggle taking place in which you have to decide to be on the side of change or to offer excuses for the status quo, and that leads to a second wave of anti-Tomism."

Uncle Tom's Cabin continued to be a stage favorite right up to the Depression. Mary Pickford got her start playing Little Eva. In the 1920s, a vaudeville show called *Topsy and Eva,* performed by the Duncan Sisters, was a smash hit; it would be revived on TV in the 1950s. If you count all the various productions, *Uncle Tom's Cabin* was the longest-running show in the history of the American stage. A notice in *The New York Times* of December 31, 1930, lamented: "The epoch-making run of five years for 'Abie's Irish Rose' pales before 'Uncle Tom's Cabin.' Its run is now ended, after a continuous showing of seventy-seven years. For the first time since 1853 there is now not a single company in the country playing it."

Ironically, Stowe never approved of staged versions of her book. As a good Puritan, she thought theaters were dens of iniquity (and, as we've seen, they often were). To counter the many vulgar productions over which she had no control, she wrote the text for a dramatic reading of the work, and hired Mrs. Mary E. Webb, a mulatto actress and daughter of a fugitive slave, to present it. Mrs. Webb would follow this with selections from Longfellow's *Song of Hiawatha,* for which she donned an Indian costume. Apparently this more tasteful presentation of Stowe's work met with limited success.

IN THE DECADES AFTER THE CIVIL WAR, THE NORTH'S guilty nostalgia for the Old Plantation not only gave rise to the giant minstrel-show spectacles and Tom Shows, but also spurred a national craze for Negro-dialect literature, assuaged in reams of populist poetry and short stories that fed a meteoric postwar boom in the magazine industry. Many of the writers were Southern Whites, only too happy to polish the South's tarnished image.

Irwin Russell (1853–1879) was a Mississippi writer who was inspired by Robert Burns' work in Scottish dialects to experiment with Southern White, British and Irish idioms before settling on a "Negro" style. Joel Chandler Harris, author of the Uncle Remus stories, credited Russell as a major inspiration, and his influence can be seen in work as late as Roark Bradford's (see later in this chapter)—

especially in Russell's negrified reworking of biblical material, as in these stanzas from his poem "De Fust Banjo":

"Dar's gwine to be a' oberflow," said Noah, lookin' solemn—
Fur Noah tuk de "Herald," an' he read de ribber column—
An' so he sot his hands to wuk a-clarin' timber-patches,
An' 'lowed he's gwine to build a boat to beat de steamah Natchez.

Ol' Noah kep' a-nailin' an' a-chippin' an' a-sawin';
An' all de wicked neighbors kep' a-laughin' an' a-pshawin';
But Noah didn't min' 'em, knowin' whut was gwine to happen:
An' forty days an' forty nights de rain it kep' a-drappin'.

Now, Noah had done cotched a lot ob ebry sort o' beas'es—
Ob all de shows a-trabbelin', it beat 'em all to pieces!
He had a Morgan colt an' sebral head o' Jarsey cattle—
An' druv 'em 'board de Ark as soon's he heered de thunder rattle.

Thomas Nelson Page was born in 1853, a Southern gentleman, scion of a Virginia plantation family. He grew up in classic antebellum privilege, saw the ravages of the Civil War and the upheavals of Reconstruction, and eventually became a Jim Crow propagandist. Page was an unapologetic Southern nostalgist for the old plantation days. Early in his best-known (though now rarely read) story collection, *In Ole Virginia, or Marse Chan and Other Stories* (1881), Old Sam, a freed slave, sighs, "Dem wuz good ole times, marster— de bes' Sam ever see! Dey wuz, in fac'! Niggers didn' hed nothin' 't all to do—jes' hed to 'ten' to de feedin' an' cleanin' de hosses, an' doin' what de marster tell 'em to do; an' when dey wuz sick, dey had things sont 'em out de house, an' de same doctor come to see 'em whar 'ten' to de white folks when dey wuz po'ly. Dyar warn' no trouble nor nothin'.'"

Then again, Page did sometimes let a Negro character slip in a sideways comment about White folks, as in this uncharacteristically charming scene:

> Entirely oblivious of my proximity, the negro went on calling "Whoo-oop, heah!" until along the path, walking very slowly and with great dignity, appeared a noble-looking old orange and white setter, gray with age, and corpulent with excessive feeding. As soon as he came in sight, his master began:
>
> "Yes, dat you! You gittin' deaf as well as bline, I s'pose! Kyarnt heah me callin', I reckon? Whyn't yo' come on, dawg?"
>
> The setter sauntered slowly up to the fence and stopped, without even deigning a look at the speaker, who immediately proceeded to take the rails down, talking meanwhile:
>
> "Now, I got to pull down de gap, I s'pose! Yo' so sp'ilt yo' kyahn hardly walk. Jes' ez able to git over it as I is! Jes' like white folks— think 'cuz you's white and I's black, I got to wait on yo' all de time. Ne'm mine, I ain' gwi' do it!"

One of the best, and most enduringly popular, post Civil War dialect authors was Joel Chandler Harris, purveyor of the Uncle Remus tales. When I was growing up in the 1950s and into the 1960s, Uncle Remus and his fables about Brer Rabbit, Brer Fox and Brer Bear were still beloved fixtures of American popular culture. Harris' books were favorite reading, and the 1946 movie adaptation *Song of the South* was still one of Disney's most popular. Every kid knew the stories of the Tar Baby, who enraged and eventually engulfed Brer Rabbit, and the briar patch, where Brer Rabbit cleverly evaded Brer Fox.

In the post–civil rights era, Uncle Remus became yet another embarrassment, and though the stories remain in print, they are now something of a guilty pleasure. *Song of the South*, meanwhile, is forbidden knowledge, circulating only on a kind of politically incorrect black market (pun acknowledged). Some years ago, I began to notice that if I said that some intractable problem had become "a real Tar

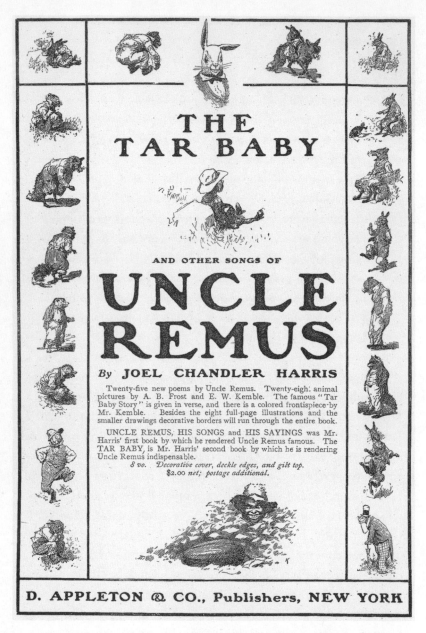

An advertisement for Joel Chandler Harris' second volume
of Uncle Remus lore, from *Scribner's Magazine,* 1904.

Baby," people under the age of thirty tilted their heads quizzically. That's because the Tar Baby came to be mistaken for a racist joke, when in fact Harris was simply transmitting a folktale that has its roots in Africa and is told throughout the lands of the diaspora. Today, "Zip-a-dee-doo-dah" is the only remnant of Uncle Remus lore that's universally recognized, and I doubt many young people know its controversial provenance. Probably just as few see Brer Rabbit's lineage in his wisecracking twentieth-century descendant Bugs Bunny.

Harris, of course, did not invent Brer Rabbit and his fellow creatures. Their lineage goes all the way back to the fables of Aesop, the legendary dark-skinned slave (Aesop = Ethiopian) whose animal allegories instructed the Greek world in the sixth century B.C. There are many similarities to Yoruban tales, and in fact to trickster lore around the world. Africans brought these tales with them to the Americas, where they became a feature of Southern Black oral culture.

"Indeed, for generations black southerners had been using the Brer Rabbit tales at the heart of Harris's narratives to teach their own children lessons about survival in a decidedly brutal and unjust world," writes Jennifer Ritterhouse. "As the quintessential trickster, Brer Rabbit proved that the weak could outsmart and overcome the strong. His victories provided important psychological benefits." Blacks identified with Brer Rabbit because he was, to mix animal metaphors, the ultimate underdog, and used his wits and wiles to get over or around figures of power and authority.

Harris was born out of wedlock to a poor seamstress in the town of Eatonton, Georgia, around 1845. As a teenager he came under the wing of a nearby plantation owner, reputed to be one of the most kind and gentle massas in the region. It was there, Harris said, he first heard Brer Rabbit tales from the slaves. Later, he would gather many more of them from other Black sources, as well as secondhand from Whites. After wandering the South as a journeyman journalist, he landed a permanent spot at *The Atlanta Constitution* in 1876. It was in its pages that Harris' Uncle Remus stories first appeared, and they were soon being reprinted nationally and collected in books that were cherished around the world.

Harris was writing popular fiction, not ethnography, and he freely adapted the lore he gathered from Black informants for a readership he could assume was largely White. The folktales he'd heard survive in his stories of the loose-tongued, mischief-making Brer Rabbit, constantly talking himself into and out of trouble with the always famished Brer Fox and the slow-witted Brer Bear. Harris' stroke of genius was to create an appealing frame tale for a White audience, set on a Southern plantation after the Civil War. The owners, Marse John and Miss Sally, are the last word in Southern White gentility, flawlessly kind and loving to their Negro charges. Uncle Remus, their most trusted and loyal retainer, has chosen to stay with them after emancipation. It's Miss Sally's seven-year-old boy to whom Uncle Remus (sometimes aided by Aunt Tempy, Tildy and Daddy Jack) relates his tales.

Today, it might take readers a while to get into the rhythm of Harris' dialogue. But not long. Of all the White writers assaying Negro dialects, he was the smoothest and easiest to follow:

"One day atter Brer Rabbit fool 'im wid dat calamus root, Brer Fox went ter wuk en got 'im some tar, en mix it wid some turkentime, en fix up a contrapshun w'at he call a Tar-Baby, en he tuck dish yer Tar-Baby en he sot 'er in de big road, en den he lay off in de bushes fer to see what de news wuz gwine ter be. En he didn't hatter wait long, nudder, kaze bimeby here come Brer Rabbit pacin' down de road— lippity-clippity, clippity-lippity—dez ez sassy ez a jay-bird. Brer Fox, he lay low. Brer Rabbit come prancin' 'long twel he spy de Tar-Baby, en den he fotch up on his behime legs like he wuz 'stonished. De Tar-Baby, she sot dar, she did, en Brer Fox, he lay low.

"'Mawnin'!' sez Brer Rabbit, sezee—'nice wedder dis mawnin',' sezee.

"Tar-Baby ain't sayin' nuthin', en Brer Fox, he lay low.

"'How duz yo' sym'tums seem ter segashuate?' sez Brer Rabbit, sezee.

"Brer Fox, he wink his eye slow, en lay low, en de Tar-Baby, she ain't sayin' nuthin'.

"'How you come on, den? Is you deaf?' sez Brer Rabbit, sezee. 'Kaze if you is, I kin holler louder,' sezee.

"Tar-Baby stay still, en Brer Fox, he lay low.

"'You er stuck up, dat's w'at you is,' says Brer Rabbit, sezee, 'en I'm gwine ter kyore you, dat's w'at I'm a gwine ter do,' sezee.

"Brer Fox, he sorter chuckle in his stummick, he did, but Tar Baby ain't sayin' nothin'.

"'I'm gwine ter larn you how ter talk ter 'spectubble folks ef hit's de las' ack,' sez Brer Rabbit, sezee. 'Ef you don't take off dat hat en tell me howdy, I'm gwine ter bus' you wide open,' sezee.

"Tar-Baby stay still, en Brer Fox, he lay low."

It's telling that Uncle Remus emerged just as the Reconstruction period was ending and the harsh backlash of the Jim Crow era was getting started. Reconstruction efforts to integrate Whites and freed Blacks as equal citizens were declared a dismal failure; the two races, it was decided, had to be "separate but equal." Much of the propaganda bolstering the new apartheid system flogged lurid images of Blacks as violent sexual predators, still too wild and "primitive" to mingle freely with civilized Whites. Around the turn of the century, Thomas Nelson Page contributed to this propaganda with his books *Red Rock: A Chronicle of Reconstruction* and *The Negro: The Southerner's Problem*. D. W. Griffith would be inspired by a novel with a similar theme, Thomas Dixon, Jr.'s *The Clansman*.

Into this context strolled kindly old Uncle Remus with his sweet demeanor and childlike fables. Although Harris set his tales after the Civil War, it was inevitable that White readers, Southern and Northern alike, would see in Uncle Remus another beloved archetype of the antebellum plantation, the happy and unthreatening darky of the Old South, the same smiling figure who was striding the minstrel stages of the era.

But then, it's neither Uncle Remus nor the little boy with whom children identify in these stories, but Brer Rabbit himself. Smaller than most of the other creatures, constantly preyed upon by the ever "hongry" fox and bear, he has only his wits and cunning to defend himself. You don't need to be a Black child to empathize and to cheer every time little Mr. Rabbit outwits his larger predators.

Harris' genuine admiration and affection for Southern Black culture are quite evident in his writing. His attitude is easily contrasted to the glib paternalism of Russell or Page. For a White Southerner, he was unusually outspoken in his opposition to the racism of his time. He wrote against lynching, preached tolerance and brotherhood, and championed the achievements of Blacks. It's true he did not convey the passion of a John Brown or the moral convictions of a Harriet Beecher Stowe, but he did his best.

Critics see problems in Harris' work that have little to do with his apparently innocent intentions. They argue, for example, that his reworking Negro folklore under his own byline was what today would be called cultural theft. Novelist Alice Walker, also from Eatonton, is one of many who've leveled this charge against Harris. It's also said that by situating the tales as he did in sweet, nostalgic settings, where they're being passed down not from one Black generation to the next but from a Black man to a privileged White boy, Harris stripped them of the subversive subtext described above.

Well, maybe. Yet Harris always made it clear that he was not the creator of the stories but only a "dull reporter," expressly stating that "my purpose has been to preserve the legends in their original simplicity, and to wed them permanently to the quaint dialect—if, indeed, it can be called a dialect—through the medium of which they have become a part of the domestic history of every Southern family; and I have endeavored to give to the whole a genuine flavor of the old plantation. Each legend has its variants, but in every instance I have retained that particular version which seemed to me to be the most characteristic, and have given it without embellishment and without exaggeration."

Also, the label "theft" implies that Harris rendered Black culture bereft of the stories, but there's ample evidence that this wasn't the case. When Zora Neale Hurston collected lore from Blacks in Florida and along the Gulf Coast in the 1920s and 1930s, she heard many variants on the Brer Rabbit tales, still obviously very much alive and in circulation. Besides, you can't steal what someone doesn't own, and the argument that Blacks, or anyone else, held sole or privileged right to the lore they passed down is unconvincing. All Harris did was move some of these tales from oral transmission to print—from orality to literacy. "Dull reporters" have been doing that with orally transmitted stories since whoever wrote down the Gilgamesh tales and the Old Testament stories, up through *Beowulf* and the Grimms to today's ethnographers. Do the stories lose some of their flavor and their meaning in the translation to the page? Maybe. But through print they are preserved and disseminated to the culture at large. Harris learned the Brer Rabbit tales from Black culture, and made them American culture.

And in so doing, I'd argue, he made them subversive in a different, perhaps unintended, way. Launched into popular culture at the very time when Blacks and Whites were being forcefully and legally segregated, the Uncle Remus stories presented an opposite image of Blacks and Whites living together in harmony, mutual respect and love. At a time when Whites were being warned against any contact with Blacks, Harris had Uncle Remus putting "Miss Sally's little boy on his knee, and stroking the child's hair thoughtfully and caressingly." That may be a "false" image of interracial togetherness—this is fiction, after all—but as I argue elsewhere in this book, it's also an ideal, and I can't believe that it didn't in some way mitigate segregationist lore in the minds of millions of children, not to mention the parents who read to them. It can be seen as yet another example of popular culture offering an alternative to present reality.

In his gentle, if patronizing, portraits of plantation Negroes and their doting White bosses, Harris found a natural ally in Maria Howard Weeden (1846–1905), a fragile flower of Southern maidenhood who lived her whole life, save for a brief remove to safer territory during the Civil War, in her parents' home in Huntsville, Alabama. A self-taught artist of considerable skill, she's best known for her portraits of Negroes, which are extraordinarily realistic, sympathetic and sometimes even insightful, especially given that they were executed toward the end of the century, the height of coon songs and vulgar caricatures. Writing as Howard Weeden (she also used "Flake White"), she penned some of the sweetest, most genteel and weepily nostalgic of all Negro-dialect verse, published in four slim volumes, illustrated with accompanying portraits, between 1898 and 1904. *Bandanna Ballads* (1899) is dedicated "to the memory of all the faithful mammies who ever sung Southern babes to rest," and saintly mammies indeed abound (one even wears a halo in her portrait), as in "Mother and Mammy":

Among the ranks of shining saints
Disguised in heavenly splendor,
Two Mother-faces wait for me,
Familiar still, and tender.

One face shines whiter than the dawn,
And steadfast as a star;
None but my Mother's face could shine
So bright—and be so far!

The other dark one leans from Heaven,
Brooding still to calm me;
Black as if ebon Rest had found
Its image in my Mammy!

Numerous familiar stereotypes find their way into Weeden's ditties, especially those employing dialect—possum, "watermilion," bright-eyed dusky maidens, de ole banjo and de steadfast hoe, wistful old Uncle Toms jest waitin' for de day kindly Ol Massa call 'em to Heaben:

Dem was mighty big plantations
Dat he owned before de war
An' he, de kindes' master
Dat darkies ever saw.

But de care of dem was heavy,
Makin him de slave, not we—
An' often I have heard him say
He wished dat he was me!

Weeden's verses retained some popularity well into the twentieth century—a friend of mine has a Southern-style cookbook, issued by a Pennsylvania publishing house in 1938, that quotes from her poem "Beaten Biscuit." But in its day the treacly sentimentality was too much for some readers, leading Joel Chandler Harris to defend Weeden's honor in his courtly introduction to *Bandanna Ballads.* "A new generation has arisen, and it has become incredulous and skeptical in regard to the traditions and legends of the old plantation in general, and of the old-time quality negro in particular," he wrote. "If there were negroes in the old days so quaint and gentle, so tender-hearted and devoted . . . what has become of them?" Assuring his reader that these folks did indeed exist, he sighs, "Alas! that the successors and descendants of these old negroes should now everywhere answer to the name of 'coons,' and that their rich melodies should be degraded into the vulgar and disgusting 'rag-time' songs!"

As Negro-dialect lit swept the land, for every sincere and gifted Joel Chandler Harris or sympathetic Howard Weeden there would be a dozen hacks who exploited the genre for low humor or the most vilely racist stereotyping. By the turn of the century it had become a kind of gentleman's pastime to record a few of one's favorite dialect stories and jokes and have them printed in a book or pamphlet to amuse friends with. The University of North Carolina website presents several examples from the low end of the genre.

Quite popular for decades and rightly forgotten now, Louise Clarke-Pyrnelle's children's book *Diddie, Dumps and Tot* (1882) has a structure similar to Harris' books—folksy tales told by plantation darkies to their massa's daughters, including an alternative version of the Tar Baby story—but it's just simpering racist trash. A plantation owner's daughter herself, the author proclaims, "I KNOW whereof I do speak," in the introduction, then trots out all the usual stereotypes. The girls' Negro playmates are listed among their puppies and other toys.

Katherine McDowell, under the pseudonym Sherwood Bonner, offered her *Dialect Tales* in 1883, complete with grinning mammy on the cover. It concerns a young man dispatched by his father to collect a debt in the remote Southern town of Sarsar. "A good many worthless negroes have congregated in the place," his father warns, "who fight, quarrel, and steal without much interference from anybody." The Negroes have names like Tiddlekins, Aunt Annicky (who "looked as if she had been dipped in ink and polished off with lamp-black") and Hieronymus Pop; the Whites are all poor White trash; and the whole thing reads like a cross between *Li'l Abner* and *The Birth of a Nation.*

Speaking of which, dialect came to its lowest ebb in the novel that inspired D. W. Griffith, Dixon's *The Clansman* (1905). Interspersed

with scenes of darkies trembling before valiant Klansmen and crying out, "Yes, Lawd, I'se er comin'. I hain't ready—but, Lawd, I got ter
come!" are passages like:

> Suddenly through the dense mass appeared the forms of two gigan-
> tic negroes carrying an old man. His grim face, white and rigid, and
> his big club foot hanging pathetically from those black arms, could
> not be mistaken. A thrill of excitement swept the floor and galleries,
> and a faint cheer rippled the surface, quickly suppressed by the gavel.
>
> The negroes placed him in an arm-chair facing the semi-circle of
> Senators, and crouched down on their haunches beside him. Their
> kinky heads, black skin, thick lips, white teeth, and flat noses made
> for the moment a curious symbolic frame for the chalk-white pas-
> sion of the old Commoner's face.
>
> No sculptor ever dreamed a more sinister emblem of the corrup-
> tion of a race of empire-builders than this group. Its black figures,
> wrapped in the night of four thousand years of barbarism, squatted
> there the "equal" of their master, grinning at his forms of Justice, the
> evolution of forty centuries of Aryan genius. To their brute strength
> the white fanatic in the madness of his hate had appealed, and for
> their hire he had bartered the birthright of a mighty race of freemen.

SO NEGRO-DIALECT LIT COULD BE ANYTHING FROM ANTI-
racist propaganda to patronizing nostalgia to psychotic negropho-
bia. And just to complicate things further, just as with minstrelsy and
coon songs, there were also a number of Blacks who wrote it.

Paul Laurence Dunbar was the first Black poet to gain national acclaim, and though his work, like that of many Victorian-era poets, is
not much read outside the classroom anymore, he's still remembered
with pride. He was born in Dayton, Ohio, in 1872. His father had
been a slave who escaped to Canada, then served in the Union army;
his mother a slave freed at the end of the war. Paul was the only Black

student in his high school, where he ran the newspaper and literary society. As a young man he founded a newsletter, the *Dayton Tattler,* with the Wright brothers among his backers. His first book of poems was published when he was only twenty. A few years later, his work was discovered by William Dean Howells, editor of *Harper's Weekly,* who helped make him a national and international literary star. He began his introduction to Dunbar's 1898 collection *Lyrics of Lowly Life*: "I think I should scarcely trouble the reader with a special appeal in behalf of this book, if it had not specially appealed to me for reasons apart from the author's race, origin, and condition. The world is too old now, and I find myself too much of its mood, to care for the work of a poet because he is black, because his father and mother were slaves, because he was, before and after he began to write poems, an elevator-boy. These facts would certainly attract me to him as a man, if I knew him to have a literary ambition, but when it came to his literary art, I must judge it irrespective of these facts, and enjoy or endure it for what it was in itself."

That's a very fine-sounding speech, but it was rather disingenuous, as I'll explain in a moment.

What's fascinating about Dunbar's work is that from the start he wrote in two very different voices. One is the classical, formal Victorian style, as in "Emancipation," which begins:

Fling out your banners, your honors be bringing,
Raise to the ether your paeans of praise.
Strike every chord and let music be ringing!
Celebrate freely this day of all days.

One of his most famous works in this style is "We Wear the Mask":

We wear the mask that grins and lies,
It hides our cheeks and shades our eyes,—
This debt we pay to human guile;

With torn and bleeding hearts we smile,
And mouth with myriad subtleties.

Why should the world be over-wise,
In counting all our tears and sighs?
Nay, let them only see us, while
   We wear the mask.

We smile, but, O great Christ, our cries
To thee from tortured souls arise.
We sing, but oh the clay is vile
Beneath our feet, and long the mile;
But let the world dream otherwise,
   We wear the mask!

But Dunbar also wrote a great deal of both poetry and fiction in Negro dialect, and outside literary circles he was far better known for this work during his lifetime. He was inspired partly by the language and the stories of his parents' slave days in Kentucky. Still, growing up Black among Whites in the North, he could adopt a rather distant stance to Southern Black culture, which he referred to as "quaint old tales and songs of our fathers," which he felt might make for him "capital literary materials." Although he spent little time in the South himself, he is known to have gathered stories from many former slaves who'd migrated north. Dialect literature being such a craze in his day, it was natural for Dunbar to show his hand at it and hope to profit from it.

White magazine editors such as Howells egged him on. It was Howells who brought national attention to Dunbar's dialect writing, declaring him, not terribly inventively, a Black American Robert Burns. Dunbar would later complain that Howells "has done me irrevocable harm" in focusing too much on the dialect work—but he'd been writing it before Howells promoted him, and he didn't stop. He might hope to base his legacy on the high-flown poesy, but the dialect verse was how he made his living.

Later critics saw definite influences of Irwin Russell and Thomas Nelson Page in Dunbar's dialect writing, though I'd say that, as with other Black writers who used dialect, there's something more sympathetic and mellifluous about Dunbar's, less a sense of struggle, than in either of those two. "A Frolic" begins:

> *Swing yo' lady roun' an' roun',*
> *Do de bes' you know;*
> *Mek yo' bow an' p'omenade*
> *Up an' down de flo';*
> *Mek dat banjo hump huhse'f,*
> *Listen at huh talk:*
> *Mastah gone to town to-night;*
> *'Tain't no time to walk.*

When Dunbar fantasized about plantation life, he could wax as nostalgic and sentimental as Miss Weeden. The speaker in "The Deserted Plantation" mourns the passing of the gold ol' days:

> *Dey have lef' de ole plantation to de swallers,*
> *But it hol's in me a lover till de las';*
> *Fu' I fin' hyeah in de memory dat follers*
> *All dat loved me an' dat I loved in de pas'.*

> *So I'll stay an' watch de deah ole place an' tend it*
> *Ez I used to in de happy days gone by.*
> *'Twell de othah Mastah thinks it's time to end it,*
> *An' calls me to my qua'ters in de sky.*

The freed slaves in "Chrismus on the Plantation" have opted to stay on the plantation with their good massa, only to be told that he must sell the place because he can't afford to run it anymore now that he has to pay them wages. "Old Ben" opines:

Well, ef dat's de way dis freedom ac's on people, white er black,
You kin jes' tell Mistah Lincum fu' to tek his freedom back.

Dunbar, as we saw earlier, also wrote the lyrics for minstrel and coon songs. His big hits included "Down de Lover's Lane (Plantation Croon)," "Evah Dahkey Is a King" and the remarkable "Who Dat Say Chicken in Dis Crowd," from *Clorindy*:

There was once a great assemblage of the cullud population,
   all the cullud swells was there,
They had got them-selves together to discuss the situation
   and rumours in the air.
There were speakers there from Georgia and some from Tennessee,
   who were making feather fly,
When a roostah in the bahn-yu'd flew up whut folks could see,
   Then those darkies all did cry.

CHORUS
Who dat say chicken in dis crowd?
Speak de word agin' and speak it loud—
Blame de lan' let white folks rule it,
I'se a lookin fu a pullet,
Who dat say chicken in dis crowd.

Writing prolifically all his short life—he was only thirty-three when he died of tuberculosis—Dunbar also churned out paeans to Frederick Douglass and to "The Colored Soldiers" ("those noble sons of Ham"), a nationalist ode to Ethiopia, harrowing depictions of lynchings in both prose and verse, and love poems, comic verses (including the funny retort "To a Captious Critic"), satires, hymns and dirges. He also wrote four volumes of short stories, often dealing with complex issues of race that were far removed from the jocularity of a minstrel ditty or coon song.

Dunbar's friend James Weldon Johnson (1871–1938) also wrote both formal verse and dialect; he contributed lyrics to musicals including *Sons of Ham, The Belle of Bridgeport* and *In Dahomey.* Today he's best remembered for the so-called Black national anthem, the lovely "Lift Ev'ry Voice and Sing." (Which I'd love to see replace "The Star-Spangled Banner." It has a much prettier tune, far easier to sing, and its lyrics encapsulate a lot more about the American ideal. And I say that even though I'm from Baltimore, Home of the National Anthem.)

The Black intellectual establishment, from Du Bois at the start of the twentieth century to Amiri Baraka at the end, has always been scandalized by Dunbar's and (to a far milder degree) Johnson's dialect writings. But the truth is, Dunbar's dialect writing reads a lot better today than his stiff and formal work, which is the kind of Victorian verse high school students are made to memorize and recite at graduation, then promptly forget. Johnson was a much better writer of formal verse than Dunbar, and even he could lapse into bombastic doggerel. ("See! There he stands; not brave, but with an air / Of sullen stupor. Mark him well! Is he / Not more like brute than man?") There's life in Dunbar's best dialect verses, music, humor, vivacity. If he can be accused of literary blackface, can't a reverse critique be made of his and Johnson's formal verse—that it was a kind of phony whiteface poesy? And shouldn't it be noted that, whether writing in dialect or with grave formality, they were doing whatever they thought was needed to reach White readers and audiences? They wore the mask. They were slumming, like Will Marion Cook and Bert Williams and countless others, and they knew it. It beat waiting tables or digging ditches.

Because Dunbar's dialect poems present happy plantation slaves who sometimes express genuine affection for Massa, and freed

slaves in the North who pine to return South, critics find them in-
authentic. But he did his "fieldwork," collecting stories from his
mother and other former slaves. And the fact is, those are sentiments that were expressed by some former slaves. From 1934 to
1941, the WPA sent out teams of interviewers to gather some two
thousand oral histories from the last surviving former slaves around
the country. A number of their stories, recorded as mild dialect, are
collected in the book *Bullwhip Days*. The vast majority of the informants describe the horrors and degradations of slavery, but a minority actually do pine for the old plantation days, in language
surprisingly similar to that of Dunbar's speakers.

Charley Williams was born on a plantation near Monroe,
Louisiana, in 1843, and in interview professes nothing but love and
admiration for his kindly "Old Master." He says that "any time de
Lord want me I'm ready, and I likes to think when He ready He going tell Old Master to ring de bell for me to come on in." And "I wants
to see Old Master again anyways. I reckon maybe I'll jest go up and
ask him what he want me to do, and he'll tell me, and iffen I don't
know how, he'll show me how, and I'll try to do it to please him."

Maybe that's an old man's nostalgia for a poorly remembered
youth. Maybe it's Stockholm syndrome. Still, the sentiment was neither ubiquitous norm nor unique. I offer it to suggest that Dunbar
may well have heard similar from his informants. The very next former slave in *Bullwhip Days*, Jack Maddox, adds a bitterly funny coda:

"Yes, I was born a slave and so was [his wife] Rosa. We got out of
the chattel slavery, and I was better for gettin' out, but Rosa don't
think so. She says all we was freed for is to starve to death. I guess
she's right 'bout that, too, for herself. She says her white folks were
good to her. But don't you expect me to love my white folks. I love
them like a dog loves hickory.

"I was settin' here thinking the other night 'bout the talk of them
kind of white folks going to Heaven. Lord God, they'd turn Heaven

the wrong side out and have the angels working to make something they could take away from them."

Charles Chesnutt (1853–1932) was a Black writer who used and subverted tropes of Dixified nostalgia more successfully and less apologetically than Dunbar. He was writing some of the best fiction in America around the turn of the century, but he doesn't have the reputation he deserves because he often incorporated Negro dialects. The grandson of a White man and the son of freed slaves, Chesnutt was very light-skinned and could easily pass for White—a topic he wrote about with piercing intelligence and great courage.

In the series of stories collected as *The Conjure Woman* (1899), Chesnutt introduced yet another storytelling "uncle," Uncle Julius, who speaks in a very heavy Carolinas dialect. When we first see Julius, Chesnutt portrays him, with what I'm sure was conscious intent, as just a farcical coon character:

> One end of the log was already occupied by a venerable-looking colored man. He held on his knees a hatful of grapes, over which he was smacking his lips with great gusto. . . .
>
> "Now, ef dey's an'thing a nigger lub, nex' ter 'possum, en chick'n, en watermill,ums, it's scuppernon's [wine]. . . . De scuppernon' make you smack yo' lip en roll yo' eye en wush fer mo'; so I reckon it ain' very 'stonmishin' dat niggers lub scuppernon'."

Having beguiled his White readers with precisely the sort of comical old darky they loved to see—complete with lip-smacking, eye-rolling, and possum en chicken en watermillyums—Chesnutt quickly starts to dismantle the stereotype, and slip in all sorts of revealing observations about the complexities of Southern society during and after slavery days. As *The Conjure Woman* progresses, Julius turns out to be a clever negotiator of roles and manipulator of often clueless White folks. The witchy hoodoo practiced by Aunt Peggy, the titular conjurer, operates on many levels throughout plantation society—as folklore, as superstition, but especially as an agency through which Blacks can work out power relations both among themselves and between them and the White folks. Sometimes the results are very funny. In "The Goophered Grapevine" (to "goopher" is more or less to put a hex on something or someone), Uncle Julius tells a long tale of how Aunt Peggy bewitched the plantation's grapes so that anyone who ate them came to a bad end—except for one old slave, whose health is linked to that of the grapes, so that every spring and summer he's virile and strong, while he just seems to wither up and grow feeble every fall and winter. Seeing this, his cunning master sells him to a different unsuspecting owner every spring, then apologetically buys him back at half-price every fall, only to sell him again to some new sucker when his strength returns in the spring. At the end of the story, we find out that Uncle Julius may be working a con of his own: it's possible that in telling the tale to a prospective new owner from the North, he's trying to scare the White man off so that he can have all the "scuppernon'" to himself.

Wheels within wheels, transfers of dominance and submission in all directions, everybody scheming and scamming or just trying to survive within the constrictions of ante- and postbellum plantation culture—Chesnutt's stories reveal layers of Southern life rarely seen in even the best of the other dialect writers. His novel *The Marrow of Tradition* (1901) delves deeper still. It's a harrowing, closely observed story of corrosive race relations in the Reconstruction South, incorporating multiple points of view: former slaves negotiating a new social order, their offspring who never knew slavery, plantation gentry ruined by the war, poor white trash who embrace and exploit supremacist trends, mulattoes caught in between. In one of many remarkable passages, a young "brown" nurse meets and is dismissive of an old Black mammy, a former slave. Chesnutt writes: "Standing, like most young people of her race, on the border between two irreconcilable states of life, she had neither the picturesqueness of the slave, nor the unconscious dignity of those of whom freedom has been the immemorial birthright; she was in what might be called the chip-on-the-shoulder stage, through which races as well as individuals must pass in climbing the ladder of life,—not an interesting, at least not an agreeable stage, but an inevitable one."

Like Dunbar, though even more wrongheadedly, Chesnutt would be accused of Uncle Tomism by twentieth-century chip-on-the-shoulder dogmatists such as Baraka. More recently, some critics have revived interest in Chesnutt "by noting [his] role as a subversive voice working quietly to dismantle the plantation tradition [in literature] from within." Chesnutt's journals make his agenda plain. He wrote to make a living: "I want fame; I want money. I want to raise my children in a different rank of life from that I sprang from." At the same time, he noted, "I shall write for a purpose, a high holy purpose. . . . The object of my writings would be not so much the elevation of the colored people as the elevation of the whites." I think his work brilliantly negotiates this tricky path.

Zora Neale Hurston was raised in the Black town of Eatonville, Florida, in the first decade of the 1900s. She traveled north as a young woman, attending Howard University and then Barnard, where she studied anthropology under Franz Boas. She went back to Florida and the Gulf States to collect the Black folklore—locally known as "lies"—that she presented in books like the wonderful *Mules and Men* (1935).

Hurston used dialect to capture how her friends and family spoke—the rhythms, the humor, the local slang and references. Compare this story Hurston heard about "Ole Nora" (Noah) with Irwin Russell's "De Fust Banjo":

Well, you know when de Flood was and dey had two of everything in de ark—well, Ole Nora didn't take on no trees, so de woodpecker set 'round and set 'round for a week or so then he felt like he just had to peck himself some wood. So he begin to peck on de Ark. Ole Nora come to him and tole him, "Don't peck on de Ark. If you peck a hole in it, we'll all drown."

Woodpecker says: "But Ah'm hungry for some wood to peck."

Ole Nora says, "Ah don't keer how hongry you gits don't you peck on dis ark no mo. You want to drown everybody and everything?"

But the woodpecker can't stop himself, until eventually Noah puts a hammer to the back of his head, "and dat's why a peckerwood got a red head today."

Hurston's "liars" were masters of the sort of ridiculous tall tales that Constance Rourke considered quintessential American humor. One informant tells Hurston about planting corn on land so rich the corn sprouted as soon as he sowed the seed. "Ah didn't want it to grow too fast 'cause it would make all fodder and no roastin' ears so Ah hollered to my brother to sit down on some of it to stunt de growth. So he did, and de next day he dropped me back a note—says: 'passed thru Heben yesterday twelve o'clock sellin' roastin' ears to de angels.'" Hurston also collected numerous examples of the same kind of animal lore that Joel Chandler Harris had heard, adapted by her neighbors to their swampy Gulf environs—how Brer Gator got his grin, how the possum lost the hair on his tail, and many more.

Hurston was a terrific folklorist, who also did important anthropological work on Southern hoodoo and Haitian Voodoo. You'd think a Black woman in the early twentieth century who showed Hurston's indomitable ambition and dazzling intelligence would have been widely praised, but the use of dialect got her into trouble with the dicty types as well. She "continually needed to defend her work from the Black purists who regarded [her stories] as misleading portrayals of African-American existence." Some of the most powerful voices in the Black intelligentsia, from Du Bois to Richard Wright, deplored her use of dialect and likened it to minstrelsy.

Their censure of her work had its effect—she died in poverty, with much of her work having lapsed out of print. Alice Walker and others helped resurrect Hurston's genius in the 1970s, but her writing remains, for all the wrong reasons, somewhat controversial.

ALTHOUGH IT HAD PASSED ITS ZENITH, NEGRO-DIALECT lit could still achieve wide popularity well into the 1900s. The works employing it included not only low humor, but some of the leading American fiction of the century, from William Faulkner's *The Sound and the Fury*, with its dialogue of Reverend Shegog and the Deacon, to Toni Morrison's *Beloved*, with its much milder usage. Whether this usage is proper or appropriate, whether it marks the writer as a racist or a self-hater, whether it renders the work unsuitable for teaching in today's "diverse" classrooms, have been endlessly debated by academics and literati, with little consensus in sight.

Porgy, a novel about Blacks by White Southern gentleman DuBose Heyward, was published with success in 1925. Heyward adapted it into a play two years later, and that was the basis for George Gershwin's hit musical *Porgy and Bess*. At about the same time, Roark Bradford saw the publication of his *Ol' Man Adam an' His Chillun*, issued by Harper & Brothers in 1928 and still being reprinted in paperback at least into the mid-1940s. It retells Bible stories, from Genesis through the tale of "Nigger Deemus," in Bradford's version of Louisiana Negro dialect. Genesis ("Eve and That Snake") begins:

> Well, a long time ago things was diffrunt. Hit wa'n't nothin' on de yearth 'cause hit wa'n't no yearth. And hit wa'n't nothin' nowheres and ev'y day was Sunday. Wid de Lawd r'ared back preachin' all day long ev'y day. 'Ceptin' on Sadday, and den ev'ybody went to de fish fry.
>
> So one day ev'ybody was out to de fish fry, eatin' fish and b'iled custard and carryin' on, to all at once de Lawd swallowed some b'iled custard which didn't suit his tas'e.

"Dis custard," say de Lawd, "ain't seasoned right. Hit's too thick."

De Lawd and Gabriel determine that there's not enough "firmament" in the recipe.

So de Lawd r'ared back and passed a miracle and say, "Let hit be some firmament. And when I say let hit be some firmament, I mean let hit be a whole heap of firmament. I'm sick and tired of lettin' hit be jest a little bitty dab of firmament when I pass a miracle."

And you jest ought to see de firmament! Hit jes sloshed all over ev'ything so de angels and cherubs couldn't hardly fly, and ev'ybody was standin' round, knee deep, shiverin' and chatterin' and squirmin' round.

"Well," say de mammy angel, "I guess I better git my cherubs and git on home and dry 'em out. They's shiverin' like they got a buck aguer, right now."

And so on.

Bradford was born in Tennessee in 1896. He was a journalist in Atlanta and New Orleans in the early 1920s, and began writing fiction in 1926. *Ol' Man Adam*, his first book, collects stories he wrote for the New York *World* and elsewhere. He wrote two other Negro-themed books, *This Side of Jordan* and *John Henry*, before his death in 1948.

Ol' Man Adam is best remembered today not as a book but in performance. It was the inspiration for Marc Connelly's highly successful if controversial Broadway play *The Green Pastures*, performed by an all-Black cast, which won a Pulitzer in 1930. The well-known film version appeared in 1936. It became one of Warner Bros.' big box-office hits of the 1930s. Among its stars was the comic Eddie Anderson, who the following year would debut on radio as Jack Benny's foil Rochester. Ironically, the movie's actors were coached by a White man in how to speak Louisiana dialect.

Reading *Ol' Man Adam* is a somewhat different experience from watching *The Green Pastures*. On the page, the heavy dialect soon grows wearisome, and the humor and charm grow stale. Connelly's lighter hand and the cast's graceful and dignified performances help uplift the film. Although it's not so easy to find copies of the film anymore, it remains a "Critic's Pick" on the *New York Times* website, which says it is "excellent for children" and remarks: "Unlike many other so-called racist films of decades past, *The Green Pastures* nearly always charms and captivates its modern-day audiences; even the most adamant of 'P.C.' advocates will probably thoroughly enjoy the experience." Even Black filmmaker Melvin Van Peebles, who can be scathing in his denunciations of Hollywood's depictions of Black culture, cuts it a break.

Black film historian Donald Bogle takes a dimmer view. "It is now evident that *The Green Pastures* rested on a cruel assumption: that nothing could be more ludicrous than transporting the lowly language and folkways of the early twentieth-century Negro back to the high stately world before the flood. . . . And in this juxtaposition of low with high, there were implied Negro ignorance and inferiority."

Really? Bradford's book, and Connelly's adaptations even more so, seem less like parody than sincere, if patronizing, attempts by White men to evoke and pay homage to Black speech and Negro spirituality. As in the Uncle Remus stories, the intent here appears to be not mockery but mimicry. No characters are maligned or lampooned; at worst, they're treated with a gentle but respectful condescension. Certainly not a single character in the film version is any more caricatured or less dignified than in the so-called race movies Blacks themselves were making at the time of its release. There's even something mildly subversive about picturing heaven and earth and the whole universe as places where Blacks don't encounter a single White person. Jack Maddox would no doubt have agreed that this would be heaven indeed.

At the height of Whites' fascination with Harlem in the 1920s, many White writers offered their readers peeks inside the nightclubs and parlors of the famous neighborhood. Some were spurious, others achieved a respectable authenticity. Octavus Roy Cohen was a Jewish lawyer in Birmingham, Alabama, who gave up his law career to write full-time, cranking out innumerable short stories for *The Saturday Evening Post* and many other magazines from the 1910s into the 1950s. He specialized in detective stories and other pulp. One of his best-known creations was Florian Slappey, a sharp-dressing but often dull-witted "colored gentleman" from "Bumminham" who moves to Harlem, where the local sharpies quickly disabuse him of his savings, thereby leading him into numerous intrigues and misadventures. The stories were collected in the books *Florian Slappey Goes Abroad* (1928) and *Florian Slappey* (1938). You have to wonder whether Cohen understood what an extraordinary affront it was to launch his Jazz Age Zip Coon into the heart of the Harlem Renaissance, where he never seems to encounter a Langston Hughes or an Arna Bontemps, but only characters straight out of *Amos 'N' Andy* (for which Cohen wrote some radio episodes), with names like Caesar Clump, Forcep Swain and Orifice R. Latimer. Probably not. Typical dialogue:

"Somethin' wrong, Willie?"

"Us is ruint!" wailed Mr. Plush. "Absotively an' posolutely bank-rumpted!"

You get the idea. Things get even more Slappey-happy when Florian goes abroad, having lied his way onto a Negro film crew, Midnight Pictures, which most implausibly travels around Europe and North Africa to shoot on location. He tells them he can speak French. The joke being, of course, that he can't even speak Standard English. There's precisely one good joke in the entire volume: Seeing Carabinieri marching all around Naples in their fancy uniforms, Florian assumes they're all lodge brothers.

Carl Van Vechten was another White author who wrote about Harlem in the 1920s, but there are more than six degrees of separation between his characters and Mr. Slappey. Van Vechten was a novelist, critic, photographer and all-around aesthete. A Jazz Age avatar of Norman Mailer's White Negro—the sort of White enthusiast for Black culture whom Zora Neale Hurston humorously dubbed "Negrotarian"—he spent a lot of time in Harlem and was an enthusiastic supporter, financial and otherwise, of the Harlem Renaissance. It was his personal intervention that got the first books published by James Weldon Johnson, Hurston and Hughes, with whom he probably had a love affair.

His personal associations with Black culture emboldened Van Vechten to write a novel with all Black characters, freely using dialect, and give it the incendiary title *Nigger Heaven.* Published in 1926, the book was a dazzling succès de scandale, quickly selling through multiple printings (my copy is from the fourteenth edition, which came out eighteen months after the first). It set off a ruckus in literary circles, where White critics tended to defend it as Black critics attacked it. Read more calmly eight decades later, we can see it as a sincere, if eccentric, attempt to depict Roaring Twenties Harlem, very reminiscent of Charles Chesnutt's work (which Van Vechten also championed). Van Vechten shows off his familiarity with various levels of Harlem society, from the dicty elite and their resentful servants to the gamblers and hoodlums. Like Chesnutt, he's especially insightful in describing the difficulties faced by mulattoes as they attempt to negotiate the color bars in both White and Black society. One pair of friends who are light enough to pass for Latin can go to any play, opera or restaurant in Manhattan; still, they're always afraid a sharp-eyed maître d' or theater manager will mortify them by inviting them up to the balcony or out to the street. Van Vechten studs the narrative with piquant hipster details. He can list the hot spots by their clientele: the Winter Palace for "ofays and jig-chasers," another for "pink-chasers and bulldikers," and so on. He informed his White readers that West 139th Street, where successful folks like Fletcher Henderson lived in big brownstones, was locally known as Strivers' Row. He puts dialect in the mouths of the lowlifers, but contrasts them with the college-educated Talented Tenth, who speak bitterly about the struggle of Black intellectuals and artists to be taken seriously in the White world.

In *Nigger Heaven*'s explosive climax, his representatives of the Talented Tenth fail to rise above the ghetto, and are dragged down by Harlem's nightlife and criminal elements. A slam-bang ending, but one that caused many critics to denounce Van Vechten for "catering to the voyeurism of whites who were already accustomed to reading about the primitive nature of Blacks and their inclination toward criminality. Leading the attack was the Black press, most notably the editor of the NAACP's *The Crisis*, W. E. B. DuBois, who in chastising Van Vechten for ignoring the average, hardworking, decent Harlemite, wrote in his scathing review: 'There is scarcely a generous impulse or beautiful idea. . . . It is the surface mud he slops in.'" There's both irony and pathos in this: Du Bois was yet another Black writer whom Van Vechten supported. Van Vechten's Black friends, including Hughes, rose to his defense, but a bit halfheartedly; the crux of their argument was that if White readers needed a White author to explain Black culture to them, better a Van Vechten than an Octavus Roy Cohen.

Old-school dialect literature petered out by 1930, but that wasn't the end of White author's creating Black characters or putting Black English in their mouths, which can still spark arguments. They range from the series of Shaft novels penned by a White man, Ernest Tidyman, to William Styron's highly controversial *The Confessions of Nat Turner* (1967), which some critics accused of trafficking in old stereotypes of Black males as oversexed and violent, to Philip Roth's no less argued-about *The Human Stain* (2000), which addressed identity politics and political correctness through the figure of a light-skinned Black professor bizarrely accused of racism.

And then there's John Howard Griffin's *Black Like Me* (1961). It's not Negro-dialect lit, but then again, its author literally wore black-face. In 1959, Griffin chemically darkened his skin and spent six weeks traveling around the South, impersonating a Black man. The book (and to a lesser degree the film adaptation) made a giant splash because a White person had "gone undercover," as it were, and reported back to White America on the daily indignities and injustices suffered by Black Americans. It was pitched as seat-of-the-pants sociology, but it was really sensational journalism. On that level, it was a rousing success. Liberal media widely championed Griffin, while rednecks and crackers lynched him in effigy in the center of the small Texas town where he lived.

Black readers were less impressed with the book than their White counterparts. They pointed out, correctly, that Griffin's experiment, while undoubtedly bold and well intentioned, was seriously flawed. In the first place, there was something inadvertently but deeply insulting in the notion that a White man had to explain to other Whites what it felt like to be Black, when there were plenty of gifted Black writers and speakers in the country who'd been trying to tell them the same thing for a very, very long time.

Also, Griffin's central claim—that he'd learned what it felt like to be Black in the segregated South—was awesomely presumptuous. Griffin could not, of course, experience or explain what it's like to be Black in America: he could describe only what it felt like to be a *White man pretending to be Black* in America. In effect, he could report only what it felt like to wear blackface. Simply darkening his skin and spending six weeks being treated rudely and hatefully by Whites hardly meant he could speak knowledgeably about what it was like to be born, live and die as a Black person. When his charade became intolerable, Griffin could always transform back into a White man, which he did several times during his experiment. How many Black people could do the same?

At his most excessive, Griffin wrote as though merely by appearing to be Black, and living briefly among Blacks, some part of him actually *became* Black during the experience. Relatively early in the book, he begins slipping into the use of "we," implying "we Black people." Even the book's title suggests this. Although Griffin lifted the title from a Negro song, the reader can't help getting the impression that the "me" refers to the author.

Even as pseudosociology, Griffin's research program was severely biased from the start. He began his project with a preconception of how awful it was to be a Black in the South, and then went looking only for experiences that would confirm that preconception. He sits in the back of many buses, he shines shoes on a sidewalk in New Orleans, he hitchhikes on lonely country roads, and so on. The Black life he reports on is one-sided, repetitious and, by the end of the book, almost as caricatured and two-dimensional as the stereotypes of Black life he was hoping to counter. He assiduously avoids any occasion of good times or fun in Black society: he never attends a church social, a barbecue or ballgame, never just sits on a stoop of an evening or plays a game of cards with other men. On Saturday nights he holes up in his tiny room in a Black YMCA, hiding from the boisterous activities he can hear booming out of the bars and honky-tonks on the street below. A devout convert to Roman Catholicism, Griffin apparently equated occasions of fun with occasions of sin. He cannot witness (even from a safe distance) Blacks having a good time without perceiving an underlying foundation of desperation, despair, degradation and violence. Had he loosened up, had a few drinks, danced with a few women, jawed with a few fellows over some beers, he might have gotten a fuller picture of Southern Black life. Put simply, the guy was a killjoy. Behind the blackface, he was just another White man with a stick up his ass. "Yeah, we got our troubles all right," Albert Murray once wrote. "But still and all, if white folks could be black for just one Saturday night they wouldn't never want to be white folks no more!"

Griffin had that chance, and he muffed it.

THE FLAGSHIP OF ALL CONTROVERSIAL NEGRO DIALECT literature remains what may have been its high-water mark. *The Adventures of Huckleberry Finn* has been scandalizing librarians, educators and other watchdogs of the moral fiber of America's youth since the day it was published in the United States in 1885—but the reason it outrages people has flipped over the years. The public library in Concord, Massachusetts, banned it upon publication as "the veriest trash," but not out of any apprehension that it was racially insensitive. They just thought Huck was a White-trash delinquent who presented a terrible role model for good little girls and boys. In the first decade of the 1900s, public libraries from Brooklyn to Denver followed suit. By the 1930s many libraries carried only edited and expurgated editions.

The charges that the book is racist are based on Twain's use of dialect, the frequent appearance of the word "nigger," and the fact that some see the runaway slave Jim as a minstrel-show stereotype. Because it's become a racial football, *Huck Finn* has been reduced to simplistic pro-or-con, good-or-bad arguments. Is it a great work of American literature that must be taught to all students, or so offensive to Black students that it must be banned?

That the argument has dragged on for decades demonstrates that neither Twain nor his book yields easily to simple political agendizing. Twain was a genius, and had the satirist's gift for observing humanity in all its glories and foibles. But he was a man of his time. He was not untainted by the racism that surrounded him. (Who is?) He was tremendously fond of blackface minstrelsy, and as Eric Lott and others have pointed out, there's a lot in *Huck Finn* that seems lifted straight from the minstrel stage, especially Huck and Jim's comic repartee, so reminiscent of Mr. Interlocutor (Huck) and Mr. Bones (Jim). Toni Morrison famously declared the characters an example of "over-the-top minstrelization." Ralph Ellison noted that the adult in the Huck–Jim relationship is really Huck, "with his street-sparrow sophistication," while Jim comes off as a big, innocent child.

And yet, as even Ellison grudgingly agreed, Twain worked those racialist conventions for complex effect, and the book builds toward a message that completely contradicts its minstrel-show trappings. Since the book is narrated by Huck, the epitome of ignunt poor White trash, it makes perfect literary sense that he should start out with what sounds like a dismissive attitude toward Blacks:

Tom said he slipped Jim's hat off of his head and hung it on a limb right over him, and Jim stirred a little, but he didn't wake. Afterwards Jim said the witches bewitched him and put him in a trance, and rode him all over the State, and then set him under the trees again, and hung his hat on a limb to show who done it. And next time Jim told it he said they rode him down to New Orleans; and, after that, every time he told it he spread it more and more, till by and by he said they rode him all over the world, and tired him most to death, and his back was all over saddle-boils. Jim was monstrous proud about it, and he got so he wouldn't hardly notice the other niggers. Niggers would come miles to hear Jim tell about it, and he was more looked up to than any nigger in that country. Strange niggers would stand with their mouths open and look him all over, same as if he was a wonder. Niggers is always talking about witches in the dark by the kitchen fire; but whenever one was talking and letting on to know all about such things, Jim would happen in and say, "Hm! What you know 'bout witches?" and that nigger was corked up and had to take a back seat. Jim always kept that five-center piece round his neck with a string, and said it was a charm the devil give to him with his own hands, and told him he could cure anybody with it and fetch witches whenever he wanted to just by saying something to it; but he never told what it was he said to it. Niggers would come from all around there and give Jim anything they had, just for a sight of that five-center piece; but they wouldn't touch it, because the devil had had his hands on it. Jim was most ruined for a servant, because he got stuck up on account of having seen the devil and been rode by witches.

But when Huck and Jim run away and begin their adventures as a pair of fugitives on the Mississippi, no reader can mistake the genuine admiration and love that come to bind them. Both grow and develop from their friendship. By the end of the novel, Jim is arguably the most fully human Black character created by a White author in the nineteenth century, not a flat symbol but a complexity of ignorance and wisdom, fear and courage, as filled with ambiguity and confusion and the potential for greatness as any human being. "Twain fitted Jim into the outlines of the minstrel tradition," Ellison wrote, but went on to say that "it is from behind the stereotype mask that we see Jim's dignity and human capacity—and Twain's complexity—emerge." Meanwhile, Huck grows from his association with Jim. At the story's pivotal point, when Jim is captured and returned to slavery, Huck steps up to his duty and risks his own freedom to help his friend escape again. "Huck Finn has struggled with the problem posed by the clash between property rights and human rights," Ellison argued, and "has made his decision on the side of humanity."

Ellison wrote that in 1946. It did not help *Huck Finn* get around complaints of racism from groups like the NAACP, which began its campaign against the book's presence in public school classrooms in 1957. It's worth noting that the national headquarters of the organization has never advocated the outright banning of the book, though many more hotheaded state offices have. Since the 1970s, not a year has gone by without reports that some library or school system somewhere in the country is facing demands from students, parents or a local NAACP office to remove the book from the classroom and the stacks. In the 1980s a school administrator took it upon himself to rewrite the book deleting the word "nigger."

In 1996, *Huck Finn* topped People For the American Way's list of most frequently challenged books, but that needs to be put in proper context. In 2000, the American Library Association ranked it fifth—just above *Of Mice and Men* and the Harry Potter series, but below *Daddy's Roommate* and Maya Angelou's *I Know Why the Caged Bird Sings*. Others high on the ALA list were *The Catcher in the Rye*, the Goosebumps series, *Heather Has Two Mommies*, Madonna's *Sex*, and *The Color Purple*. Charges of racist content rank a lowly ninth in terms of frequency, far exceeded by complaints about sexually explicit material, "offensive language" or the promotion of homosexuality or the occult.

The complaint of Black students that they are made to feel uncomfortable by *Huck Finn*, especially from hearing passages read aloud in the classroom, cannot be shrugged off easily. A number of school systems have simply dropped the book from their curricula, prompting many citations of a famous Twain observation: "In the first place God made idiots. This was for practice. Then he made School Boards." Others negotiate a settlement whereby the book is taught with a lot of contextual materials and discussion.

6

BLACK & WHITE FILM, REEL ONE

Uncle Tom's Cinema

Topsy was soon a noted character in the establishment. Her talent for
every species of drollery, grimace, and mimicry,—for dancing, tum-
bling, climbing, singing, whistling, imitating every sound that hit her
fancy,—seemed inexhaustible.

— HARRIET BEECHER STOWE, *Uncle Tom's Cabin*

Blackface made an effortless leap from the stage to the movie
screen virtually the moment the moving picture was invented.
No medium is more American than movies. So it should be no sur-
prise that American movies have often been obsessed with matters
of race and images of Blackness. From the instant Thomas Edison
introduced his peep-show Kinetoscope in 1889, American motion
pictures began capturing images of Blacks on film. His brief footage
of Black kids from 1893 is the earliest known. For almost a century,
since the cameras were almost always in the hands of White people,
those images were almost always of Blacks, and others, as White
people saw them. A stroll through early film strips turns up a wealth
of ethnic imagery. Some of it is documentary and ethnographic, like
Edison's views of Mexican washerwomen, Japanese acrobats, shy
"pickaninnies" and "Esquimaux." Other strips document the ethnic

and lower-class stereotypes that so amused vaudeville audiences. Coon-show antics make up only a small part of this rogues' gallery, which included bearded, hook-nosed Jews (American Mutoscope & Biograph's 1903 "A Gesture Fight in Hester Street"), drunken Irishmen (Mutoscope's "A Wake in Hell's Kitchen," in which the deceased sits up in his coffin and enjoys a last mug of ale), glum Injuns, "Turkish" dancing girls, the "French" clowns Alphonse and Gaston, ragged Bowery boys and so on.

Donald Bogle, one of the most influential and dyspeptic of Black film historians, sees Black film caricatures falling into five archetypes, indicated in the title of his best-known book, *Toms, Coons, Mulattoes, Mammies, & Bucks.* Toms and mammies are obvious—they're the kindly older Negro house servants, Uncle Tom, Uncle Remus, Uncle Mose, Uncle Ben, Aunt Chloe, Aunt Jemima (Ain'tcha Mama). We may call them uncles and aunts, but they're really the nation's grandparents, the granddads and grandmas we all wish we had but only wealthy folks could afford to buy. Coons are the shuffling black clowns like Stepin Fetchit. Mulattoes and mulattas are the light-skinned, Caucasian-looking hunks and hotties, from 1930s cowboy star Herb Jeffries to Lena Horne and Halle Berry, who—even in many Black-made films—often get the lead over darker performers. The buck is the big, dangerous, sexual male, from the rampaging hordes in *The Birth of a Nation* to John Shaft, Jim Brown and Samuel L. Jackson. (Black film critic Armond White writes off Jackson's entire career as "Scary Negro" shtick.) Bogle sees mortifying examples of these archetypes littering the early decades of American moviemaking, from Edison's *Ten Pickaninnies* of 1904 through *The Wooing and Wedding of a Coon, How Rastus Got His Turkey, Coon Town Suffragettes* and *The Birth of a Nation* to Shirley Temple movies, *The Green Pastures* and *Song of the South.*

Political scientist Michael Rogin noted the oddly telling fact that three of the most important films in this developmental period of American movies use stories that centrally feature Blackness. The

1903 Edison–Porter adaptation of *Uncle Tom's Cabin* is considered one of the first "full-length" American films (at fourteen minutes) to tell a more or less fully developed story, and the first to use title cards. D. W. Griffith's 1915 *The Birth of a Nation* was really the first feature-length Hollywood epic, establishing a language for making and watching films that Hollywood follows to this day. And in 1927, *The Jazz Singer*, with Al Jolson's renowned blackface scenes, was the first talkie.

Edwin S. Porter was a mechanic who went to work for Thomas Edison as a cameraman in 1900. He's considered the first American film director, the pioneer who took Edison's 1894 invention of moving pictures and figured out the rudiments of using the new technology to create entertainment for the masses. In 1903 he premiered two of the most significant works of early cinema—the ten-minute *Great Train Robbery* (which, though brief and primitive, established a remarkable number of the tropes cowboy movies would employ, to this day) and his fourteen-minute redaction of *Uncle Tom's Cabin*. Fittingly, both debuted at a venue of low entertainment—Huber's 14th Street Museum in Manhattan. Huber's was a dime museum. It displayed a grab bag of odd items (including, most famously, a forgery of Abraham Lincoln's touching condolence letter to Mrs. Lydia Bixby, who had lost five sons in the Civil War), and hosted vaudeville and circus and sideshow acts (a seventeen-year-old Harry Houdini honed his routine there), and could reasonably claim to be America's first movie theater, although the first nickelodeon, or space devoted specifically to screening movies, wasn't created until 1905. Huber's would screen short films as part of a larger revue of live acts. The debut screening of *Uncle Tom's Cabin*, for instance, shared the bill with a team of "colored comedians."

Donald Bogle would probably disagree, but I find that Porter's *Uncle Tom's Cabin* remains a film of immense charm. He shot it in Edison's studio in New Jersey, a tiny space where actors were crammed together before flat backdrops and bits of cheap stage set.

Porter is thought to have hired a passing Tom Show, and it certainly looks that way—as though a traveling road show simply backed its caravan into the studio, dropped the back gate, and started to perform while Porter cranked his single, stationary camera. To squeeze Stowe's epic story onto one reel of film, Porter reduced it to fourteen brief, iconic vignettes—not unlike the images in those magic-lantern shows. He knew that his audience would be thoroughly familiar with the story, so he could dispense with virtually all exposition and shoot just the high points—Eliza on the ice floes, Topsy's dance, Eva's and Tom's death scenes and so on. Porter used title cards, for the first time ever, to introduce each vignette. He ingeniously integrated traditional stage tricks—the river Eliza "crosses" is a billowing cloth—with new filmic special effects that must have been eye-popping in 1903, a time when a cowboy unloading his six-gun at the audience of *The Great Train Robbery* could incite panicked rioting. One can only imagine how the Huber's crowd—reputedly made up mainly of prostitutes, pickpockets, assorted other lowlifes, and immigrant laborers—reacted when the glowing angel appeared to the dying Tom, or the toy steamboat burst into flames.

The featured Negro roles were all performed by blackfaced Whites, with Blacks only as extras. Somehow this fits all the other road-show gimcrackery: with all the sets and effects so cheap and patently unrealistic, why not black up White folks to portray Negroes?

Film had made tremendous strides in the decade between Porter's short and William Robert Daly's 1914 version of *Uncle Tom's Cabin*. In effect, movies had become movies. Much of the cinematic language Griffith is often said to have introduced in *The Birth of a Nation* is visible, if sometimes in a more primitive form, in Daly's film. Daly's version is in every way an expansion of what Porter had been able to do. At roughly fifty minutes, he had space to tell Stowe's whole story, if still in a compressed version. He shot some scenes with more than one camera, so that he could edit between points of view. Where

Porter's version is basically a filmed stage performance, Daly took his cameras outdoors for many location shoots for "realism." Some location shoots are stunningly lensed—a gunfight in a rocky canyon is shot from several precipitous angles. Cinematic special effects had come a long way as well, and Daly made fine use of double exposure to show angels and ghosts in the same frame as living characters.

For our purposes, Daly's most impressive and bold directorial choice was to use actual Black actors in all featured Negro roles. Uncle Tom was played by none other than the minstrel and vaudeville star Sam Lucas, said to be the first Black to play the lead in an American movie. At seventy-four, he was a well-loved celebrity. In 1877, he'd been the first Black performer to integrate the formerly all-White Tom Show, and in decades of touring the country he established a reputation as the finest Uncle Tom of them all. A very popular song, "Uncle Tom's Gwine to Stay," was written for him in the 1880s after lyricist George Russell Jackson had been moved to tears by a Lucas performance. Lucas incorporated the song in his performances, and it became identified solely with him.

Oh, de old man's so tired dat he can't hardly walk,
But its here he's a-gwine for to stay.
And so now honey Liza you may cease yer talk,
For de old man he can't run away.
Oh, I've worked 'round de place for a great many years,
I'se always been honest and true;
Oh, de massa may sell me, but dry up your tears,
Fo' old Tom will be faithful to you.

CHORUS
Uncle Tom, Angels call,
And the old man am ready to go.
Dear dry your tears and for me hab no fears,
For de good Lord will help me I know.

Lucas didn't get to sing his signature song in Daly's silent film, of course, but he displayed some fine acting, as did several other Blacks in key roles. The most notable blackface role is that of Topsy; maybe Daly didn't feel up to bucking tradition on this score. Lucas had accustomed White audiences to seeing an actual Black man play Uncle Tom, but the blackface drag Topsy was one of the best-loved and most familiar figures of the American stage at the time. It was a critics' axiom of the day that when it came to playing the more outlandish or comic Negro characters, actual Blacks couldn't hold a candle to a blackfaced White man.

There were many other versions of Stowe's book on film. A 1927 version starred James B. Lowe, another fine Black actor, and the studio, Universal Pictures, proudly ballyhooed him and itself for it. The film's director had played Tom in blackface in an earlier version. An obscure 1976 version was, as far as I can tell, Blaxploitation; its star, Marilyn Joi (aka Tracy-Ann King, Ineda King—why not Ineda Mann?), also appeared in *Blazing Stewardesses, The Happy Hooker Goes to Washington, Cheerleaders' Wild Weekend* and *Ilsa, Harem Keeper of the Oil Sheiks.* A 1987 TV adaptation featured Phylicia Rashad, Samuel L. Jackson, Bruce Dern and, perhaps most odd, Avery Brooks (better known as Commander Sisko on *Star Trek: Deep Space Nine*) as Uncle Tom. But for some folks, probably the best film version of all was the one staged Thai-style in the 1956 Cinema-Scope adaptation of Rodgers and Hammerstein's *The King and I.* Somehow, the translation of the Civil War story of evil massas and runaway slaves to a "Siamese" setting brought its universal themes to the fore. Besides, it's the most charming set piece in the entire oeuvre of fifties movie musicals.

D. W. GRIFFITH'S *THE BIRTH OF A NATION* IS ONE OF THE two most controversial films of the twentieth century. The other is Leni Riefenstahl's *Triumph of the Will.* They're so controversial because they present us with the same ethical dilemma: how to assess and respond to a work of art when its artistic and technical genius are at the service of repugnant ideology. Both films offer heroic images of widely reviled political organizations: Riefenstahl glorifies the Nazi Party, Griffith makes heroes of the KKK. (Griffith's film is said to have been Adolf Hitler's all-time fave.) Ideologically, then, both films evoke revulsion. Yet aesthetically and technically, both are works of undeniable virtuosity, and milestones of cinema history. How we deal with that is a question that is still hotly debated, a century after Griffith's film appeared.

On one side are those who argue that these films are so offensive that they should be banned, destroyed, erased from the cultural record. Any artistic, technical or film-history value they may have is far outweighed by the repulsive ideologies they champion. They are perfect examples of history that's "best forgotten." Thus the Library of Congress left *Birth* off its archive of "cinema's wondrous first century," despite its enormous importance. The Museum of Modern Art similarly deaccessioned it for a time, as no doubt have many other archives. One user of the online Internet Movie Database (imdb.com) proudly reported that he found *Birth* so offensive he went into his local DVD store, bought all the copies he could find, and destroyed them. Another user noted how counterproductive and just plain dumbass this was, if everyone who found the film offensive imitated this action, stores would rush to restock their shelves and the movie would become a bestseller all over again.

The opposing view is that *no* history is best forgotten. It's foolish and dangerous to censor historical events we're not comfortable remembering. The impulse to erase the historical record of books, films, TV shows and other cultural products of the past because people find them offensive or embarrassing today is a totalitarian urge that results only in ignunce. Hitler did it, the Soviets did it, and George Orwell described it as a key tool of thought control in *1984*.

Triumph of the Will and *The Birth of a Nation* are important precisely because they were such powerful propaganda. They need to be studied as outstanding examples of how film can be used to promote ideology. That we find the ideology repulsive makes them all the more worth our attention. "*The Birth of a Nation* is not bad because it argues for evil," film critic Roger Ebert has written. "It is a great film that argues for evil. To understand how it does so is to learn a great deal about film, and even something about evil."

Griffith was a White Southerner, born and raised in rural Kentucky. His father had been a hero of the Confederacy in the Civil War. (Henry Walthall, the actor who plays the hero of the film and founder of the Klan, was also the son of a Confederate officer.) Griffith started out in theater, then went to work as an actor for Thomas Edison's studio (Edwin Porter directed him in some roles there) before becoming a prolific director of short films for American Biograph. It was there that he invented or honed the many revolutionizing techniques that film historians praise in *Birth of a Nation:* the enormous, wide-angle battle scenes and crowd scenes; the painstaking historical authenticity of the sets and tableaux; the use of the close-up reaction shot to prompt emotional responses in the audience; the way the film is edited to follow two or three simultaneous narrative lines; the iris shot; the flashback. Film buffs sometimes go overboard in claiming that all of these innovations suddenly appeared in *Birth,* when many of them can be seen, if sometimes in more primitive stages, in earlier films by Griffith and others. But it can certainly be said that Griffith both created new techniques and brilliantly incorporated the innovations of others, assembling everything in a whole that was far greater than the sum of its parts.

With *Birth of a Nation,* Griffith undeniably invented the Hollywood blockbuster. At twelve reels and three hours in length, with a cast of thousands, it was an enormous project by any standard of its day. It is the prototype of the big, long, expensive, much-ballyhooed box-office smasheroo that grips the attention of the entire nation and divides audiences and critics along clear love–hate lines. It's a formula Hollywood has tried to repeat as often as possible ever since.

It is also, as even its most ardent supporters readily admit, stunningly racist. Griffith reworked and expanded the story from Thomas Dixon's *The Clansman*. Both Griffith and Dixon were exploiting—and Griffith did much to spread—nativist, White supremacist sentiments that had spread among White Americans since Reconstruction. Nativists attacked not only Blacks but also Catholics, Jews, other ethnic immigrant groups and trade unionists, all of whom they accused of diluting and perverting the pure WASP heritage and spirit of this great nation. Blacks made the easiest and most favored targets. The NAACP estimates that between 1889 and 1918, some 2,500 Blacks were lynched by White vigilantes; the practice peaked in the years surrounding Griffith's film, probably not by coincidence.

Griffith's film blatantly championed the nativist view of the Civil War and its repercussions. In *Birth,* the defeat of the Confederacy floods the South with rampaging freed slaves and the Northern carpetbaggers (led by a mulatto) who egg them on. The idyllic, peaceful order of antebellum Southern society—a plantation system in which both the Whites and the darkies knew their place, and all were content to keep it—is rent asunder, and chaos (i.e., Reconstruction) ensues. Shiftless coons infest the hallowed halls of Southern statehouses. Bad-tempered bucks patrol the streets, saying and doing rude things to White folks. Formerly docile, obedient servants put on airs. Finally, the ultimate violation of Southern civil order: Blacks and mulattoes assaulting and raping Southern White women. This is too much for the Southern Gentleman to bear, naturally, and so he forms a noble organization of White self-protection, the Ku Klux Klan, which rides to the rescue like a cavalry of White knights, routing the loutish Negro and his carpetbagging mulatto friend, restoring order, civility, segregation and Jim Crow law: the Birth of a Nation.

Griffith was both a filmmaking genius and a master propagandist, and he fired *Birth* straight into the heart of America's psychosis about race. America responded, passionately pro or con. *Birth* packed moviehouses throughout the land, Hollywood's first box-office boffo. When periodic re-releases are added on, it is still among the highest-grossing films ever.

Birth of a Nation had a huge impact outside the box office as well. The KKK enjoyed a fabulous rebirth and growth spurt, in both publicity and membership, that has been attributed directly to the film; Klan members actually patrolled the aisles of theaters in some places, trolling for new sign-ups. It also drew protesters en masse. The young NAACP, founded in 1909 by Du Bois, Ida Wells-Barnett and other activists, mobilized picketers outside theaters in several cities. Other civic and religious organizations joined in. Violence sometimes ensued, persuading some cities and states to ban the film. No doubt that banned-in-Boston notoriety sold even more tickets in places where it was shown. Many newspaper editorials denounced the film as well. It was re-released to further uproar in 1921. "In 1950, there were renewed outcries when word leaked out that a Hollywood company was to remake the movie in sound," Bogle writes. "The remake plans were quickly aborted, as were the 1959 proposals to present it on television."

Today, *Birth of a Nation,* like many other racially embarrassing documents from the past, is one of those films that's talked about more than it's seen. It's screened mostly in film classes or library/ museum series, where, as with *Huck Finn,* presenters can carefully surround it with appropriate contexting materials and discussion. Presumably, the fear is that audiences won't be able to recognize the racist content for themselves. Even then, it continues to draw complaints and protests from those who believe it should simply disappear, period. In 2004, a Los Angeles movie theater that specializes in screening silent films with an accompanying organist canceled a screening because of what the proprietor said were threatening phone calls. It was the second time the theater had announced a screening and then withdrawn the film. That same year, a local chapter of the NAACP flipped when a public library in the Quad-City region of Iowa scheduled a screening as part of a "Movies That Changed Us" series. "People could not believe it was being shown in our community," an NAACP spokesperson said. "Our first thought was, 'You cannot show that movie.'" The organization and library staff reached a limp compromise: rather than the entire film, they screened selected excerpts as part of a discussion about racism.

That year saw an even more highly, but confusingly, contextualized screening when New York artist DJ Spooky showed his multimedia presentation *Rebirth of a Nation* at Lincoln Center. Spooky screened edited and digitally played-with versions of the film on three screens, with a thumping sound track of electronic dance music. As an audience member, I found it very hard to discern what Spooky was trying to say about the film, or race, with *Rebirth*. Maybe the point was simply that as a Black artist he was reclaiming Griffith's work as a species of Negrobilia. Whatever he was trying to say, as a retort to Griffith it was, as one *New York Times* critic put it, a "feeble" effort.

Griffith went to his grave in 1948 disingenuously proclaiming his innocence of any ill intent. He followed *Birth* with films like *Intolerance, The Greatest Thing in Life, Way Down East* and the stilted *Abraham Lincoln,* which can all be seen as his way of apologizing for *Birth* and demonstrating himself to be a great humanitarian.

Some of the most amazing scenes in *Birth of a Nation*—the Civil War battles, Lincoln's assassination—look uncannily "realistic." Griffith went to great lengths to achieve historical accuracy in these scenes, and it shows. They look like documentary newsreel footage.

The problem, at least for modern viewers, is that the apparent verisimilitude of these scenes makes the more staged scenes look all the more mawkishly melodramatic or historically bogus, and often just plain silly. To us today, the silliest-looking are the blackface actors. In this sense, Griffith wasn't innovating, but merely following stage and film convention. All the important Black roles are played by Whites in blackface. Indeed, virtually whenever Griffith needed a darky to act, even in a tiny role, he used a blackface actor. When he needed darkies merely lolling around or, of course, dancing, he used Blacks. In crowd scenes, Black people and blackfaced Whites rarely appear together; a crowd will usually be all Black extras or all black-face ones.

But whether they're standing next to real Blacks or in the frame alone, it's ludicrously obvious that they're White men in blackface. The shape of their heads, their ears, their noses, their flat butts, the way they move—except when executing the broadest minstrel-show pantomime gestures—none of it is remotely authentic to the way Black people would look or move. They are transparently White men in blackface. They're not even trying to look or act like Black people. It's as though they're intentionally *not* acting Black; as though the last thing they want the viewer to think is that they're real Black people. Interestingly, the only ones who even try to move and act like real Negroes are the fat White guys playing mammies. Which makes a certain sense. If blackface is a form of racial cross-dressing, leave it to the drag artists to pull it off the best.

The use of blackface reaches the height of the ridiculous in the pivotal chase scene where Flora, the virginal flower of Southern womanhood, is pursued through a primordial-looking forest by the lustful former slave Gus. The man playing Gus is patently not a Black man but a White actor in blackface—Walter Long, a lunk-headed tough-guy character actor who had an incredibly lengthy career in Hollywood, seen in nearly two hundred films, from *The Fugitive* in 1910 to the 1990 TV show *Dick Tracy,* in which he appeared as an old man named, ironically, Whitey. Long was a terrible blackface performer. He looks and moves like a heavyset White man who has somehow gotten himself very sooty. There's not a thing about him that would convince you he's a Black man. To the viewer today, this plays havoc with Griffith's intentions for the scene. We're supposed to see a young White female throw herself off a cliff rather than submit to the advances of a rampaging Black. But what we're watching is a young White female throwing herself off a cliff rather than submit to the advances of . . . a coal miner? an escapee from a minstrel show?

According to Lillian Gish, who starred in the film, Griffith's excuse for using so many blackface actors was that he couldn't find enough actual Black performers to fill the roles. That's not at all convincing. Daly had found plenty of Black actors when he filmed *Uncle Tom's Cabin* a few years earlier. Black filmmaker Oscar Micheaux, working at the same time as Griffith, filled his movies with Black casts. Why couldn't Griffith find any? I suspect he didn't look very hard. Griffith had lived through the era he evoked in the film. Born at the tail end of Reconstruction in 1875, he grew up White in the Jim Crow South, while America was busily deconstructing Reconstruction and establishing itself as an apartheid nation. Also, he'd lived most of his life at a time when the minstrel show was the dominant form of popular entertainment. Like all White Americans, he understood and liked blackface. And he was making a film in which the Black characters are almost all evil, loathsome savages. So, despite all the groundbreaking ingenuity and vision he displays in other realms of the film, he stuck to familiar minstrel-show conventions in this aspect.

Nineteenth-century minstrels claimed that when they toured the boondocks, the local Whites often mistook them for actual Black people. W. T. Lhamon, a most astute reader of historical documents, takes this claim at face value. Of course, there were plenty of frontier towns where White people may never have seen a Negro, or at least were not in any way familiar with Negroes. I suppose it's possible that some White moviegoers were similarly unaware that they were watching blackfaced Whites in Griffith's evil-Negro roles, but they also must have been out in the boonies.

Al Jolson in the familiar pose.

Birth of a Nation stimulated such a storm of protest over its negative Negro stereotypes that, except for a few weak-sister attempts at imitation, it shamed and scared Hollywood completely away from using blackfaced White actors imitating Blacks. This was good for Black actors and extras, though they were almost universally confined to demeaning or silly roles for decades. Blackface did not disappear from the screen, but after Griffith it was seen only in movies about vaudeville or when White characters decided to put on a minstrel show.

This was not by a long shot the end of other kinds of "ethnic drag" in Hollywood, of course. White folks in bad makeup and goofy costumes continued to play Hollywood Indians, Hollywood Asians,

Hollywood Arabs, Hollywood Latinos, even Hollywood Europeans, in film and on TV, for the rest of the century. Most of these portrayals would be as cringe-makingly stereotyped, as clumsy and just plain *wrong* as the worst blackface. And when Indian, Asian or Latino actors did get to play these roles, like Black actors they were often still playing their ethnicity as Hollywood saw it. (Latino actor-playwright John Leguizamo, for example, speaks wryly of being asked to play in many "Spixploitation" films in the 1990s.)

RELEASED IN 1927, *THE JAZZ SINGER* IS REMEMBERED NOW mostly as the movie that killed the silent film, "the first talkie"— although the first "singie" might be more accurate, since almost all of the sound in it is in the form of songs. It's hardly a talkie at all, but more of a hybrid of a traditional silent movie for the bulk of its running length, with a few isolated moments of sound dropped in.

As Michael Rogin noted, *The Jazz Singer* is at least as remarkable for the story it tells as for the technical revolution it signaled. Jake Rabinowitz grows up in the Jewish immigrant ghetto of the Lower East Side of Manhattan. His stern, resolutely Old World father (Warner Oland, a Swedish-born character actor who would soon switch from Jewish drag to Chinese drag and find enormous success in the long-running Charlie Chan series, sidekicked by Black comic actor Mantan Moreland) trains him to become the sixth generation of Rabinowitz men to sing as cantors in the synagogue, but little Jakie is far more interested in singing that newfangled American music called jazz. They fight; Jake leaves home; and when we next see him he's an adult, a jazz singer performing as Jack Robin. Back in New York to make his debut on Broadway, he has a fiery reunion with his outraged father and a tender one with his more open-minded, long-suffering mother. Jake's continued insistence on pursuing his jazz career sends his father to his deathbed. Jake/Jack is then forced to choose: Sing on Broadway on opening night, or in his father's place at the synagogue on Yom Kippur. He agonizes— missing his Broadway debut could kill his career, while missing Yom Kippur could kill his father. He ends up singing the Kol Nidre in the synagogue. This allows his father to die a happy man, thinking that his son has finally chosen the prayer shawl over blackface. But with his father now out of the way, Jake returns to the stage and gets his big Broadway debut after all, in the iconic scene where, in blackface and white gloves, he goes down on one knee to sing "My Mammy" to his mother in the front row.

Jake's story is nothing less than a microcosm of the entire American project: the creation of an American Culture out of the disparate elements of many ethnic and racial subgroups. Jake is Jewish, and he's also American. He sings Hebrew sacred music, but also jazz, Tin Pan Alley and Irish-tenor ballads. He unites the synagogue, Broadway, the vaudeville stage and Hollywood. He engages not only in the interracial mixing implied by the blackface, but also in interfaith romance—his purported love interest is, as his Jewish mother observes with some alarm, a "shiksa." Jake's story is the whole assimilationist agenda put on view. He's a one-man melting pot, negotiating the social conflict faced by all new immigrants to America: to remain true to one's ethnic roots, or to become an assimilated American.

In most recent scholarly readings of *The Jazz Singer*, Jake ends the film a failure, an immigrant's son who has repudiated his heritage in his headlong rush to be accepted as an American. Rogin, for example, insisted Jake's embrace of American culture is a "flight" from his ethnic heritage; he becomes a "cultural schizophrenic." In wearing blackface, he rises in American culture by symbolically keeping Blacks down. Rogin went so far as to brand Jake a traitor to the American labor movement in which so many other immigrant Jews were then involved, because he's obviously out only for himself.

This is academic-lefty nonsense. The other way to look at this story's message is exactly as the (Jewish) filmmakers intended us to: Jake is a model of how to preserve your Old World roots but still participate as a citizen in the New World. While he does not submit to his overbearing father's demands, he does not fully reject his Jewishness, either. He even delays his Broadway debut and jeopardizes his career to fulfill his father's dying wish to hear him sing the Kol Nidre. Only after he has thus fulfilled his filial duties—as he, if not his father, understands them—does he black up and sing "My Mammy." (It's also worth noting that "Kol Nidre" is the most attractive song in the film, and Jolson's best performance in it. He does much better as a stand-in cantor than in what his father appropriately calls his "raggy-time" rendition of "Blue Skies," for instance.)

So Jake successfully navigates the social conflict faced by all immigrant Americans. He is able to have it both ways: He's a Jew, and a cantor's son, but he's also an American, and a jazz singer. He's a Jewish-Irish-Black-shiksa-loving, jazz-and-Hebrew-singing American cultural mutt. He chooses the New World over the Old, but he doesn't turn his back on his ethnicity or religious affiliation; he merely assigns to those preset definitions of his identity as a tribe member less priority than to his own self-created identity as an American individual.

Even multiculturalists would have to agree that this is the central point of the American cultural project, what sets it apart from all other social systems: In America, the individual is not assigned a fixed position in a rigid social hierarchy dominated by caste or class or family lineage, but is free to choose and create his/her own identity—theoretically, at least.

Which still leaves the bedeviling problem of the blackface to contend with. It's startling to us now when we first see Jolson, midway into the film, casually applying blackface in his dressing room. When he completes the disguise by slipping on a nappy-haired wig, he rolls his eyes and cracks a wide grin in a stereotypical minstrel-show caricature. For us today, it's a jarring, ridiculous, and/or repugnant moment. Movie audiences in 1927 most likely accepted the transformation as casually as Jolson performs it. They were likely much more flabbergasted by those first bursts of sound from the moviehouse speakers. Griffith's use of blackface had outraged critics a decade earlier because he'd used White actors to portray Blacks in a demeaning way in a serious dramatic film. By contrast, the vaudevillian Jolson's blacking up to sing "My Mammy" seemed just harmless, old-timey stagecraft.

And even today, when we watch Jolson do blackface in this film, there's barely a hint of the racist mockery that's supposed to be the corrupt heart of blackface entertainment. It's much more like watching Mick Jagger or Eminem—not mockery, but the sincere mimicry of a non-Black artist who loves Black culture (or what he thinks is Black culture) so dearly he can't resist imitating it, even to the ridiculous point of blacking up. If anything, there's only self-mockery in it. Jolson doesn't even get around to singing the supposedly Negro "My Mammy" until the very last scene. The first song he sings in blackface is in fact a schmaltzy Irish-tenor tearjerker, expressing more nostalgia for the Old Country than the Old South.

Nevertheless, the blackface scenes remind us again of the cruel flaw in the American cultural experiment as it was still being worked out in 1927: The one American subgroup who were not invited or allowed to assimilate, who were in fact rigorously confined by a rigid caste system, were Black people. The very people Jake emulates in his successful attempt to fit in were still outcasts, America's untouchables. The moviehouses where *The Jazz Singer* was screened were segregated. Black audiences either came to special all-Black matinees or sat up in nigger heaven.

Still, *The Jazz Singer*'s blackface is a world away from its use in *The Birth of a Nation*. Griffith's Hollywood was largely White; the Hollywood of 1927 was almost entirely Jewish-run. And Jews, even if they were using late-model blackface minstrelsy as a way to get ahead in show business, were also far more sympathetic to Negroes than Griffith had revealed himself to be.

If *The Jazz Singer* plays up any ethnic stereotypes, they're all Jewish. Jake's father and mother are the Jewish equivalents of Uncle Mose and Mammy—the latter association is made literal in the final scene. Jake's relationship to them provides a bizarre psychosexual subtext, an Oedipal conflict straight out of Freud's notebooks. As played by Jolson, Jake epitomizes the stereotype of the effeminate Jewish male, which was quite popular in the anti-Semitic literature of the day. Small and slight of build, swinging and twitching his narrow hips, rolling and batting his heavily made-up eyes, Jolson hardly cuts what you'd call a manly figure. Jake's effeminate carrying-on literally kills his father—leaving the field open for Jake to woo his mother. The film makes it unsettlingly obvious that his true love interest isn't his shiksa girlfriend, but his mom. Two of the half-dozen secular songs he sings are about "mother." Their reunion is the film's central love scene. They caress, kiss and hug each other. In the film's longest bout of recorded sound, Jake sings to her and goes on and on about how she's the only girl for him. They're billing and cooing, carrying on like two flirting lovebirds, when Jake's father bursts in, looks irate (or jealous?), and shouts, "Stop!" In Warner Oland's Jewish-drag pronunciation, it comes out as "Schtop!"—just a vowel away from *schtup*. It's a very strange scene fraught with squeamish-making suggestion.

There was already a whiff of nostalgia about blackface when *The Jazz Singer* debuted. Jolson's Mammy routines evoked a vanishing era. And since nothing succeeds like pushing moviegoers' nostalgia buttons, many Hollywood musicals of the 1930s and 1940s repeated the formula. A good old-fashioned minstrel routine reminded viewers of a supposedly simpler time, a gaslit era before the two world wars, the Great Depression, the workers' revolts and all the other turmoil the twentieth century had brought with it. It didn't hurt that some large segment of these movies' audience had not been around to see this supposedly golden era themselves; nostalgia works best when your audience has only the dimmest grasp of the Golden Age you're evoking for them.

Jolson, naturally, flogged his blackface routines for all their worth in many of his films after the smash success of *The Jazz Singer*. The 1930 *Mammy* is overtly nostalgic for the good ol' days, with Jolson playing an endman in a traveling minstrel troupe. The 1934 musical *Wonder Bar*, adapted from a Weimarish Viennese play and clearly a model for *Cabaret*, includes a campy fantasy sequence of a blackface Negro heaven complete with pork chops hanging from the trees. It makes *The Green Pastures* look like *The Color Purple*. Because of their blackface scenes, both *Mammy* and *Wonder Bar* are obscure collectors' items now.

Jolson also starred in the remarkable musical *Hallelujah, I'm a Bum!* (1933), based on a story by Ben Hecht, with music—including much sung dialogue—by Rodgers and Hart. He plays Bumper, the hobo "mayor of Central Park," whose inseparable companion is a young Black man, Acorn, played by the diminutive Edgar Connor (who also appeared in the 1933 musical short *Rufus Jones for President*, which starred Ethel Waters and child prodigy Sammy Davis, Jr.). This Black–White duo does everything and goes everywhere together, at least until a blonde hussy catches Bumper's eye and temporarily breaks them up. Acorn calls Bumper "Papa," Bumper calls him "Son." While this makes the White–Black paternalism of the era terribly obvious, the warmth and affection between the two characters, and evidently the two performers, is touching. Jolson does not do blackface in the movie.

Eddie Cantor, the Other Jolson, was a real-life up-from-the-Lower-East-Side Jewish vaudevillian (born Isidore Itzkowitz), who made his bones with the Ziegfeld Follies, where for a long time he dueted with Bert Williams—both of them in blackface, doing a humorous-yet-sentimental father-and-son routine. Like Jolson's, Cantor's films combined blackface turns with eye-rolling, hand-patting, sissy camp. In George S. Kaufman's *Roman Scandals* (1933), Cantor even finds an excuse to do a blackface number in ancient Rome. It's a lavish Busby Berkeley set piece that many people today

Eddie Cantor in *Roman Scandals,* 1933.

would find both racist *and* sexist—a precursor to Shirley Q. Liquor, maybe? Yet even when he's not blacked up, it can be a struggle today to imagine how audiences could be charmed by Cantor's mugging and prancing. It's telling that the "apostle of pep" even once said of his own stage persona, "You know, I can't stand that pop-eyed baboon."

Buster Keaton put on blackface to get a job as a "colored waiter" in a brief routine in the silent film *College,* released the same year as *The Jazz Singer.* But after Jolson and Cantor, no movie star worked blackface to better effect than Shirley Temple. Audiences just couldn't get enough of the golden-haired, moonfaced little poppet putting on the burnt cork to shuck 'n' jive with Negro performers like Bill "Bojangles" Robinson in movies such as *The Little Colonel* and *The Littlest Rebel,* both released in 1935. As with Jolson's and Cantor's routines, you'd have to watch Temple's movies from a particularly touchy point of view to see them as examples of vicious racist mockery. The affection between the kid and her Black costars

Little Shirley Temple blacked up often.

may have been stagey and condescending, but in their own naive way the films portrayed an image of racial harmony—an ideal of Whites and Blacks meeting amicably through the medium of popular culture—that was not such a terrible message to be sending movie audiences in their segregated theaters in the 1930s.

Later movie musicals that milked the old-timey nostalgia to the last drop include the 1939 *Babes in Arms* and 1941 *Babes on Broadway,* with teen stars Mickey Rooney and Judy Garland blacking up; both films incorporate lavish minstrel-show routines. The big minstrel finale in *Babes on Broadway* failed to move audiences at early screenings, for a funny reason. Originally, the movie didn't show Rooney and Garland applying the burnt cork, it just went straight into the routine. Confused viewers didn't recognize the pair in black-face, so they didn't get why they were watching the scene. With a new backstage scene showing them blacking up, the movie was a hit.

Fred Astaire blacked up for a sincere and well-meaning tribute to

Bill Robinson in the 1936 *Swing Time*. In the smash wartime hit *Holiday Inn*, the 1942 vehicle for Astaire and Bing Crosby that launched Irving Berlin's "White Christmas" into the stratosphere (it also spawned "Happy Holiday" and "Easter Parade," and inspired the name of the hotel/motel chain, founded a decade later), Crosby, his blonde love interest Marjorie Reynolds and the entire staff of the inn black up to do a retro minstrel number in honor of Lincoln's birthday. Crosby's gotten up as a gray-haired Uncle Tom who croons lines like "Who dat?" Reynolds does Topsy. Astaire, who's also pursuing her, fails to recognize her in blackface. Disconcertingly, the scene cuts back and forth between the blackfaced Whites and the actual Black staff in the kitchen. To the popular Black actress Louise Beavers—who, as she often did, plays the bighearted cook—goes the dubious honor of singing a line about how Lincoln "set de darkies free." Yes, and *Holiday Inn* set Hollywood race relations back twenty years. It won an Oscar anyway.

The last gasp of movie-minstrel sentimentality came in a spate of self-referential showbiz tribute movies in the World War II and postwar years. They include the 1939 Stephen Foster biopic *Swanee River* and the 1943 *Dixie*, a tribute to the monarch of minstrelsy Dan Emmett, as well as a series of Jolson and Cantor tribute flicks—*The Jolson Story, Jolson Sings Again, The Eddie Cantor Story*—culminating in a dreadful 1952 remake of *The Jazz Singer* with Danny Thomas. By then, the only rationale for such movies seemed simply the excuse to show blackface on the big screen, and the practice died as the civil rights era dawned. (Neil Diamond's even more mind-bogglingly awful 1980 remake of the film ingeniously, if disingenuously, got around the blackface taboo by having him black up to help a friend, a Black singer who's too sick to perform.)

Today, it's likely that most people have seen these movies only on television, in which case they wouldn't know they ever included blackface scenes—they were long ago edited out for TV. If the minstrel-show content is too integral to be cut, the films just

Blackfaced Judy Garland in
Everybody Sing, 1938.

aren't televised. A couple of generations of Americans have now grown up being *told* about the shamefully racist antics some beloved movie stars got up to in the Bad Old Days, without ever seeing the evidence.

Blackface didn't disappear from the screen in the 1950s, but instances were rare and ever more self-conscious. There was the excruciatingly preachy spectacle of James Whitmore blacking up in the 1964 adaptation of *Black Like Me.* A couple of decades later, Hollywood felt emboldened to flip that formula on its head and use blackface in a satire about affirmative action, the 1986 *Soul Man,* wherein a White youth blacks up to get a minority scholarship to Harvard.

On TV, there was the famous two-part episode of *All in the Family* during the 1975–1976 season, when Archie blacked up for his lodge's minstrel show, then forgot to remove the blackface when he rushed to the hospital for the birth of his first grandchild. The show got away with it because of its impeccable liberal credentials, and because Archie is thoroughly embarrassed to be caught out. More recently, Tracey Ullman has blacked up as Sheneesha the airport security guard. In 2006, FX aired *Black. White.*, a reality show featuring a White family in blackface and a Black family in whiteface.

A KIND OF AURAL BLACKFACE ONCE INVADED RADIO, WITH great success, and then moved to film and TV. Debuting in 1928, *The Amos 'N' Andy Show* was an enormously popular radio program written and performed by two white men, Freeman Gosden (Amos) from Richmond, Virginia, and Charles Correll (Andy) from Peoria, Illinois. Despite some protest from the Black community, it was a staple in as many Black households as White ones (even a great liberal figure like FDR was a fan), and it became the longest-running show in the history of radio, with a life span of almost thirty years. In the antics of Amos, Andy, the Kingfish, Sapphire, Lightnin' and other characters, some heard only mockery and racist stereotypes. Others found it harmless fun, and praised it for at least attempting to present a microcosm of a fully developed Black society, ranging from porters and janitors to doctors and lawyers, from smooth-talking criminals to upstanding citizens, from dull-witted coons like Lightnin' to the smart and skeptical Sapphire and her mama, who saw through every scheme and ruse.

In 1930, the show was adapted for the screen as *Check and Double Check*, with Gosden and Correll in blackface. It's a horrible film, utterly bereft of the warmth and wit of the radio broadcast, and entirely forgotten today except when Duke Ellington is taken to task for his cameo appearance in it. Some cartoon Amos 'n' Andy shorts appeared around the same time, and were almost as bad.

The show's enormous popularity also spun off imitators, like *Pick 'n' Pat* (originally *Molasses 'n' January*), with "two dusky delin-

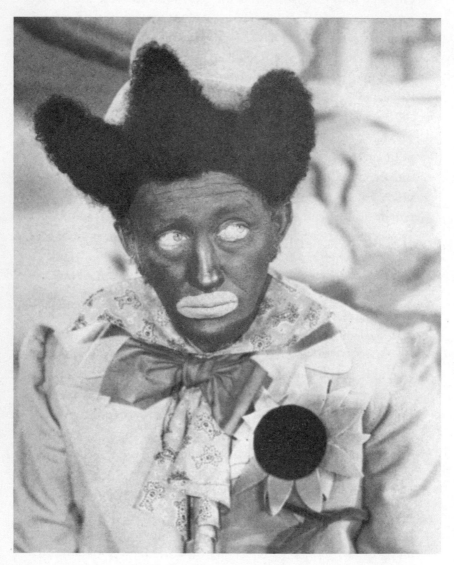

Bing Crosby as Dan Emmett in *Dixie*, 1943.

eators of devastating dumbfoolery," "two dark clouds of joy." Broadcast from the 1930s through World War II, it stuck close to the old coon-show model of insult humor. Still, the writers were not incapable of jokes that must have sounded pretty funny on the radio:

PICK: Well, Pat, I want you to meet my gal friend, here, sweetsmellin' Bethesda.

BETHESDA: Hello, short, dark and repulsive.

In 1951, CBS began airing *The Amos 'N' Andy Show* as a TV sitcom, produced by Gosden and Correll but now starring an all-Black cast of gifted comedians and accomplished actors. (Evidently the notion of using blackfaced White actors was originally discussed and wisely shelved.) They included Spencer Williams, Jr., as the eternally bamboozled Andy, and Nick Stewart (billed as Nick O'Demus) as the slow-moving Lightnin'. But the real star was Tim "Kingfish" Moore, a veteran comic who'd started out doing sideshow and blackface vaudeville (sometimes teaming up with the comic Mantan Moreland) at the turn of the century, and what sounds like a remarkable solo version of *Uncle Tom's Cabin,* in which apparently he played all the characters in profile, half his face chalked white and half blackfaced. He is said to have written W. C. Fields' "Ain't a Fit Night Out for Man nor Beast" skit. Moore had retired from show business when he was tapped for the Kingfish role, which he made one of the best-loved in television history, and one of the most widely imitated. Americans both White (for example, Dean Martin) and Black (Flip Wilson) enjoyed doing Kingfish impersonations.

It's been said, correctly, that early fifties television was effectively "radio with pictures." But it was also a kind of neo-vaudeville, and much of its comedy recycled the same ethnic, immigrant and working-class types that had been popular fodder a half-century earlier. *Amos 'N' Andy* aired along with several now long-forgotten comedies, including *Life with Luigi, The Goldbergs, The Life of Riley,*

Pick 'n' Pat.

and *Beulah,* in which the 1930s film star Hattie McDaniel reprised for the last time her role as a domestic servant with more sense than any of her masters. They can all be seen as precursors to Jackie Gleason's more successful *The Honeymooners.*

Amos 'N' Andy proved to be as popular on TV as the radio version had been, among Blacks as well as Whites. Still, although the overall tenor of the humor was warm and gentle, it contained too many old-fashioned caricatures, like the shufflin' Lightnin' and the Zip Coonish Kingfish, to survive in the burgeoning civil rights era. The NAACP went to federal court to try to block the show from airing, and other groups denounced it. Meanwhile, Southern Whites attacked it from the opposite direction, because of its Black cast. The negative attention began to scare advertisers, and CBS pulled the show in 1953. It would be two decades before the next all-Black show appeared in prime time. Yet *Amos 'N' Andy* remained popular, and controversial, in syndicated reruns until the mid-1960s, when it was removed from circulation. It now has a sort of underground afterlife, being passed around among fans in bootleg videos and DVDs.

Why should I complain about making seven thousand dollars a week playing a maid? If I didn't, I'd be making seven dollars a week actually being one!   —HATTIE MCDANIEL

AT THE SAME TIME ALL THOSE WHITE VAUDEVILLIANS WERE preserving minstrelsy on film in the 1930s and 1940s, many Black performers from the vaudeville and minstrel stages were making their way to Hollywood. The now Jewish-run studios were hungry for Black talent—there were far more Black faces on the big screen than blackface ones. Part of the impetus was the introduction of sound in 1927. With their "natural" singing and dancing talents, Blacks were thought to be uniquely suited to the new technology.

Before World War II, the roles Blacks were offered in Hollywood were almost all restricted within Bogle's stereotypes. Black actors played maids, cooks and manservants; kindly old Toms and Jemimas; sleepy, shuffling coons; pickaninnies, golliwogs and Topsies. Often they danced and sang; just as often they donned leopard-print loincloths and carried spears through fake jungles; and once in a great while they got to play a romantic lead, or even God. Filmmaker Melvin Van Peebles sums up his view of the era succinctly. Before the war, he has declared, "if you were a Black actor in Hollywood, that meant you tossed a spear, cooked somebody for dinner, or took a bullet. Or you brought a drink, or carried a plate."

True, as far as it goes. But prewar Hollywood also created a lot of highly lucrative work for Black entertainers. That some of that work was mortifying cannot be denied. Yet for a mass entertainment industry operating within the context of segregated 1930s America, Hollywood took a notably progressive stance on race (just as TV later would) by showing Blacks and Whites together on the big screen in ways that can be seen as pop-culture models of behavior for the mass audience to adopt, or at least unconsciously absorb. Many studio bosses, like David O. Selznick (who produced *Gone With the Wind*), were liberal Jews who saw it as their duty to project uplifting Black images and characters. And within the limited, stereotyped roles offered them, Black performers—and the overwhelmingly White scriptwriters who supplied their lines—found many opportunities to present Black characters ennobled with wit, grace, intelligence and wisdom. In fact, it's no exaggeration to say that in many Hollywood films of the period, the only character with a lick of sense is a Black one.

The antics of the coon-show clowns, spooks and fake Africans are the hardest to justify, and have themselves become the stereotypical examples of Hollywood's embarrassing treatment of Blacks. Stepin Fetchit (born Lincoln Perry) became a very wealthy man portraying "the laziest human being in the world," the quintessential coon figure, shuffling, mumbling, slacking and dozing off whenever he could, his heavy eyelids and loose lower lip forever dangling, scratching his shaved head in befuddlement whenever a White actor upbraided or barked orders at him, as they did all the time. He was a living cartoon coon—and the animated cartoons of his day often featured a thinly veiled Stepin Fetchit caricature that was hardly more exaggerated than his own shtick. He also spawned a legion of imitators. He was the first Black actor to share star billing with Whites, he made and spent a fortune, and his apparently effortless ability to steal a scene made him much admired, and feared, by Charlie Chaplin, Lionel Barrymore, John Wayne, Will Rogers and other stars.

Like Bert Williams, Perry was of Caribbean descent, and in private held himself somewhat superior both to the Black Americans he caricatured and to the ignunt White folks who laughed at his routines. As docile as Fetchit was on screen, Perry himself was demanding and argumentative with directors and producers. His penchant for drunken brawls and teenage girls made for lurid tabloid copy and earned denunciations from Black civic and church leaders. Despite his huge popularity with audiences, White and Black, he had made himself a Hollywood pariah by 1936. In 1942, when the NAACP's executive secretary, Walter White, lobbied the studios to end demeaning portrayals of blacks, he specifically cited Stepin Fetchit. Perry declined through decades of bitter obscurity, watching the name Stepin Fetchit become a slur akin to Uncle Tom. By the time he died in 1985, many of his films had been quietly removed from general circulation or edited to cut him out. Only the insult of his name remained.

It's a measure of how effectively he was made an unperson that despite his being Hollywood's first Black superstar, the first book-length biographies of Lincoln Perry / Stepin Fetchit weren't published until 2005, when two appeared simultaneously: Mel Watkins' *Stepin Fetchit* and Champ Clark's *Shuffling to Ignominy.* Both sought to rescue Perry from obscurity and infamy. Watkins argued that "the comic image Lincoln Perry projected was not nearly as harmful, deleterious, and degrading as the images projected by many of to day's black comedians, rap artists, and even television sitcom stars." Clark compared Fetchit to trickster figures like Brer Rabbit, in following a centuries-old subversive tradition whereby Blacks played the fool to fool Whites. He noted how often Fetchit, by pretending to be too lazy and addled to understand the simplest directions, avoided doing the White characters' bidding, all the while muttering subtle sarcasms in a drawl that was indecipherable to Whites but clear and hilarious to Black audiences.

Mantan Moreland (Spike Lee would borrow his name for one of his characters in *Bamboozled*) provided comic relief in numerous all-Black "race films" of the period, but was known best to White filmgoers as Birmingham Brown, Charlie Chan's chauffeur. His clowning was the opposite of Fetchit's; where Fetchit was Hollywood's favorite coon, Moreland was its jumpiest spook. His characters were nervous as cats, ready to leap through the ceiling at the slightest noise. He could pop his bulging eyes and had a way of making his entire body quake with ludicrous, teeth-chattering tremors. He was also such a gifted comic that he often stole films right out from under his White costars. The 1941 *King of the Zombies,* ostensibly a horror film starring two bland White guys, is entirely a Mantan Moreland vehicle.

And there were the legions of Black extras who put on loincloths and bone jewelry to portray African savages in countless adventure pictures like the long-running Tarzan series. Their role was usually just to make the White actors look noble, brave, God-fearing and intelligent, in stark contrast to their bestial, cowardly, pagan and cannibal ways. If they were carrying the Whites' luggage, they were always ready to drop everything and run away at the slightest sign of trouble. If they were attacking the Whites, they were ever prepared to give themselves up by the score to varieties of grisly deaths; no African adventure flick was complete without having at least one Black savage come to an ignoble, screaming end in the jaws of a lion or crocodile, or under the foot of an elephant, or in the embrace of a python or a pit of quicksand. These films were the inspiration for the racial slur "spearchucker."

The 1931 *Trader Horn,* the *Godfather* of Great White Hunter movies, was one African adventure film that deviated in some significant ways from the spearchucker norm. Unlike the Tarzan series and countless other B movies where "Africa" was a Hollywood backlot and the "natives" were all Black American extras, it was shot on location in Africa, the first Hollywood film made there, at a time when, hard as it is to believe now, parts of the continent's interior were still unknown to and uncharted by Whites. The natives are all Africans, and director W. S. Van Dyke lavished his camera on them in documentary travelogue style. Noble Masai warriors stare inscrutably, bare-breasted lasses giggle shyly, elders with saggy earlobes and teats bicker with one another in front of their grass huts.

It was also surely the first Hollywood film to recruit a tribe of Pygmies as extras. But the effect is somehow less than authentic—it looks like Van Dyke was documenting one of those world's fair African villages than a real one. For all that, in terms of preserving their dignity, Van Dyke's Africans were light-years ahead of the pot-bellied fake Africans who ooga-boogaed among the potted jungle plants in so very many adventure pictures.

Given all the trouble and expense the filmmakers went to in providing an authentic setting, it's surprising what a Saturday-matinee fantasy the story is. Grizzled old Trader Horn (Harry Carey) shows the ropes to his protégé, Peru (a young Duncan Renaldo, later TV's much-loved Cisco Kid). They meet various native tribes, of whom Peru remarks, "You're wrong about these people. They're not savages, they're ignorant children." Apparently those were the only options for African people—deadly savages or ignorant children. When any of these natives is killed—as several are, usually screaming hysterically—Horn lights his pipe and shrugs it off with a stoic "Well, that's Africa for ya" nonchalance. That is, except for his trusty native gunbearer, Rencharo, sternly, almost silently and very buffly played by Mutia Omoolu. Their relationship is the film's central love affair. You don't have to be a professor of queer theory to be struck by the scene where the faithful African servant takes a spear intended for his crusty White boss and dies in his arms while they hold hands and Horn sheds a tear. Call it *Hallelujah, I'm a Great White Hunter!* Horn's affection for Rencharo doesn't mark him as a humanitarian. He explicitly states that the great mass of Africans are worthless Black savages; Rencharo is unique among them for being as good as any White man.

Before Rencharo dies, the trio comes upon a tribe whose leader turns out to be—wonder of wonders—a gorgeous blonde, the White Goddess, sort of a female Tarzan. Sadly, starring in the film proved to be bad juju for Edwina Booth, the White Goddess. She contracted a near-fatal infection while on location, referred to as "jungle fever" at the time. Which is hilarious when you consider that Booth was a Mormon, one of those American Aryans for whom jungle fever is a very definite no-no. Instead of being her big break, *Trader Horn* almost killed her, and while she survived her long bout with the disease, her career did not.

Black extras with fake bones in their noses would go on grimacing murderously and dying comically through countless reels of African-adventure films. White comedians often traveled to backlot "Africa" for some cheap jokes at the expense of the "natives." In *Call Me Bwana* (1963), Bob Hope hoodwinks a silly chief by saying things to him like, "Ooky ooky. Nooky nooky. They went thataway." You could still see plenty of these movies on TV when I was a kid, but by the mid-1960s embarrassed studios began pulling the worst offenders from circulation. What was once one of the best-known *Our Gang* episodes circulates now only in bootlegged copies. In "The Kid from Borneo," from 1933, the gang mistakes a sideshow runaway, Bumbo, the Wild Man from Borneo, for Spanky's long-lost uncle. Why he's called a "kid" in the title is a mystery. He's an adult Black actor, John Lester Johnson, who had bit parts in a number of 1930s movies, as a porter, an African witch doctor, a Nubian slave and, in the 1941 *Mr. Washington Goes to Town*, as a headless figure who gives Mantan Moreland the teeth-rattling heebie-jeebies. As Bumbo, Johnson wears the familiar loincloth and a bone in his 'fro; he has a mean sweet tooth and chases the gang all over town, trying to get his hands on Stymie's bag of candy. His only dialogue became a universal tagline: "Yum yum, eat 'em up!" (The gang, naturally, thought he meant to eat *them* up.) It was not, let us say, the most dignified role a Black actor was ever asked to play. Although few people are likely to know where it comes from anymore, "Yum yum, eat 'em up" still has a fixed place in the pop-culture lexicon, gracing cookie recipes, comfort-food-restaurant menus and an electro-dance track by the Beat-Box Boys.

The spearchucker movie reached its apotheosis in 1964—not in a Hollywood epic, as it happens, but in the British production *Zulu*. Based on a historical event, in which 139 mostly Welsh soldiers withstood a siege by some four thousand Zulu warriors in 1879, the movie pits Michael Caine and a gaggle of British character actors against an army of actual Zulus, led by an actual chief, Mangosuthu Buthelezi, a descendant of the man he portrays in the film. For all its historical fidelity, it's hard to get around the fact that *Zulu* features more Blacks literally tossing spears and taking bullets than any movie Hollywood ever made. Wave after human wave of warriors crashes against the soldiers' battlements, the men dying by the hundreds, until their dark bodies are stacked up like cordwood. Faithful to the Hollywood tradition, *Zulu* treats every scratch and splinter suffered by a White soldier as a tragic catastrophe, while the hundreds of Africans dying anonymously outside are noted with dispassion. Dead darkies strewn all over the plain? That's Africa for ya. By the end of the film they've come to look less like an army than a swarm; in all their buzzing darkness, they press down on the besieged Whites like a plague of locusts.

The Zulus would get theirs back in the fine 1986 TV miniseries *Shaka Zulu*, starring the regal South African Henry Cele in the title role. Another follow-up to *Zulu* appeared that same year—*Aliens*, the second Alien movie. It might just as well have been called *Zulus in Space*. Was the resemblance totally unintentional? White soldiers-in-space circling their wagons and blasting away, while instead of the corpses of large, anonymously threatening, dark-skinned humans piling up at the barricades, it's the husks of large, anonymously threatening, dark-skinned humanoid insects? Hmmm . . .

In their roles as maids and mammies, cooks and man Fridays, some fine Black actors got to play characters who were altogether smarter, wiser and kinder than the White folks who were their ostensible betters—a tradition, recall, that went back to the earliest blackface theater in America. The classic example is Hattie McDaniel as Mammy in Selznick's 1939 *Gone With the Wind*. She is the

Jack Benny makes eyes at Rochester in *Man About Town* (1939).

only sensible person in the entire epic film, and the only one you come out of the film liking. She knows that Scarlett is a slut, that Ashley is too good for her, that Rhett's a cad and Prissy's a twit. As the White folk make a mess of the world all around her, she serves as the audience's moral compass, "an all-seeing, all-hearing, all-knowing commentator and observer. She remarks. She annotates. She makes asides," Bogle writes. At the same time, she's the only real mother Scarlett has, protecting and nurturing her like a wayward daughter even though the silly White girl rejects her sage counsel time and again. It's pure old-fashioned mammy nostalgia, pulled straight from the plantation literature of the nineteenth century and given a few ironic spins by screenwriters Sidney Howard, Ben Hecht and Selznick himself. And it's played with enormous wit by Mc-Daniel, who steals the film and who received the first Oscar given to a Black performer.

Then there was the original Odd Couple, Jack Benny and

Rochester. The son of a minstrel singer, Eddie Anderson started out in vaudeville and had appeared in a number of films when he debuted as the voice of a Pullman porter on Benny's popular radio show in 1937. Audiences responded with such enthusiasm that the canny Benny soon made Rochester his man Friday and inseparable sidekick, and the duo starred together on radio, in movies and on TV for twenty-three years. It often seemed less a boss–servant arrangement than a long-term relationship between a pair of closeted, middle-aged gay men. Benny was the feminine one—silly, flighty, hysterical, demanding, flouncing, prissy and limp-wristed. Rochester was deep of voice and manly, competent, calm, organized. He wore not only the apron but also the pants in the relationship; he may have been the servant, but he was surely the top. Benny's long, never consummated relationship with his gal pal, the rarely seen and aptly named Mary, was patently a beard. Like Mammy in *Gone With the Wind*, Rochester was the audience's voice of reason, offering wry asides and cutting commentary whenever his boss or his boss' movie-star pals said or did something foolish, as was their fairly constant behavior. It's true that Benny bossed Rochester around with no compunction. *Rochester, answer the phone. Get the door. Make some sandwiches for my guests. Fan my brow.* But the power dynamic between them was less like a White bossman and his yassuhing house nigger than like a drama queen diva and her devoted man. Think *La Cage aux Folles*.

Three young Black comic actors turned what could have been demeaning pickaninny roles into their own indelible characters, and earned permanent niches in American pop culture. Farina, Stymie and Buckwheat enlivened the *Our Gang* (aka *Little Rascals*) shorts from the silent era (1922) through the Depression years. With his nest of dreadlocks in pickaninny bows and his unisex ragdoll outfits, Farina (Allen Clayton Hoskins) was a close impersonation of the traditional blackface drag Topsy. What would you call a young Black man imitating blackface drag—meta-blackface? Stymie

Buckwheat.

(Matthew Beard), in his trademark derby, was more slick and street-wise, a ragged Zip Coon. He handily outsmarted his White pals on occasion. In one of my favorite episodes, he gazes longingly at a plate of fried eggs and bets the other kids that he can make those eggs talk. When they challenge him, he promptly devours the eggs and then crows, "Those eggs are sayin' hello to my stomach riii-iight now!" (I'm quoting from ancient memory; it was one of my favorite jokes as a kid.) Little Buckwheat (Billie Thomas) presented the most primitive of the three characters; sexless as a tadpole and shiny-black as a golliwog, he enriched the American vernacular with the undying "O-tay!" Barely remembered now, there was also Pine-apple, Farina's older brother, who appeared in a handful of the silents. He was played by Eugene Jackson, who also appeared in the musical *Hearts in Dixie*, and on a few episodes of *Sanford and Son*, and toured vaudeville billed as "Hollywood's most famous colored kid star."

Our Gang and *Little Rascals* episodes were in constant rotation on TV when I was growing up, before they were declared offensive and sightings of them became much rarer. I well remember that one of the strongest impressions they made on me was the way the Black and White kids were perfectly integrated in the gang, all ragamuffins together. They never commented on it and never even seemed to notice. I didn't see this in my hometown Baltimore, where Blacks and Whites lived elbow to elbow and yet at some considerable psychic distance from each other. You have to wonder what sort of subconscious effect these images had on their original audiences.

Every now and again in the prewar years a Hollywood studio would get adventurous and produce an all-Black film—always a musical, of course. *Hearts in Dixie* (1929), the first all-Black movie musical, was basically a minstrel show on film, with actual Blacks in what would have been the blackface roles, complete with a rendition of "Massa's in de Cold Ground." It starred Stepin Fetchit (as a slave named Gummy) and the dignified Clarence Muse, who would go on to a very long career in Hollywood (he was Jim in the 1931 *Huckleberry Finn*) and in independent Black film. *Hallelujah,* which followed that same year, was a somewhat more realistic story about sharecroppers, directed and cowritten by the great King Vidor, for whom it was a pet project. It was filmed in the South, a place alien and forbidding to most of its Black actors, sophisticates from New York and Los Angeles. Neither film did well at the box office, especially in the South, and Hollywood didn't attempt another all-Black feature until *The Green Pastures* in 1936. It did well enough to embolden Hollywood to produce a few great wartime musicals, like *Cabin in the Sky* and *Stormy Weather,* which both appeared in 1943.

MEANWHILE, IN ADDITION TO BLACKS AND THE OCCA-
sional blackfaced White appearing in feature films, there were the
cartoons that ran before them. Some of us are old enough to remember when animated shorts routinely preceded the feature film
in movie theaters, back before owners got wise and started using
that time to dun us with commercials and endless coming attractions. Some of us who are really ancient may even remember when
these cartoons might feature racial or ethnic caricatures. Of the
thousands of animated shorts cranked out in the first, say, seventy-
five years of cinema, some hundreds included characterizations that
today would be considered offensive; it has been estimated, for example, that about a third of the cartoons released by MGM alone in
the late 1940s included a blackface, coon or mammy figure.

As with much of the material discussed in this chapter, the studios that produced or sometimes corporately inherited these cartoons began to withdraw them from public circulation in the
mid-1960s. There's a lively black market for them on the Internet,
often dupes of dupes of dupes transferred from film stock so old
and faded that those offensive images are barely visible now. I suppose there's poetic justice in that.

I've watched several dozen of them, and with a few noteworthy
exceptions I can't say their disappearance was a great blow to Saturday-
morning TV. Cartoon Africa was invariably populated with big-
lipped, bone-through-the-nose cannibals, as in *Plane Dumb,* an
RKO toon of the 1930s. A couple of comic white characters, Tom
and Jerry (not the famous cat and mouse), fly their biplane to
Africa, where they don blackface to blend in with the natives. The
blackface transforms them entirely into coons, who undergo a few
classic misadventures. They wander into a haunted cave, where even
the skeletons are black (and sing a spiritual), and end up running
from spear-chucking natives. It's a shame that the racial material

renders the cartoon unwatchable today; the rest of the animation is lively, funny and inventive. In *Robinson Crusoe, Jr.*, the uncharted island on which Porky Pig finds himself is inhabited also by spear-chucking stereotypes, and Porky's man Friday is a classic coon with a Rochester voice.

Inki, a little African boy hunter created by animator Chuck Jones, appeared in several cartoons from 1939 to 1950. Although Inki has the big lips, the loincloth and the bone through his hair, the humor is much gentler than in many other cartoons. Inki's neither a gibbering savage nor a lazy coon; he's just another cute and silly Looney Tunes character, fitting in the same pantheon as Elmer Fudd or Marvin the Martian. Indeed, the Inki cartoons were better known for another weird and ingenious character, a mysterious mynah bird who hops like Jim Crow to the tune of Mendelssohn's *Fingal's Cave Overture*.

As he was a descendant of Brer Rabbit, it was probably inevitable that Bugs Bunny's toons would sometimes delve into race imagery. In *All This and Rabbit Stew* (1941), the role usually filled by Elmer Fudd is taken by a shufflin', big-lipped, sleepy-eyed country coon (voiced by Mel Blanc), whom Bugs ultimately outwits by luring him into a game of craps, which the Black character cannot resist. Bugs briefly dons blackface and does an Al Jolson in the wartime propaganda toon *Any Bonds Today?* As late as 1953, in *Southern Fried Rabbit*, Bugs could be seen putting on blackface and playing at being a Southern Black slave.

Warner Bros.' *Coal Black and de Sebben Dwarfs* (1943) is a negrified retelling of the Snow White tale, complete with big lips and a "Prince Chawmin'" who's a zoot-suited hepcat. It's hip, jazzy and beautifully drawn, which makes it all the sadder that its racial content doomed it—contested by the NAACP on its release, it was later disappeared. As were *Goldilocks and the Jivin' Bears* (1944), and cartoons that riffed on *Uncle Tom's Cabin*, *Little Black Sambo* and *The Green Pastures* (*Clean Pastures*).

Animators couldn't resist evoking the Old South, with happy

darkies plucking cotton and strumming banjos to minstrel tunes. The 1941 *Scrub Me Mama with a Boogie Beat* is a jaw-dropping concatenation of plantation tropes. A steamboat on the Swanee River pulls into Lazytown, where all the colored men are so shiftless they can barely stir themselves from sleep, leaving Mammy to do all the work, including bathing her baby child, then powdering his black behind with black talcum. (Mammy figures of one sort or another would continue to appear in cartoons well into the 1950s.) The peaceful torpor is disrupted when a racy mulatto torch singer, à la Lena Horne, steps off the boat and gets the whole town jiving to her jazzy song.

As in vaudeville, Blacks were not the only minority caricatured. Savage Injuns, torpid Mexicans, prissy Frenchies, squinty Asians et al. abound, almost always the butt of a comic hero like Bugs. Cartoons made during World War II reveled in Japanese and German stereotypes as they propagandized theater audiences to support the war effort. The "Jap" and "Nip" soldiers in *Bugs Bunny Nips the Nips* (1944) and in the Popeye cartoon *You're a Sap, Mr. Jap* (1942) are uniformly slit-eyed, bucktoothed, gibberish-speaking ethnic slurs. Looney Tunes' *Tokio Jokio* (1943) is a cartoon "newsreel" of life in wartime Japan that viciously and violently lampoons the entirety of that society.

German characters—being, after all, European White folks—seem to have lent themselves less readily to ethnic caricature. The "Natsies" Daffy Duck outwits in the wartime *Daffy the Commando* and *Scrap Happy Daffy*, while lampooned as Heil-Hitlering dummkopfs, are merely comic buffoons, much like Klink and Schultz in the later *Hogan's Heroes*. Hermann Goering, drawn as a grotesquely fat man in lederhosen, plays the Elmer Fudd hunter role in the 1945 Bugs Bunny toon *Herr Meets Hare*, which also manages to make fun of Richard Wagner's music. Bugs outwits both Goering and Hitler in the end by impersonating Stalin.

Several wartime propaganda cartoons took an *Animal Farm* approach, rendering the enemy as barnyard types. Hitler and Hirohito are ducks and Mussolini a goose in the 1942 Warner Bros.' parable *The Ducktators*. Hitler is a pompous pig who rants in fake German and tosses peanuts to his pet monkey Mussolini in the amazing Terrytoons *The Last Round Up* of 1943, which also features Heil-Hitlering ants and caterpillars. In one brilliantly surreal scene, when Mussolini picks nits out of the Führer's hair, they're in the shape of little swastikas. In Tex Avery's beautiful *Blitz Wolf* (1942), Hitler is the Big Bad Wolf. He violates a nonaggression pact with the Three Little Pigs by attacking Pigmania. One of the pigs' houses has a "No Dogs Allowed" sign on which "Dogs" is crossed out and replaced by "Japs." In a spookily prescient scene, the pigs take a moment from fighting the wolf to blow up the nation of Japan with a single bomb. Disney's *The Thrifty Pig* took a very similar if less ingeniously executed tack.

These toons were also eventually removed from circulation. Speedy Gonzales was quietly retired, too (only to reemerge in dog drag as the Taco Bell Chihuahua), as were some cartoons with Chinese or American Indian characters. A host of Tom and Jerry cartoons that are still shown on TV were edited to remove scenes with blackface or a mammy-like maid. Dozens of other older toons that make it onto TV were edited to render them less violent, as well as to censor out scenes with cigarettes or alcohol. Thus a generation of young Americans who were too sensitive to see Wile E. Coyote light a stick of dynamite could grow up to be avid gangsta rap fans.

George Pal's "puppetoons" of the 1940s stand out both in style and content. They were not cartoons but stop-motion animations, with hand-carved wooden puppets moving through often gorgeous sets and backdrops. The great stop-motion animator Ray Harryhausen worked in Pal's studio in the 1940s. The effect in these films is similar to Art Clokey's Gumby and Davey and Goliath animations of the 1950s. Later, Eddie Murphy would close the circle by portraying a Black Gumby on *Saturday Night Live*.

Today, probably the most familiar puppetoon is Pal's *Tubby the Tuba* of 1947, but in the 1940s he was best known for working with

Black characters in his Oscar-nominated *John Henry and the Inky-Poo* of 1946 and his more controversial Jasper series. The former is probably unique among animations of its era in presenting a Black figure who is noble, manly, hardworking and heroic. Handsome and muscular, the puppet was carved with none of the stereotypical "Negro" features—he looks like a buff Sidney Poitier. Pal plays the familiar story straight and reverently. *John Henry* was widely praised by critics and civic leaders in both the White and the Black press.

It's likely that in making *John Henry,* Pal was trying to atone for the charges of racism he received for the Jasper series. Considering the era, Jasper was a rather sweet and mild caricature, a little boy who's innocent and gullible, and who tries to be good and obedient even though he's led astray by the scheming, dialect-speaking Scarecrow and his sidekick Crow. The stories are set in the usual Old Plantation South, on sets lovingly carved and gorgeously shot for a lush, 3-D effect.

Jasper debuted in the 1942 *Jasper and the Watermelons,* about which *Variety* raved, "George Pal's puppetoons ringing the bell with a fantasy about colored lad who loves watermelons not wisely but too well. Kid is led into watermelon land by a talkative scarecrow with astonishing results. Magnificent color, neat gagging and superb choral and music backgrounding help greatly. New peak in this variation of outright cartoons." The Black press was less happy. *Ebony* accused Pal of "perpetuating the myth of Negro shiftlessness, fear, and childishness."

Pal also released *Jasper and the Haunted House* in 1942. Sent by his mammy to fetch some gooseberry pies over to Deacon Jones, little Jasper is waylaid by Scarecrow and Crow and misdirected to a haunted house. "Oh, dat house ain't haunted no mo," Scarecrow lies to him. "Dem hants, deyz all been drafted." But the hants are there, and they scare the trio so badly they all go flying out the door and smack into a big roadside billboard for "Spook's Gooseberry Pie."

Pal, a Hungarian who'd fled the Nazis and arrived in the United States only in 1939, claimed not to understand the Black protests against Jasper. In his defense, it was noted that unlike many other animations, puppetoons used only Black actors for voices, and favored Black singers and musicians. By the end of the war, Pal was not only working on *John Henry* but also making serious changes to the last few Jasper toons. In *Jasper's Derby,* Jasper plays the violin like a budding Paganini (another Jim Crow echo?), never pops his eyes or licks his lips at a watermelon, and befriends an old racehorse, Hi Octane, who speaks in a Kentucky-colonel drawl. In *Jasper in a Jam,* Pal moves the boy from the watermelon patch to the streets of Harlem, beautifully rendered in the hand-carved sets. Some of the old elements are unchanged: instead of a haunted house, Jasper finds himself stuck in a haunted pawnshop, where a ghostly chanteuse sings (the voice is Peggy Lee) and musical instruments come to life to form a spectral jazz band. Jasper's eyes pop and his wooden limbs quake, but this time the ghosts turn out to be friendly.

In trying to get away from the embarrassing Southern stereotypes, these later Jaspers also lose a lot of the quasi-folkloric charm, and all the humor, of the earlier toons. *Jam* may be less embarrassing than *Haunted House,* but it's also less entertaining. And it failed to mollify Pal's critics anyway. The series was killed in 1947.

As upsetting racial images were dehistoricized and erased from cultural memory, Pal's Jasper toons and even *John Henry* were all but forgotten. He is remembered today far more for producing or directing special effects–heavy science fiction films of the 1950s and early 1960s, including *The War of the Worlds, The Time Machine* and *When Worlds Collide.*

Arguably the least offensive, and yet somehow one of the most controversial, convergences of animation and Black images came from Disney, of all places: the 1946 feature film *Song of the South,* a rather stodgy but enduringly popular adaptation of the Uncle Remus tales. A technically brilliant experiment in integrating live actors and animation, it's gorgeous, though also dull. The cartoons featuring Brer Rabbit and his cohorts are marvelous but get surpris-

ingly short shrift, while the live-action frame-tale about Uncle Remus and the other plantation folk is too long, too involved and too
stiffly acted by everyone but Hattie McDaniel, as Aunt Tempy, and
the charming James Baskett as Uncle Remus (he also does the voice
of Brer Fox). Baskett was a Hollywood unknown at the time. He had
performed onstage with Bill Robinson, done voices for *Amos 'N'
Andy* on radio, and appeared in some independent Black movies. He
originally auditioned as the voice of one of the talking butterflies,
when Walt Disney tapped him for Uncle Remus, a role he made his
own. Baskett was given a special Oscar in 1948, making him the first
Black man to win an Oscar—not Sidney Poitier, as one sometimes
reads. Which makes both the Black leads in this film Oscar winners.

Disney said he had loved Joel Chandler Harris' stories since boyhood and had always dreamed of animating them someday. It was
unfortunate that he waited until the postwar era, by which time
Black intellectuals and groups like the NAACP had grown very
weary of movies about Blacks grinnin' and singin' on de ole plantation. *Song of the South* was a box-office smash, was soon considered
a classic of American cinema, did very well in periodic theatrical re-
releases for no less than forty years, and spun off what's still one of
the most popular entries in the American songbook, "Zip-a-dee-
doo-dah." But the objections to its minstrelsy content tainted its
reputation all along. Under no specific pressure, the Disney organization finally decided to retire it from public viewing after a last theatrical run in 1986, and has never made it available in the United
States on video or DVD. This fostered numerous urban legends—
that the film had been "banned in the U.S.," that Bill Cosby had
bought the rights so he could keep the movie from ever being seen
again. As with most "banned" material, there is an active underground of devoted fans, who circulate bootleg European copies like
splinters of the True Cross, and continually petition Disney to bring
the film back into circulation.

7

BLACK & WHITE FILM, REEL TWO

From Race Movies to *White Chicks*

Did you hear that the KKK bought the movie rights to *Roots*? They're going to play it backwards so it has a happy ending.
—Joke found on the Internet

Throughout the early decades of American filmmaking, just as there was a separate Black vaudeville, there was Black filmmaking that operated outside Hollywood. The history of Black filmmaking can be seen as a kind of parallel universe to Hollywood, with actual Black faces instead of blackface, as Black artists and entrepreneurs tried, not always with success, to put more fully realized and sensitive images of Black life on the screen.

As early as the 1910s, small, independent Black film studios were starting up in a number of cities around the country, from Los Angeles to New York, Chicago to Philadelphia. Luther J. Pollard, who founded Ebony Film Corporation, offered films that, he said, were "clean and without those situations which are usually attributed to the American Negro. We proved to the public that colored players can put over good comedy without any of that crap shooting, chicken stealing, razor display, watermelon eating stuff that the colored people generally have been a little disgusted at seeing."

The best-known pioneer of Black filmmaking, and one of the

most prolific, was Oscar Micheaux. He was a remarkably industri-
ous and resourceful man. Born to former slaves in small-town Illinois in 1884, he was at various times in his youth a homesteading
farmer, a Pullman porter and a budding novelist who self-published
his books and then sold them door-to-door. Seeing that the future
was in film, he founded the Micheaux Film & Book Company in the
mid-1910s. Operating outside the growing Hollywood studio system, Micheaux was an early practitioner of do-it-yourself "independent cinema." He wrote, produced and directed all of his films,
raising the capital in small amounts from anyone who'd invest, film-
ing on the run in friends' houses and on the streets, splicing together
the tail-ends of mismatched film stock into lowest-budget features
and shorts. Some films were six weeks from the first day of shooting
to the moviehouse. Micheaux had no time for retakes and no
budget for elaborate editing, so he screened his films with line-flubs
and continuity problems intact. "Distribution" meant throwing the
reels of a completed film into his car and driving around to moviehouses where he'd cajole the management into special midnight
screenings for "colored" audiences.

At first, those theater owners would always be White, the moviehouses segregated. But in the twenties and thirties, as the Great Migration drew five million Blacks from the rural South to the big cities,
a national network of Black-run (though not always Black-owned)
moviehouses developed in Black neighborhoods. By the end of the
1930s, there were more than four hundred around the country;
some estimates cite a peak of around seven hundred. An entire industry of Black cinema—dubbed "race movies"—developed to feed
them.

Micheaux completed his first feature-length silent film, *The
Homesteader* (adapted from his novel of the same name), in 1919.
His second, *Within Our Gates*, followed in 1920. It was Micheaux's
direct retort to Griffith's *Birth of a Nation*. The rather intricate plot
revolves around a pretty, young Black woman from the South who

helps run a school for poor Black kids and travels North to seek funds for it from a sympathetic Yankee grande dame. She returns with the money to the South, where her plans are almost thwarted by a nefarious Black man, but she triumphs. The film is known best for its lengthy flashback that includes harrowing—and for the time, almost foolhardily bold—scenes of a White lynch mob and a White man whose attempt to rape the pretty heroine is foiled only when he realizes she is his daughter by a poor Black woman. Many White theater managers refused to show the movie because of these scenes.

Unlike any White filmmakers for a very long time, Micheaux sought to show Black society in all its facets. There are good Black characters and wicked ones, sharp ones and clowns, rural folk and city slickers, Black professionals and schoolteachers, preachers and police chiefs. Some Blacks work together to uplift the race, while others collude with bad White men to keep the Negro down. Micheaux did not flinch from showing that there was racism and class conflict within Black society. In one of his early talkies, a light-skinned Negro scholar has graduated from Harvard and returned to the South. One morning a dark-skinned maid brings him breakfast, and is shocked and disgusted to realize that she's waiting on a Black man—never mind that he's high-yellow (light-skinned enough to pass for White). "You is just as much a spook as I am," she sneers, "and this the last mouthful I fetch you or any other jig!" Micheaux also portrayed good and kindly White folks as well as evil, hateful ones.

The indefatigable Micheaux made dozens of films between 1919 and 1948. Sadly, many have been lost or are known only in fragments. At a time when even the big Hollywood studios were often careless about preserving and archiving their product, no one was concerned with saving a Negro DIYer's work for posterity. For a long time, *Within Our Gates* was known to film historians only by reputation; all copies were presumed to have been lost. Then a print with Spanish intertitles was discovered in Madrid in 1990.

As they developed in the 1930s, race films followed a devolutionary pattern familiar in American popular culture. What film historians eulogize today as the first flowering of "independent Black cinema" was in fact often funded, written, directed and distributed by Whites. Quite often the cast and the target audience were the only "Black" aspects of a race movie. The only difference between many of the race films and Hollywood's all-Black movies is the vast discrepancy in budgets. Inevitably the product was watered down and dumbed down. Even Micheaux's later work conforms. The bulk of race films are just lower-budget B-movie imitations of Hollywood's low-budget B movies. Light-skinned Black actors and actresses in romantic leads were promoted as "the Black Valentino" or "the sepia Mae West." Black comedian-clowns like Mantan Moreland played characters in race movies who were no less bug-eyed and easily spooked than those they played in Hollywood.

Plots were usually legible. There were lame mysteries, including some based on the stories of Octavus Roy Cohen. Black westerns, such as those starring singing-cowboy matinee idol Herb Jeffries, were typical Saturday-matinee pictures that just happened to have all-Black casts—a sort of blackface western. Many others—including *The Duke Is Tops* (1938), *Sunday Sinners* (1940), the Mantan Moreland vehicle *Tall, Tan, and Terrific* (1946) and *Boarding House Blues* (1948)—were little more than excuses to put chitlin-circuit variety shows on film, organized around the barest wisp of a plot. Some race movies were proto-MTV platforms for popular Black entertainers like Cab Calloway or Louis Jordan. *Look Out, Sister* (1947) featured Jordan and his band performing an album's worth of songs, strung together by a plot that took him out to an Arizona dude ranch.

A few Black filmmakers struggled to inject a bit of social commentary. Spencer Williams, Jr., who would become known to White TV audiences as Andy in *The Amos 'N' Andy Show* in the early 1950s, acted in numerous race movies through the 1930s and 1940s.

He also wrote, produced, directed and costarred in a few of the most charming films of the genre, including *The Blood of Jesus* (1941), *Go Down, Death!* (1944) and *The Girl in Room 20* (1946). *Girl* follows the typical variety-show format: an innocent songbird from the country comes to Harlem to take a nightclub job, and falls in with various low types. But Williams used the formula to tell a cautionary tale close to his heart: a simple Christian moral about how the Great Migration from the rural South to the big cities threatened to corrupt the country virtues that had been the foundation of Southern Black culture. Williams, who had grown up a poor country boy in Vidalia, Louisiana, knew this story firsthand.

The Blood of Jesus and *Go Down, Death!* treat this theme in Christian parables as simple and vivid as a Baptist preacher's sermons. In *The Blood of Jesus*, Williams plays a country husband who's not a bad man but not religious. In a freak accident, his hunting rifle goes off and wounds his pretty, young wife, a churchgoer. As she lies in a coma, an angel (with cardboard wings) visits her bed and takes her spirit to a crossroads, where she must decide between heaven and hell—a sign at the crossroads literally points "To Zion" and "To Hell," with a crucifix above it. She chooses hell—the wicked city, with its jitterbug nightclubs and dance halls.

Go Down, Death! (a "Harlemwood Studios production") was inspired by a funeral poem of James Weldon Johnson's that was well known to the movie's audience:

Weep not, weep not,
She is not dead;
She's resting in the bosom of Jesus.
Heart-broken husband—weep no more;
Grief-stricken son—weep no more;
Left-lonesome daughter—weep no more;
She's only just gone home.

Go Down, Death! pits the Black church against the Black nightclub, a familiar theme in race movies. The evil nightclub owner (played by Williams) hires a trio of hoochie girls to trap the handsome young preacher in a somewhat compromising position—he's photographed holding a glass of liquor. The nightclub owner's saintly adoptive mother gets wind of his plan and confronts him, and in a tussle he accidentally kills her—leading to the long, lugubrious deathbed scene inspired by Weldon's poem. Haunted by guilt, the nightclub owner flees to the wilderness, where he experiences terrible visions of hell and dies.

Where many race movies were shot on cheap sets, Williams took his camera out into the fields, down by the riverside and into actual dance halls, capturing some of the best moments of these films: a preacher conducting baptisms in a river; a bunch of black youths showing off their spectacular jitterbug moves in a low-ceilinged dance joint; a man behind a plow in a dusty field. It's beautiful black-and-white footage with a documentary feel. These authentic moments are juxtaposed with high Christian fantasy—visions of heaven and hell, Satan (in a cheap Halloween costume) and the angels. In one marvelous scene, Satan arrives at that crossroads driving a flatbed truck with a jazz band on it—a kind of mobile juke joint that draws the rural rubes down the road "To Hell."

You wouldn't call Williams' films great cinema, but they do qualify as Outsider Art. Writing of Micheaux, film scholar Thomas Cripps, one of the first to bring his work to wide attention, in the 1977 book *Slow Fade to Black,* sums up the entire genre: "He was important to Black filmmaking, while at the same time much of his work is a historical and cultural treasure rather than an aesthetic one."

Race movies petered out after World War II. Movie theaters were progressively desegregated, and the need for Blacks-only theaters vanished. Meanwhile, Hollywood went into its "New Negro" phase, supplanting race films with fancier integrated fare. In the documentary *Classified X,* Melvin Van Peebles describes the period from a characteristically jaundiced point of view:

> What had happened was that to win the war, the government needed everybody's help, not just white folks'. Besides, Hitler had given racism a bad name. Anyhow, in the effort to win the war, the government had done a lot of flag-waving to unite the nation. There was a lot of talk about the United States being a melting pot with liberty, equality and justice for all, regardless of race, creed or color, et cetera. A little social engineering to get blacks and women accepted in jobs formerly all-male, all-white preserves. In the flush of victory over the Nazis, America actually bought into its own propaganda. In short, the U.S. was experiencing a flood of democracy, a wave or two of which lapped up on the shores of Hollywood. Hence the promise of movies depicting Negroes more honestly, more dignified—i.e., the New Negro.

In its sincere efforts to present Negroes in a new, more humane and sympathetic way, Hollywood, being Hollywood, often went overboard, and simply replaced the old, negative Negro stereotypes with new, positive stereotypes that were just as unrealistic and awfully patronizing. Sidney Poitier rose to superstardom portraying endless minor variations on his Black superman trademark, as stereotypically positive as any Stepin Fetchit routine had been stereotypically negative. Like Bert Williams and Lincoln Perry, Poitier was of Caribbean descent, so it could be argued that there was a whiff of at least conceptual blackface every time he played a Black American. Interestingly, while conducting interviews for *Shuffling to Ignominy,* his 2005 biography of Fetchit, Champ Clark was told by Poitier that "it would be beyond my capability as a white man to understand and write about the life of Stepin Fetchit. The thought that I might try seemed to anger him."

Achingly well-intentioned films like *Lost Boundaries, Pinky, Home of the Brave* and *Black Like Me* managed simultaneously to address issues of race and be entirely trivial. Even such late efforts as Spielberg's *The Color Purple* (jokingly referred to as *The Colored People*) and *Amistad* can be seen as fitting this mode. Some great Black plays did make it to the screen as Hollywood pursued this earnest course, for instance *Nothing But a Man* and *A Raisin in the Sun*. But even this type of film became formulaic with repetition, such that Black playwright George C. Wolfe, in his 1986 play *The Colored Museum*, could lampoon them as "mama on the couch" dramas.

WATCH OUT . . . A baad asssss nigger is coming back to collect some dues . . .   —*Sweet Sweetback's Baad Asssss Song*

INDEPENDENT BLACK FILMMAKING LANGUISHED THROUGH the 1950s and 1960s. Then, in the late 1960s, Melvin Van Peebles, a young writer-actor-director and American expatriate in France, released his first feature film, *La Permission* (1967). Impressed, Columbia Pictures invited him to Hollywood—and realized only when he arrived that he was a young *Black* American expatriate. Van Peebles instantly set to work on a brilliant racial satire, *The Watermelon Man* (1970)—the title copped from a famous nineteenth-century minstrel routine. It is still the best whiteface movie ever.

Van Peebles says that the studio originally wanted a White movie star in blackface, but he reversed that concept and cast Godfrey Cambridge to star in full-body whiteface. Cambridge plays Jeff Gerber, an obnoxious, casually bigoted insurance salesman who gets up to pee in the middle of the night and discovers he's turned Black. Clearly riffing off *Black Like Me*, the film follows the downward spiral of Gerber's life as the literally blackfaced White man must enter and experience the world as Black people knew it in 1970. After failing at various ridiculous methods to turn himself White again, Gerber slowly accepts that his Blackness is a permanent condition. He learns what it's like to be barred from his former club because of his color, and how it feels to be the object of White women's jungle fever, and eventually how to exploit the White guilt of neighbors and colleagues for personal gain. He gradually immerses himself fully in Black culture—to the point where, in the film's bitter and chilling final scene, he has embraced the violence of the era's Black revolutionary politics. Van Peebles says this was another deviation from the studio's wishes: originally, the whole thing was to turn out to be a nightmare.

The rage boiling under the surface of this ostensible comedy erupted in Van Peebles' next movie, the one that came to over-shadow it: *Sweet Sweetback's Baad Asssss Song.* After *Watermelon Man* did well enough, Columbia offered Van Peebles a three-picture deal. Uncomfortable and unhappy in the Hollywood system, he walked away from the offer and set about writing, producing, di-recting and starring in the low-low-budget *Sweetback,* a film he hoped would "get The Man's foot out of my ass." Meanwhile, in New York, another Black director, Gordon Parks, was making *Shaft,* and his son, Gordon Parks, Jr., would soon get to work on *Superfly.*

These three films went off like serial explosions in 1971 and 1972. They're often cited as the first three Blaxploitation flicks, though *Sweetback* was an anomaly, really "a European art film set in Watts." Still, all three films did establish many tropes that would be repeated ad nauseam over the short life of the Blaxploitation craze. All pre-sent a strong, quiet Black man as hero. (Sweetback is almost literally silent. He utters only six lines of dialogue in the full-length film.) They're all Donald Bogle's bucks, violent Black renegade males who stand up to The Man. They represent a Black reversal of the White mythos, White power, White law; Sweetback's a hustler and killer, Superfly's a dope dealer, Shaft's a private eye but he fights the White cops as much as he fights the criminals. Sweetback and Superfly, and in his much more muted way even Shaft, are models of a new revo-

Italian movie poster for *Shaft*.

lutionary Black man, icons of Black Power. It's hardly coincidental that the Black Panthers would make *Sweetback* required viewing as a training film. The three are also the quintessence of the Black male as walking phallus—Shaft's and Sweetback's names say it loudly and proudly—as irresistible to White as to Black women. It's no exaggeration that these three movies changed forever how Black men saw themselves and how the rest of America saw them.

When *Sweetback* received an X rating, Van Peebles ingeniously exploited the publicity value, trumpeting that his film had been "rated X by an all-white jury," presumably because of its frightening message of impending Black revolution. Getting a "political X" was not unheard of; Haskell Wexler's *Medium Cool*, a withering critique of American politics and the media, earned an X in 1969. But *Sweetback* is filled with explicit sex scenes that surely would have earned it an X without any of its "revolutionary" politicking. *Midnight Cowboy*, sexually explicit but apolitical, earned an X in the same era.

Artistically and politically, *Shaft* is the least adventurous of the three movies, the most like a conventional Hollywood B movie—and thus the most Blaxploitational. No doubt that has a lot to do with the fact that it was based on a pulp novel by a White writer, Ernest Tidyman, a direct 1970s descendant of Negro-dialect lit. *Shaft* is just an updated race movie, a hard-boiled detective story in which the characters happen to be Black, giving the term "film noir" a new meaning. Nelson George dubs Shaft the "sepia Sam Spade." *Shaft* is probably best remembered now for its magnificent score and Oscar-winning theme song by Isaac Hayes. It spawned a weak sequel, *Shaft in Africa*. In *That's Blaxploitation!*, Darius James wonders why Hollywood never adapted the third novel in Tidyman's series—*Shaft Among the Jews*.

Superfly falls somewhere between the two, not as radical as *Sweetback*, but edgier than *Shaft*. It also featured a majestic sound track, this one by Curtis Mayfield. It was Gordon Parks, Jr.'s first feature film, made on a shoestring budget legendarily raised by producer Sig Shore from two Black dentists, Gordon Parks, Sr., and various gangstas and hoodlums in Harlem. (The Jewish Shore had previously distributed in the United States the 1968 Italian film *Seduto alla Sua Destra*, renamed *Black Jesus* for American audiences. Sometimes mistaken for proto-Blaxploitation, it's actually a leftist, anticolonial screed that boldly conflates the life of Christ with the story of Congolese political hero Patrice Lumumba. The film clearly makes its point that the only "savages" in Africa are the White colonials.)

In *Superfly*, as the reluctant but defiant dope dealer Youngblood Priest, Ron O'Neal comes off like a sepia Sean Connery; with his light skin, not very African features, and long, straight Jesus hair, he is undeniably, as one character puts it insultingly, "white-looking." Carl Lee, upstaging O'Neal as Priest's sidekick, encapsulates the film's message that in the White man's world, the Black man has the right to do whatever he needs to do to get by. "You gonna give all this up?" he scoffs when Priest expresses doubts about the dope-dealing profession. "Eight-track stereo, color TV in every room, and can snort half a piece of dope every day? That's the American dream, nigger."

At a time when Hollywood was in a stupor, bankrupt of ideas and struggling mightily to get Americans into theaters, *Sweetback, Superfly* and *Shaft* played to packed houses and generated tremendous hoopla. While the NAACP and others in the Black establishment responded with dismay or outright condemnation—it was they who called the films "Black exploitation"—Black audiences were overjoyed. For the first time since the death of race movies, Black people were piling into Black moviehouses to see Black role models in Black-made films.

One of the best films of the genre, and one of the best ever made about pimps and The Life, was *The Mack* (1973), written by a man named Robert J. Poole, who was reputedly behind bars at the time (and who clearly knew the writings of Iceberg Slim, the Original Gangsta of Black gangsta lit). Shot on the streets of Oakland, *The Mack* was produced and directed by White men (Harvey Bernhard, who also produced the Omen series, and Michael Campus), and featured another Jesus-haired, not-terribly-Black-looking star, Max Julien.

Noting the extraordinary profits these small-budget films were making, Hollywood was quick to jump on board. After *The Mack,* as Hollywood became increasingly involved in the production of Blaxploitation films, the genre would quickly abandon most of its oppositional and revolutionary sentiments. It would, in short, become truly Blaxploitational, following the same sort of downward arc that race movies had followed once White folk got involved. The budgets grew, the production and acting became slicker and more "professional," while the social and political commentary were either leached out or simplified to comic-book depictions of Black heroes and heroines kicking the asses of evil, oafish White villains.

Still, a lot of them were fun, and a few did play a larger social role. *Coffy* (1973) and *Foxy Brown* (1974) catapulted Pam Grier to fame and success, making her one of the most bankable female stars in 1970s Hollywood. Both were written and directed by a White man, Jack Hill, an all-purpose B-movie auteur whose other credits include *The Swinging Cheerleaders, Switchblade Sisters, Spider Baby* and two other Pam Grier vehicles, *The Big Doll House* and *The Big Bird Cage.* Though most of her films were highly forgettable and trashy, Grier—and to a lesser extent Tamara Dobson (*Cleopatra Jones*) and Vonetta McGee (*Hammer, Shaft in Africa, Thomasine & Bushrod*)— presented Black moviegoers with strong, independent Black females in starring roles, and audiences responded enthusiastically.

The climax of the 1973 *Black Caesar* is one of the most amazing blackface scenes ever filmed. Until then, the movie—written and directed by another prolific B-meister, Larry Cohen—is a by-the-numbers Blaxploitation yarn about Tommy Gibbs, a good boy in Harlem who's turned into a hardened gangsta by The System and who returns from the penitentiary to become the biggest, baddest crime lord in Da Hood. It ends with Gibbs, played by Fred Williamson, beating a crooked White cop with his boyhood shoeshine box, then plastering black shoe polish over his face and forcing him to sing "My Mammy." Similarly, a bad White guy in *The Spook Who Sat by the Door* (1973), a cult favorite among Blaxploitation fans, is kidnapped and drugged by Black revolutionaries, then reappears in public, riding a bicycle in blackface while singing a silly song.

As these films continued to generate admirable box-office receipts, Hollywood hurried to keep filling urban moviehouses with Black product—any Black product. For a few years, Blaxploitation became the B-movie genre that threatened to devour all other B-movie genres. There were Blaxploitation westerns like *The Legend of Nigger*

Charley (1972) and *Bucktown* (1975). The making of Blaxploitational kung fu films, inspired by Bruce Lee's giant success in urban moviehouses, became a mini-industry unto itself. There were Blaxploitation women-behind-bars flicks like Jack Hill's *The Big Doll House* (1971) and *Black Mama, White Mama* (1972), the latter cowritten by Jonathan Demme, which teamed Pam Grier with Aryan demigoddess Margaret Markov. Grier and Markov were also paired as big-bosomed gladiatrices in Roger Corman's Blaxploitationish toga movie *The Arena* (1973).

Blaxploitation devoured all B-movie genres.

There were numerous Blaxploitation horror films, ranging from the rather suave *Blacula* (1972) and its sequel *Scream, Blacula, Scream* (1973) to the wonderfully wack *Thing with Two Heads* (1972), in which NFL vet Roosevelt Grier and B-movie vet Ray Milland play two heads with one body. It would be the ultimate Black–White buddy movie, except the two heads hate each other. Zora Neale Hurston tells us that hoodoo conjure men are often said to be two-headed, because they have double the knowledge of the rest of us. That would make this movie one of the wackier instances ever of a lore cycle popping up unexpectedly.

Further still down the pike was the awesomely psychotronic *Blackenstein* (1973), one of those low-budget movies where all the actors appear to be the producer's investors, neighbors, dentist et cetera. Then there was *Abby* (1974), a Blaxploitation "homage" to (i.e., rip-off of) *The Exorcist*. Darius James dubs it *The Blacorcist*. (The producer of both *Blacula* films, as well as *Abby*, was B-movie titan Samuel Z. Arkoff, than whom no White man leaped into the Blaxploitation genre more energetically. He also had a hand in *Coffy*, two *Slaughter* films, and *Hell Up in Harlem* and *Cooley High*.) Other Blaxploitation "homages" include *Black Shampoo, Black Lolita, Black Godfather, Dr. Black, Mr. Hyde* and, of course, *The Wiz*. As Black film critic Elvis Mitchell once quipped, it was surprising no one ever thought to make one called *Count Chocula*. Dave Chappelle later did a Blaxploitational skit featuring himself in *Blackzilla*.

Some of the funniest Blaxploitation films are those of chitlin-circuit comedian Rudy Ray Moore, aka Dolemite, who hijacked the genre to make low-budget extravaganzas that were basically promotional vehicles for his stage act and recordings. In the self-produced *Dolemite* (1975) and *The Human Tornado* (1976) he plays himself as the world's baddest man, a mackin', drug-dealing, wife-stealin', kung-fu-fighting, um, nightclub comedian, with a stable of bitches, a fleet of Caddies and closets full of fur-trimmed pastel, superfly weeds. Moore's a wild comedian who tells X-rated stories in verse—

a sort of next-generation Redd Foxx. As an action figure and auteur he's more like Leon Spinks, which lends these films considerable Z-movie charm. Dolemite whups copious honky butt while delivering much of his dialogue in rhyming couplets like "That motherfucker caught me in the bed with his wife, / Now he want to try to take my life! / Drive, nigger, drive! Drive, nigger, drive!" Raw and totally ghetto, these films would later be adopted by young rappers ("Nigger, please!" is a line from *Dolemite*), a phenomenon captured in the 1994 documentary *The Legend of Dolemite*.

About the only B-movie genre that, to the best of my knowledge, did not provide fodder for Blaxploitational adaptations was science fiction. *Space Is the Place* (1974), the Sun Ra movie, is certainly an homage to sci fi and Ra's outer-space mythologizing, but it could be called Blaxploitation only by virtue of its date. Uniquely weird in a way reminiscent of *El Topo*, it's really a psychedelic art film wherein a San Francisco hippie vibe and a hint of Mitchell Brothers porn cuddle up with some questionable Black separatist cant, all set to Ra's cosmic jazz. But there were no real Blaxploitation-in-space movies, and by the time *Star Wars* was released in 1977, the Blaxploitation craze had run its course. Too bad. A sepia *Star Wars* or *Dolemite on Uranus* might've been classic. The world had to wait until 2004 for the closest equivalent—*The Old Negro Space Program*, Andy Bobrow's short mockumentary about the Blackstronauts who went to the moon for NASSA.

As Darius James notes, one of the strangest, most controversial and misunderstood of all Blaxploitation films was and remains one of the least seen: Ralph Bakshi's 1975 mix of animation and live action, *Coonskin* (later released on video with the more anodyne title *Street Fight*). Bakshi, a White filmmaker who'd grown up in the Black and Jewish area of Brownsville, Brooklyn, brought a gritty urban reality to the feature-length cartoon format. Coming off the enormous success of his X-rated *Fritz the Cat* (1972), he was emboldened to venture much further into streetwise social commentary with his next projects, *Heavy Traffic* (1973) and *Coonskin*.

With the latter he strayed too far. *Coonskin* stars Scatman Crothers, Charles Gordone, Barry White and Philip Michael Thomas (Tubbs from *Miami Vice*), live and doing voices for the cartoon characters. The story, written by Bakshi, is a shotgun wedding of *Superfly* and the Uncle Remus tales. Call it *Song of the South Comes to Harlem*. Brother Rabbit, Brother Bear and Brother Fox flee the modern-day South for 125th Street, where they encounter, and blow away, a phony Black revolutionary, crooked cops and a Mob family. Bakshi's trademark aesthetic is in full view, with numerous very bloody shootings and stabbings, and nubile cartoon hotties who make Jessica Rabbit look like Hello Kitty. Most notable among the latter is Miss America, a blonde, buxom, button-nosed White girl wearing a skintight American flag. She teases one Black character, then cries rape and giggles when he is instantly lynched. She entices another Black suitor and then blows him away with the gun in her crotch.

Coonskin is a satire of American race relations in the 1970s, a parody of Black stereotypes in films and fiction (complete with its own version of the Tar Baby), and a loving tribute to the Blaxploitation movies of its day. The problem with satire and parody, especially when they play with "offensive" material, is that they require a sense of humor of the viewer. In this case, representatives of the Black establishment proved to be completely humorless, and missed the point of the film entirely. The civil rights organization CORE vehemently denounced *Coonskin* as racist, with members staging a noisy protest at an early screening at the Museum of Modern Art. Although the NAACP guardedly supported the film, CORE's preemptive exhibition of cultural ignunce ensured *Coonskin*'s demise. Paramount dropped the film overnight. It was picked up by a tiny distributor, which barely got it into some theaters before going out of business within two weeks. *Coonskin* was then buried as an embarrassment best forgotten. Although it did see video release, copies are hard to find in the country to this day, assuring *Coonskin,* like *Song of the South,* which it lampoons, an enduring cult allure.

Too bad the film did not reach young Black audiences, who would surely have gotten its message, its anger and its humor. *Coonskin* is not a racist film—it's blatantly, and often viciously, antiracist. Black people and urban culture are its heroes, White people and White culture are its savagely satirized villains. That it was completely misread in its day and remains effectively banned demonstrates how self-defeating hair-trigger hypersensitivity can be.

Coonskin is in some ways a fitting coda to Blaxploitation, which by the mid-1970s had begun to collapse under the sheer weight of its volume: at its peak, one in four American films could be called Blaxploitation. It didn't help that, generally, the quality of the films decreased as the volume ballooned. Also, with the release of *The Exorcist* in 1973 and *Star Wars* in 1977, Hollywood was back big-time. It didn't need to rely on Black movies to fill theaters anymore; as much as a third of the audience for these films was Black.

Thus, as the ultimate irony, the genre that Melvin Van Peebles unintentionally inspired when he abandoned Hollywood had saved Hollywood. It's funny to think of Van Peebles, the angry Black Marxist and godfather of independent cinema, as The Man Who Saved Hollywood, but there it is.

THE 1970S ALSO SAW A SPECTACULAR RETORT TO *THE BIRTH of a Nation*—the 1977 six-episode TV miniseries *Roots,* which ABC aired for a record-breaking 130 million Americans. It was based on a 1976 book of historical fiction—or "faction"—by the master Black journalist Alex Haley. He'd also written *The Autobiography of Malcolm X* and conducted a number of seminal interviews for *Playboy,* but *Roots*—both the book and the TV show—made him a household name.

Roots was informed by the twelve years Haley spent tracking down his mother's family lineage, which led back to an eighteenth-century Mandingo youth named Kunta Kinte, who was born and raised in Gambia. The story follows Kunta as he is captured and manages to survive the deadly Middle Passage aboard a slave ship to Maryland. There he is quickly bought at auction and given the "American" name Toby, and he spends the rest of his life as plantation chattel. The brutally dehumanizing treatment of slaves is depicted in detail. At one point Kunta/Toby escapes; he is then recaptured and crippled to keep him from running away again. The story passes to his daughter, who is born and lives her life a slave. Her son, "Chicken George," becomes a freeman and joins the Union Army in the Civil War. During Reconstruction, he joins his family and leads them off the plantation to escape the murderous reprisals of White vigilantes.

The televised version was a huge undertaking, and treated the story with a gravitas, and a production budget, rarely seen in a miniseries. It assembled an extraordinary cast of luminaries, including Maya Angelou, Cicely Tyson, Louis Gossett, Jr., Lorne Greene, Sandy Duncan, Leslie Uggams, Ben Vereen, Edward Asner, Yaphet Kotto, O. J. Simpson, Scatman Crothers, Vic Morrow, Moses Gunn, LeVar Burton, Raymond St. Jacques, Carolyn Jones, George Hamilton, Richard Roundtree, Lloyd Bridges, Burl Ives, Chuck Connors and Richard Farnsworth.

Roots was an enormous popular and critical success. The book was a megabestseller, and earned Haley a Pulitzer, a National Book Award and numerous other honors. The miniseries riveted the nation's attention the way only a few television events ever have. (That list includes, for better or worse, JFK's funeral, the moon walk, *Holocaust*, "Who shot J.R.?," the white Bronco and the World Trade Center massacre.)

Roots was aptly dubbed the *Uncle Tom's Cabin* of the twentieth century. Like Stowe's work, it had an explosive impact on the American consciousness and conscience. It popularized the history of slavery for a mass audience, with a simple story line, unmistakable heroes and villains, and large portions of melodrama, sentimentality and moral outrage. *Uncle Tom's Cabin* had challenged White readers with the then startling notion that slavery was inherently evil because Blacks were human beings, endowed with all the faculties, desires, dreams and rights of any White person. *Roots* presented TV viewers with an equally stunning idea: that the practice of slavery was not the aberrant behavior of a small set of Southern plantation owners, but an economic system woven into the very foundation and development of the nation. Amazingly for television, virtually all the White American characters are depicted as either open collaborators with or tacit beneficiaries of the institution of slavery. The unmistakable message was that slavery could not merely be shrugged off as shameful history, but had to be confronted for its lasting relevance and impact on the very shape and character of American society in 1977.

Lincoln's blandishment that *Uncle Tom's Cabin* had started the Civil War may have been a coy exaggeration; still, Stowe's work, widely read and produced on many stages around the country and in other lands, did much to foster a sense that war against the slaveholding states was a moral imperative. Its effectiveness as Union propaganda cannot be overstated. *Roots* also had a social impact well beyond that of most books or TV shows. One of the most pernicious psychosocial practices of slavery had been to strip Blacks of their history, their families, their cultures and languages. In 1977, more than a century after slavery was officially abolished, Black Americans were still well used to being written out of, or at least severely played down in, mainstream American history. *Roots* offered them back their place in history, and encouraged them to explore and take pride in their personal and family legacies as well. A huge surge in interest in genealogy, not just among Blacks, can be directly attributed to *Roots*. It lofted Africanicity into a national craze. What had begun in the 1960s with dashiki fashion and the invention of Kwanzaa now went into high gear. Both serious African studies and its loonier fringe cousin, Afrocentrism—what Debra J. Dickerson derides as "carpetbagging Afrocentrists" who invoke "impossible ancestors"— found permanent places in school and university curricula.

Rewatching *The Birth of a Nation* and *Roots* back to back, I was struck by a strange congruence I'd never noticed before: In many ways, *Birth* and *Roots* are mirror images of each other. They are almost the same film, in reverse. Both are historical fictions that stretch many truths and work many stereotypes to win political and sentimental points with mass audiences. Both are, unabashedly, propaganda. If *Birth* is the American *Triumph of the Will*, then *Roots* was the Kwanzaa of television—a well-meaning, uplifting but largely artificial celebration of Africanness.

Both work a Paradise Lost theme, presenting the past as an idyllic and mythical Garden of Eden. In *Birth*, that Garden is the plantation of the antebellum South, where darkies gaily toil in the cotton fields and seem delighted to shuck and jive for Massa when he strolls past their shacks. Peace reigns supreme, because both the darkies and the Whites know their place in the perfect social system, and both are content. The Civil War casts them all out of the Garden, by freeing the darkies and importing a host of carpetbagging scalawags from the North, who incite the freed slaves to riot, rampage, rape and pillage.

In *Roots*, the Garden is Africa, the Motherland, an equally idyllic and mythical land where young Africans happily gambol on the savannah. In the Garden, all Africans are happy, healthy, noble, wise, beautiful and courageous. Like Hebrews in Hollywood Bible movies, they speak a perfect formal language, employing an Edenic etiquette uncorrupted by slang, curse words or even contractions. Children all address their parents as "Mother" and "Father," and the parents are likely to respond with lines like, "Yes, my son? What is it you wish to say to me?" This Paradise was lost when the White Devil arrived and dragged them all off in chains.

Stereotypes abound in both. In *Birth*, the Southern Whites are uniformly good, the freed slaves evil, duplicitous beasts. In *Roots*, the slaves are uniformly good, the Southern Whites all evil beasts. (Yes, there are a few "good" darkies in *Birth*, and there are a few "good" White folks in *Roots*, like Edward Asner, typecast as a guilt-ridden White liberal.) In *Birth*, most of the darkies are impersonated, poorly, by blackfaced White guys. In *Roots*, most of the Africans are impersonated, poorly, by African-Americans like Cicely Tyson and LeVar Burton (Geordi LaForge to younger readers)—a kind of virtual blackface as false, in its own way, as that of Griffith's film.

Both *Birth* and *Roots* made much of their historical accuracy. Griffith worked closely from period photographs, lithographs and other sources to create scenes and sets that almost look like documentary footage. His intertitle cards constantly remind the audience of this fidelity to historical "fact." Alex Haley claimed that *Roots* was based on his painstaking and pioneering research into his own family's legacy.

But as we know, both *Birth* and *Roots* strayed far from history, and the more their makers protested their adherence to fact, the more they revealed their indulgence in fiction. Much of Griffith's "history" came from his own perfervid imagination, a novel and a play. Much of Haley's "true" family history was also imaginary—and the rest, scandalously, was alleged to be plagiarized from other authors' novels.

In 1977, Margaret Walker sued Haley for lifting from her 1966 novel *Jubilee*. Her case was thrown out of court, but it was soon followed by another, far more convincing, from a White novelist, Harold Courlander, whose 1967 book *The African* contained plotlines, characters and whole passages to which elements in Haley's book of a decade later were suspiciously similar. Haley settled that suit of court, but the damage to his reputation was irreparable, and he was forced to admit in public that *Roots* was a mix of fact and fiction—much of the fiction written by other, previously unattributed authors. (A third suit was brought by another novelist in 1989.)

Since his death, Haley has become a sort of intellectual O.J., his legacy sharply divided between his hagiographers, who don't even mention the scandal, and those historians and journalists who see it as "the most egregious example" of how the lure of fame and fortune can tempt one of their own away from his principles.

A THIRD GENERATION OF BLACK FILMMAKERS, BOTH "Indie" and Hollywood, arrived on the screen with Spike Lee's charming feature debut *She's Gotta Have It* in 1986. By 1989 and *Do the Right Thing*, he was firmly established as the new Melvin Van Peebles, the most controversial and outspoken Black filmmaker of his generation. But Lee's politics are far murkier than Van Peebles' stridency, and his narratives are usually messy, giving credence to the charge that he's more in fact the Black Woody Allen. Critical response to *Do the Right Thing* was all over the map. Stanley Crouch pronounced it an "Afro-fascist" gimmick and the "sort of rancid fairy tale one expects from a racist." Denouncing the film's lack of a coherent political message, Amiri Baraka wrote of Spike's "rawest opportunism," declaring, "Spike Lee expresses for me a recognizable type and trend in American society. He is the quintessential buppie, almost the spirit of the young, upwardly mobile, Black, petit bourgeois professional." Donald Bogle, on the other hand, proclaimed him "the black Spielberg."

In *Bamboozled* (2000), his fifteenth feature film, Spike directly addresses the legacy of blackface minstrelsy. A bourgie Black television exec creates *The New Millennium Minstrel Show,* complete with Black performers in blackface, named Mantan and Sleep 'n' Eat. As film critic Andrew Sarris noted, the *Minstrel Show* scenes were brilliant performance art, with both the performances and the production ingeniously quoting a wealth of historically accurate details. The multiracial audience's enthusiastic response to all the chicken-stealin', watermelon-eatin' stage antics—culminating with the entire audience's donning blackface and proudly declaring themselves "niggers"—was masterfully squirm-inducing.

As a young filmmaker, Spike had been quick to lash out publicly at colleagues who he felt were "selling out" their Blackness to make it in the entertainment industry, along with carpetbagging White co-conspirators. "He regularly ripped Whoopi Goldberg's blue contacts, Steven Spielberg's *The Color Purple,* Rae Dawn Chong, Arsenio Hall, Eddie Murphy, and others whose work or behavior he found objectionable," Nelson George notes. Interviewed about *Bamboozled,* Lee said that his targets included "Ving Rhames, Cuba Gooding Jr., Whoopi Goldberg, Diana Ross, Will Smith, President Clinton, Mother Teresa, malt liquor, the Rev. Al Sharpton, Johnnie Cochran, *In Living Color,* UPN, the WB, Quentin Tarantino, D. W. Griffith, the NAACP, athletes, rappers and myself." Pierre Delacroix, the exec who produces *The New Millennium Minstrel Show* (played, interestingly, by Damon Wayans, formerly of *In Living Color*), stands for all "self-hating" Blacks who create or consume demeaning racial images. He speaks a torturously stilted "educated" English, despises rap music and other "low" forms of Black culture, and collects Negrobilia, which crowds his office, mutely condemning him. Unfortunately, *Bamboozled* is as politically indecisive and narratively confused as all Spike Lee films—and ultimately, a squandered opportunity.

John Singleton was only twenty-three when he released *Boyz N the Hood* (1991), which inspired a number of keeping-it-real ghetto movies for the 1990s. *Boyz* was not the first entry in the new ghetto-rap-'n'-guns genre; *New Jack City* (whose premiere in several cities sparked violent incidents) and *Straight out of Brooklyn* preceded it. But *Boyz* remains one of the best and purest of the genre, which soon devolved into repetitious self-mimicry and sometimes self-parody.

Perhaps inevitably, In Da Hood movies soon looked like Blaxploitation: The Next Generation. The Hughes brothers' hearts were in the right place—South Central—when they made *Menace II Society* (1993), and it was hugely popular with younger audiences, but it was a film hampered by clichés and stereotypes, overwrought and melodramatic. Its loose-fitting plot machinations came straight out of the Hollywood scriptwriters' playbook, and its characterizations were as lousy with newjack forms of Black caricatures as any White movie from the bad old days. The narrator's grandparents were an Aunt Jemima and Uncle Ben for the 1990s, and the opening sequence, in which a Black youth calmly murders the Asian couple who run the local deli, succeeded in shock value but also plunged the film into exploitation. The advertising tagline—"This is the truth. This is what's real"—deserved an appended "Well, in Hollywood anyway."

Menace II Society was a film crying out to be parodied, and it got its comeuppance when the Wayans brothers spoofed it mercilessly a few years later in *Don't Be a Menace to South Central While Drinking Your Juice in the Hood*, which derived the bulk of its humor from *Menace*.

The Wayans family represents a Black film industry unto itself. From *In Living Color* and the Blaxploitation spoof *I'm Gonna Get You Sucka* through *Don't Be a Menace* and the *Scary Movie* franchise to *White Chicks*, they unabashedly direct their *Mad*-magazine style of parody at Blacks, Whites, Latinos, Asians and various Others. They spoof Black culture in much the same way that Shirley Q. Liquor does. How far is Shirley Q.'s infamous "Who Is My Baby Daddy?" sketch from the joke in *Don't Be a Menace* in which Ashtray meets Dashiki's seven children and she says, "Now what do we say to the nice man?" They reply in unison, "Are you my daddy?" (Similarly, how far is Shirley Q.'s notorious Ebonics Airways skit—see chapter 9—from the 2004 *Soul Plane*? Not surprisingly, both the Wayanses and the makers of *Soul Plane* were accused of trafficking in modern minstrel-show humor.)

The Wayanses brought everything full circle in 2004 with *White Chicks*—Black comedians spoofing White culture in whiteface drag. Sadly, they also squandered the opportunity; *White Chicks* says nothing about either race or gender in twenty-first-century America. It is, one reviewer wrote, "a surprisingly standard drag comedy." *The Washington Post*'s Stephen Hunter agreed: "Think of 'White Chicks' as a crude parody of Billy Wilder's 'Some Like It Hot'; it could be called 'Some Like It White.'"

In the end, all it proves is that Black filmmakers can have as much trouble bringing believable White characters to the screen as White ones have had creating credible Black characters.

8

BLACK MARKET
Negrobilia and Black Americana

O whitened head entwined in turban gay,
O kind black face, O crude, but tender hand,
O foster-mother in whose arms there lay
The race whose sons are masters of the land!

It was thine arms that sheltered in their fold,
It was thine eyes that followed through the length
Of infant days these sons. In times of old
It was thy breast that nourished them to strength.

So often hast thou to thy bosom pressed
The golden head, the face and brow of snow;
So often has it 'gainst thy broad, dark breast
Lain, set off like a quickened cameo.

Thou simple soul, as cuddling down that babe
With thy sweet croon, so plaintive and so wild,
Came ne'er the thought to thee, swift like a stab,
That it some day might crush thine own black child?

—James Weldon Johnson, *"The Black Mammy"*

One of the most effective metaphors in *Bamboozled* is the antique coin bank that sits on the desk of the ultimate buppie, Pierre Delacroix. It represents a jolly Negro who happily flips coins into his wide, grinning mouth—a popular theme for mechanical banks from the nineteenth century into the twentieth. As the movie proceeds, the jolly Negro's mute reproach haunts Delacroix's conscience, driving him mad with guilt.

For once, Spike Lee was making an unequivocating social statement. When Delacroix's bank was originally made and sold, it was for the use and amusement of Whites. But by the time of *Bamboozled,* such Negro kitsch had become antique "Black Americana" or "Negrobilia," and a large portion of the collectors' market for it comprised well-off Blacks like Delacroix. In the ongoing debate over whether Blacks should be trading in such memorabilia, with all the issues of identity, race and class the practice entails, Spike was clearly on the disapproving side.

When former slave Nancy Green portrayed Aunt Jemima at the 1893 Columbian Exposition, the nostalgia for the Old South that had fueled the spread of minstrelsy and Negro-dialect literature also permeated American advertising, marketing, toys, novelties and kitsch. For a century, White Americans who had little contact with actual Black Americans were surrounded by stereotyped images of Blacks, often humorous and always nonthreatening. It was yet another kind of virtual blackface, a blackface transformed into print or three-dimensional imagery that saturated White America, from the corporate boardroom to the kitchen.

Although actual Black Americans like Nancy Green would sometimes be employed to pose, the creators of these images more often drew their inspiration from blackface than from Black faces. The same sorts of caricatures and stereotypes that animated blackface performance can be seen in Aunt Jemima and Uncle Ben, in mammy cookie jars and Uncle Mose sugar bowls, in postcards of pickaninnies eating watermelon or about to be eaten by alligators, in the Gold Dust Twins and the Cream of Wheat chef, and in the grinning Negro heads used as commercial logos for everything from tobacco companies to restaurant chains. These images came with the same range of emotional messages that blackface conveyed, from the comforting presence of Aunt Jemima as the nation's nanny and "foster-mother" to viciously cruel nigger jokes, from Uncle Tomism to coon-show shufflin' and jivin'.

It's worth noting once again that, as on the vaudeville stage, blackface and Black faces are far from the only ethnic signifiers that have been used for commercial purposes, even into the twenty-first century. Images of American Indians have adorned everything from tobacco tins to bicycles, from Land O Lakes butter to innumerable professional and scholastic sports teams. A stereotyped Italian man, usually fat and mustached, has entered millions of American homes on pizza boxes; variations on the beret-capped Frenchman in his striped jersey have sold wine; Chinese figures have appeared on packets of rice, lazy Mexicans snoozing under their giant sombreros have advertised red beans and tortillas, a leprechaun still pimps for Lucky Charms, the pigtailed Swiss Miss sells hot chocolate, stereotyped English butlers have promoted men's haberdashery. Even stereotyped images of matronly White women like Betty Crocker and Mrs. Butterworth—the paleface equivalents of Aunt Jemima— have been used to give products a particular ethnic (or perhaps in their cases unethnic) spin and a homey glow. It's hard to think of an ethnicity or nationality that at some point or other hasn't been distilled to an instantly recognized stereotype and used to sell some product or service.

It is probably true, however, that none of the others was as ubiquitous, or as neurotically charged, as the Black imagery. It has been suggested that relegating Blacks to the status of commercial mascots was a way for Whites to feel in control of them again after slavery was abolished. It's certainly true that though Blacks began appearing as commercial icons, logos, mascots and spokespersons before the Civil War, the practice really proliferated as plantation nostalgia spread in the postwar decades.

A few of the most successful Black commercial icons came straight off the blackface minstrel stage and/or out of the pages of Negro-dialect literature. (Recall that there were no copyright infringement laws back then.) Thus Uncle Tom and Topsy were familiar advertising figures, pushing root beer, breakfast cereal, salted peanuts, tobacco, thread, sweets and numerous other goods. Uncle Remus also shilled for various products.

According to media professor Marilyn Kern-Foxworth, the creators of the beloved Aunt Jemima character also drew directly from minstrelsy. Missouri entrepreneurs Chris Rutt and Charles Underwood were seeking a distinctive mascot for the self-rising pancake flour they had perfected, when, in 1889, they attended a minstrel show and heard the song "Old Aunt Jemima," a signature ditty of the Black performer Billy Kersands, who popularized the soft-shoe. Although Rutt and Underwood soon ran out of capital and sold out to a company that eventually was bought by Quaker Oats, their idea for the jolly, kerchief-wearing icon lived on. Nancy Green's promotional appearance at the Columbian Exposition is thought to be the first use of a living person to portray an advertising logo. She was just the first of many Black women to portray the universally recognized figure.

Aunt Jemima became more than a corporate logo; backed by decades of clever promotion by Quaker Oats, she became a character of American pop-cultural mythology, her popularity rivaling that of her White counterpart Betty Crocker (who to this day many believe was an actual person). The company invented a backstory for Aunt Jemima, linking her directly to the mythological world of minstrelsy and Uncle Remus: The "original" Aunt Jemima, according to this story, was a beloved mammy back on the Old Plantation in the halcyon days before the Civil War. There were Aunt Jemima restaurants, Aunt Jemima rag dolls, Aunt Jemima kitchenware and

The mammy as commercial logo.

cooking utensils. It's a sign of Aunt Jemima's enduring strength as a logo—at least among White consumers—that her straight-off-the-plantation look remained remarkably unchanged even years after the civil rights movement, despite much unhappiness among Black consumers who found her an offensive throwback. It wasn't until 1989, her hundredth anniversary, that Quaker deigned to update her look substantially. (Betty Crocker's look, by contrast, has undergone many periodic updates since she was invented in 1921. Now she doesn't even look so White anymore; she's become a darker-skinned, more multiculti American mutt.).

Even though she's been updated, to call someone an "Aunt Jemima" remains the equivalent of saying "Uncle Tom." In 1993, the Black magazine *Emerge* portrayed Supreme Court Justice Clarence Thomas on its cover, wearing an Aunt Jemima kerchief on his head, to characterize his subservience to the White conservative power structure. The following year, Gladys Knight took heat from Kern-Foxworth, among others, for "perpetuating the stereotypes that go along with the trademark" when she starred in some Aunt Jemima TV commercials. And in 2004, a Black radio host called Condoleezza Rice an Aunt Jemima for participating in George W. Bush's Republican administration.

Jemima's male counterparts Uncle Ben and Rastus, the Cream of Wheat chef, have had similarly long and successful careers. Unlike hers, their familiar faces are derived from photos of actual people—both of whom, interestingly, worked in Chicago restaurants. The broadly grinning Rastus was based on a waiter for whose photograph the company paid five dollars in 1925. The very Uncle Remus-y Uncle Ben was a maître d' in another Chicago establishment.

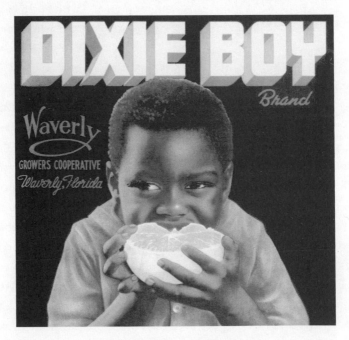

The Black child as commercial logo.

Innumerable less famous, and usually unidentified, Black figures graced the advertising and labels of a galaxy of products before the civil rights era. The term "Nigger Head" (or "Niggerhead"), usually accompanied by a caricature or silhouette, was a familiar nineteenth-century brand name and/or logo for everything from stove polish to tinned oysters. Well into the twentieth century, advertisers were so infatuated with images of Black children eating watermelon that they would slap them on even the most inappropriate-seeming products, as in a 1941 campaign for Shell Oil. Manufacturers of soaps, detergents and bleaches, meanwhile, frequently worked the joke that their product was so strong it could turn Black people, usually children, White. Ivory Soap introduced its famous tagline "It Floats" with an 1891 ad of a cute little Black girl who's made a toy sailboat out of a cake of Ivory. Goldie and Dustie, the Gold Dust Twins, appeared on their first box of washing powder in the 1880s and remained familiar household figures for fifty years.

You are justly *very* particular about your refrigerator. That's why you should clean it with

GOLD DUST

It cleanses, sterilizes and sweetens everything.

5c and larger packages.

THE N.K. FAIRBANK COMPANY
CHICAGO

"Let the GOLD DUST TWINS do your work"

Goldie and Dustie.

The name Sambo, which has West African roots, was applied to Black males from early slavery days. Apparently it amused Portuguese and Spanish slavers because it sounded like *zambo,* referring to a type of monkey; Anglophones adopted it as a funny-sounding diminutive of "Sam." Sambo was an all-purpose nickname to denote any smiling, servile Black male, from Pullman porters to hotel bellhops to restaurant waiters and cooks. Though advertisements didn't always specifically name him, everyone knew him when they saw him, whether he was grinning and pitching Armour Star ham ("The ham what *am!*"), coffee, cigars or biscuit mix.

The story of Helen Bannerman's popular 1899 children's book *The Story of Little Black Sambo* is more confused. The book has never gone out of print, though in recent years its illustrations have been sanitized and even its title changed in some editions to *The Story of Little Babaji*. That's because Bannerman was a British colonial in India, and though she gave her hero a Black name, everything else about him seems Indian, right down to the jungle tigers who churn themselves into butter for his pancakes. In 1957, when the first Sambo's pancake restaurant opened in Santa Barbara, California, founders Sam Battistone and Newell Bonette said the name was a combination of their nicknames, Sam and Bo, and that it was a natural to associate their establishment with Bannerman's popular book. They claimed no intention to make fun of Blacks, and the Sambo they used in their logo did in fact look like a cartoon Indian boy, not Black. Still, the chain could never elude the charge that its name was offensive and its management racist.

No claim of innocence could be put forward for the Coon Chicken Inn restaurants, founded in 1925 in—it's somehow not surprising to learn—one of the Whitest places in the country, the outskirts of Salt Lake City. The chain spread in the West and Northwest until the 1950s, when the aging founders sold its locations to new firms. Today, Coon Chicken Inn is remembered mostly for one of the most vulgar logos in the history of American business, a grinning Sambo face the owners obsessively stamped on every menu, plate, cup and napkin, creating a bustling aftermarket for Negrobilia collectors. The barbecue restaurant Smoking Joe's diligently flogged an equally grotesque logo.

Through the first half of the twentieth century, a woman who

Fan/menu from
the Coon Chicken Inn.

was of a mind to could outfit her entire kitchen, and much else in her home, in Negro-themed items. (Today, some dedicated Negrobilia collectors do.) Along with the well-known mammy cookie jar, she could buy salt and pepper shakers, sugar bowls, creamers, syrup pitchers, mixing bowls, teapots, coffeepots, mugs, glasses, bottle openers, tablecloths, tea towels, pot holders, wall clocks and other utensils in the likenesses of a mammy, Aunt Jemima or Uncle Mose, or endless variations on the pickaninny-with-watermelon and pickaninny-with-alligator. She could buy pipes shaped like Negro heads for hubby, which he could rest in an Old Black Joe ashtray.

For the kids, there were many versions of Delacroix's jolly Negro mechanical bank. The 1927 Sears catalogue offered a wind-up toy called a Chicken Snatcher. "When the strong spring motor is wound up," the description read, "the scared-looking negro shuffles along with a chicken dangling in his hand and a dog hanging on the seat of his pants. Very funny action which will delight the kiddies." Milton Bradley offered the Darky's Coon Game, the object of which was to toss a small wooden ball into the darky's grinning mouth.

The story of the lawn jockey is also a bit more complicated than that of other Negrobilia. Lawn jockeys used to adorn the front porches and lawns of homes throughout the Eastern United States, and sometimes businesses as well, like the '21' club in Manhattan. In the post–civil rights years they came to be seen as racist insults, and many were put away or destroyed, or painted over to make the jockeys look White; some amateur historians and collectors of Negrobilia suggest that this was wrongheaded. One theory is that the lawn jockey symbolizes Jocko Graves, a Black youth whose lamp lit the way for George Washington and his troops as they crossed the Delaware. Others say that the first use of lawn jockeys was to signal safe houses along the Underground Railroad. Both explanations may contain more than a hint of wishful revisionist history. A more plausible, and equally benign, version says that lawn jockeys first appeared in Southern horse country, to honor winning Black jockeys.

It is true that Black jockeys dominated American horse racing for years in the 1800s; the first thirteen jockeys to win the Kentucky Derby were Black riders.

Let's note again that Negroes were far from the only ethnic group who served as models for household kitsch. If your taste ran low enough, you could transform your home into a Great Ethnological Congress of Kitsch, filling it up with wooden Injuns and porcelain Chinamen, Irish bums and likker-swilling hillbillies, beer-guzzling Krauts, French girls showing their knickers, greasy-haired Italians rowing gondolas, Mexicans with their trademark donkeys, and so on. Pretty much whatever your ethnicity or nationality, there was kitsch out there to offend you if you were so inclined. The jolly Negro wasn't the only mechanical bank who flipped coins into his mouth; so did Uncle Sam, William Tell, Abe Lincoln, Teddy Roosevelt, Popeye, Little Lulu, Indians, Tammany Hall politicians, soldiers, ballerinas, cowboys and clowns.

Americans could flood not only their homes with this imagery, but the mails, too. It's nearly impossible now to imagine the enormous excitement generated by the invention and development of picture postcards in the 1860s and 1870s. Both sending and collecting them became instant fads and remained common pastimes for more than a century. In the later 1800s, the announcement of a new postcard could draw such crowds to post offices that police had to be called in.

Along with the travel-themed souvenir postcards we're familiar with to this day, jokey novelty ones were always a hit. As with household kitsch, ethnicity and nationality provided ready targets for the often vulgar humor, and Negro themes were rampant. The picaninny-with-watermelon and pickaninny-threatened-by-alligator jokes were explored to exhaustion. One strikingly designed card reduced the watermelon joke to its most basic graphic elements: Three red circles in a row transformed from a cut-open watermelon to a grinning Negroid face. It was labeled "Evolution." All the other familiar coon-song tropes—stealin' chickens, pickin' cotton, and so on—were rendered either in cartoons or in staged photographs. The humor could be unimaginably cruel; at their most loathsome, some postcards even showed images of Blacks who'd been lynched.

THERE ARE STILL GIFT SHOPS AND SOUVENIR STANDS, PARticularly down South, where one can buy newly printed Negro-themed postcards, plastic Aunt Jemima salt and pepper shakers, reproduction lawn jockeys and other examples of this kitsch. But by and large, new production of such materials ended in the 1960s and 1970s, when Americans became embarrassed by it all.

This created a curious situation. As new production dwindled, and many people threw away the old stuff, what was left came to be seen as rare, antique and collectible. A lively aftermarket for Negrobilia and Black Americana developed in the 1980s. A mechanical

Typical pickaninny postcard.

bank like Delacroix's could now fetch thousands of dollars; even a good mammy cookie jar might be worth over $1,000.

Reflecting the overall antique market, the majority of Negrobilia traders and collectors were originally White. But this began to change in the 1990s, as more Black Americans achieved middle- or upper-class status and had both the taste and the disposable income for antiques. Many focused their collecting on Negrobilia. It's been estimated that where the Negrobilia market was eighty-five percent White in the 1980s, it was seventy-five percent Black by 2000. Famous and successful Blacks have become avid collectors, including some surprising names: Julian Bond, Whoopi Goldberg, Otis Redding's widow Zelma, Oprah Winfrey, Henry Louis Gates, Jr., Cicely Tyson, Bill Cosby, Anita Baker and rocker Vernon Reid. Many less famous Black professionals and businesspeople fill out the collector ranks. *Black Enterprise, Essence* and other magazines published how-to articles in the 1990s with titles like "Black Collectibles—Just a Click Away," advising Black readers on how to collect Negrobilia online.

For some Blacks to be buying and selling what many Blacks find offensive reminders of a shameful past has raised a number of questions. Some collectors said they had entered the market because they didn't like seeing Whites trading in and making profits from the material; by buying up and trading these objects among themselves, they claimed, they were taking both the goods and the proceeds out of White hands. As one early Black collector put it, "Many White collectors have long appreciated and profited from selling and buying Black memorabilia. So it's about time that Black dealers and collectors profit from their own heritage." They contended that, embarrassing or not, Negrobilia is a part of the Black American heritage that must be preserved. One journalist wrote, "Collectors have come to realize that, for better or worse, these pieces represent a history better saved than destroyed."

Harvard convened a distinguished panel to discuss the issues in

1998. Professor Henry Louis Gates, Jr., joked to Julian Bond, "I don't think the NAACP [which had just elected Bond its chairman] would have wanted you if they knew you looked at Aunt Jemima all day." Bond replied, "They [Black collectibles] are reminders of who others thought and think I am. When I buy them, I do more than take them out of circulation. I give them a new life." Art history professor Michael Harris disagreed. "The negative can never be positive," he said. "I don't think it heals a rape victim to take images of the rapist home."

Some critics see the practice in terms of class as much as race. They portray Black Negrobilia collectors as self-hating Uncle Toms trying to buy their way into White society while distancing themselves from their heritage. "For as long as black memorabilia generates wealth, the artifacts will produce capital in ways reminiscent of the wealth produced by slavery," one such critic maintains. "That such wealth falls into the hands of slaves' descendants in no way diminishes its relationship to racism."

Philip Jackson Merrill is a Black collector, author and archivist, and a leading expert not only on the stereotypical Negrobilia, but on anything and everything related to the Black American experience, from slave implements and documents to Black high school yearbooks to the letters of famous jazz musicians to Blaxploitation posters. He feels no qualms about any collector, Black or White, trading in Negrobilia.

"Certain people feel that Caucasians should not collect Black memorabilia," he says. "But we live in a free country. This is a capitalistic society. If you've got the money and the interest, collect whatever you want. I have tremendous philosophical issues when people say, 'White people can't have this.'"

By the same token, he continues, "the people who are upset that Julian Bond or anyone else collects this stuff ought to take a real close look in the mirror before they come out with a comment. So many examples of Black history have been thrown away. As a people, we have not been taught to value our history. When I was lecturing at a Black college conference in North Carolina several years ago, I asked one of the archivists, 'Could you please tell me why the college doesn't have a stronger archive?' He said, 'It's plain and simple. We are in the business of educating. We are not in the business of documenting our experiences.'"

Asked whether he thinks that racist Negrobilia is really a part of Black American history, or only of White American history, Merrill replies, "It is a part of our history because we are a part of American history. We do what I call 'celebratory history,' where we want to celebrate aspects of history without looking at the complete picture. We want to just pick out pieces of a story and recognize them. But what about telling the whole story? You cannot blame Whitey, Charlie, Mr. Bobo, Cracker, Honky—Caucasians—for all the ill that is in the Black community today. You can't. We have our hand in this, and a lot of us don't want to deal with it. Going back to Africa, where we helped to sell our own relatives into slavery. And in America, we owned slaves. As my great-grandmother used to say, 'You gotta take the bitter with the sweet.' The bitter is the stereotypical memorabilia."

Merrill notes that he has caught some flak for preserving Nazi and KKK materials in his huge archives. "I think that the KKK is part of the American experience. I don't collect it because I'm some crazy Aryan-lover or Nazi. I collect it because we need to understand where we come from in order to understand where we're going. The KKK is a big part of that."

As a final irony, Merrill points out that the Negrobilia market became so large and lucrative that it spun off a whole other market in fake and reproduction Negrobilia—plastic Aunt Jemima wares newly made in Japan, for instance, and new reproductions of Coon Chicken Inn menus that are auctioned on eBay. And many an unwary collector has gone home with a fake set of slave shackles or forged slave's papers.

That's where Merrill and other collectors draw the line. The authentic items are history, he contends, and collecting them is preservation. The new ones are not history, he believes—just hate.

9

YACKETY YACK, DON'T TALK BLACK

Ebonics and American English

If the King's English was good enough for Jesus, it's good enough for me!

—MA FERGUSON, GOVERNOR OF TEXAS, 1925–1927 AND 1933–1935

In one of her most popular and simultaneously most reviled skits, Shirley Q. Liquor plays a flight attendant for Ebonics Airways, making the preflight announcements on a "Section 8 flight." When I saw Shirley Q. perform in 2004, a good portion of the audience could shout out many lines from the skit as she recited them. It's been rumored that a recording of this skit was played at least once on President George W. Bush's *Air Force One*, to general merriment.

Throughout the skit, Shirley Q. makes liberal use of stereotypical and exaggerated Ebonics pronunciations such as "aks" for "ask," "maks" for "mask," "attituve" for "altitude." The skit goes beyond mere Ebonics jokes to fantasize, à la *Soul Plane* (which it predates), about an airline that's a microcosm of poor Black society. The pilot and copilot are ministers from "Macadamia Jubilation Congregation." Shirley Q. announces, "We aks at this time that you do not spill things on our carpet, as it is not yet paid for. . . . On Ebonics Airways if you choose to smoke, that is of course your bidness, and de airline do not be responsible if the white folks on the grounds finds out about it. The smoke detectors in the rest rooms has been disconnected for your convenience. But we still aks please do not smoke clove up in here. . . . Our flight time today is whenever we get there, we get there. . . ."

A linchpin of all blackface performance is the notion that Black Americans "talk funny." Blacking up is only one aspect of the full performance. From Cotton Mather to Dave Chappelle, from "The Gold-Bug" to gangsta rap, Black American English has been singled out, above all other regional and ethnic variations of American speech, as an object of both mockery and pride.

All the special attention paid to Black American speech can obscure its vital role in the formation of a distinctly American way of speaking. To put it simply: White people taught African slaves how to speak English; then Africans helped teach everyone how to speak *American*.

We all know that American English has wandered some way from the British English the colonists brought across the ocean with them. Words, pronunciations, spellings, meanings and some rules of grammar and syntax now separate the two versions of English. Part of that drift was the lure of Black English. Black speakers not only introduced specific words and slang into what's called Standard American English (SAE), but influenced pronunciation, syntax, cadence, rhythm, even concept and meaning. Blackfaced minstrels, Black and White, surely played a role in spreading that influence as they roamed around the country through most of the 1800s— however inaccurate and exaggerated their versions of Black English might have been.

Before the civil rights era, White opinions about Black English were woefully ignunt, among scholars and intellectuals no less than the general public. They might find it amusing when lampooned in a coon song or a blackfaced stump speech, but all agreed Black English was incorrect and inferior to White English; they disagreed only on the particulars.

Joking about Ebonics
in the late 1990s.

The most egregiously racist attitude held that Blacks were simply too lazy and stupid to speak English correctly. Some Whites still hold this opinion, if we can judge from the Ebonics jokes that flourished in the late 1990s. It was once even thought that Blacks were physically incapable of proper speech because of the thickness of Negroid lips.

Others refused to acknowledge that Black English even existed. One theory held that Black English was merely an affectation Blacks adopted around Whites, to annoy and confuse them. Presumably Blacks spoke perfect Standard English when no White folks were around. This is a humorous idea, but totally daft. Even more bizarre was H. L. Mencken's apparent belief that Black English was never spoken before the minstrel shows and that the Negro-dialect authors created it out of whole cloth. Mencken never explained why Blacks would have read or heard the dialect of Negro caricatures and decided to adopt these speech patterns in real life.

Despite all the interest in Negro dialects evinced by White performers and writers from the eighteenth century on, proper analysis of Black English really got under way only in the 1960s, when a new generation of linguists began to give serious, nonjudgmental consideration to its history, development and structure. It is now understood that Black American English developed from very different roots from those of White American English. Its roots are in the early slave trade. Slave traders were happy to mix together African captives of different languages; it helped keep them from communicating with one another and possibly organizing themselves against their captors. As one slaver put it, they had as much chance of starting an uprising as of building a Tower of Babel.

That's the sort of situation in which a pidgin language arises. Pidgin is a newly created lingua franca, formed by combining bits of several existing languages, and following simplified codes of grammar and syntax that can be quickly learned and passed around. Through the new pidgin, slaves who originally spoke many different languages could communicate with one another, and with their masters. As a reflection of the nationalities of the traders, the slave industry gave rise to pidgin Portuguese, pidgin French and pidgin English, all of them mixing European and African elements. Traces of those pidgin tongues can be found in current American English. The word *pickaninny*, for example, is pidgin Portuguese. The French Creole spoken in the Louisiana Gulf region is a descendant of the pidgin French the slaves in that region developed. (A creole is a pidgin that becomes the dominant language in a region.)

In North America, slaves gradually learned to speak English— though, critically, the vast majority weren't allowed to read or write it. In *Bullwhip Days*, former slave Jack Maddox—the one who couldn't picture a heaven full of White folks—recalls that on his Georgia plantation "if a nigger was caught with a book he got whipped like he was a thief." And Tom Hawkins remembers, "When Dr. Cannon found out dat his carriage driver had larned to read and write whilst he was takin' de doctor's chillun to and f'om school, he had dat nigger's thumbs cut off."

Slaves were well aware of the multiple benefits to be accrued from learning the master's language. On the plantation, slaves who could communicate well with their White bosses earned preferred status and got the better jobs, as nannies, butlers, cooks, overseers of other slaves and so on. They could attain the relatively cushy position of "house niggers" as opposed to doing the backbreaking labor of "field niggers." Ironically, and far more important to the slave, learning English was also a key skill for escaping the plantation altogether. Newspaper notices offering rewards for runaway slaves routinely included notes like, "Speaks remarkably good English for a Negro," "Speaks very proper, and can at any time make out a plausible tale," and in one notable case, "Is thought secreted, in Lancaster County, among the Germans, as he speaks that Language well."

This makes perfect sense. The lone field hand, sneaking and shagging it across vast distances of hostile and unknown terrain on his way north, was unlikely to get very far if he spoke only "plantation creole" (think of it as the middle step between West African pidgin English and modern Black English). He'd be better off running west, to Indian territory. The runaway house servant who could communicate with any Whites he might encounter, who could read signs and maybe even forge himself a pass in his master's hand, had a far greater chance of reaching freedom. Nat Turner, the great runaway insurrectionist, is an example. Frederick Douglass' self-taught eloquence in speaking and writing helped him bluff his way to freedom on a train from Baltimore to Philadelphia.

As Blacks learned English, it was overlaid onto their original African tongues and the pidgin they'd developed, so it became their own variant of English. Or variants, actually. Black English incorporates a set of regional variants, just as White English varies from New England to South Carolina to California. A Black person raised in Louisiana spoke a variant distinct from, though intelligible to, that spoken by someone raised in, say, Tennessee.

Pronunciations, some words and many rules of grammar and syntax show that the roots of Black English are African and pidgin, not Standard English. Black English differs more from Standard than any dialect spoken by any White subgroup in the country. Yet it *is* a dialect—a variant of Standard English that is intelligible (if sometimes with difficulty) to Standard speakers. Part of the furor behind the Ebonics controversy of the late 1990s was roused by the Afrocentrism-run-amok contention that in fact Black English isn't a dialect of English at all, but a wholly separate and distinct language of West African origin. That was an overstatement, and a grievous political misstep. Still, it's important to realize that Black English isn't just an incompletely learned or lazy corruption of Standard English, either, as many Whites suppose. The apparent "mistakes" that speakers of Black English make aren't haphazard errors. As linguist J. L. Dillard pointed out in the landmark *Black English* of 1972, Black English follows rules of grammar and syntax that are every bit as complex and subtle as those of Standard English—sometimes more so. They're just different rules. Which is why when Whites try to mock and mimic Black speech, it often doesn't sound quite right. They miss the logic and the poetry, and just sound coarse and buffoonish. They don't know the rules.

Dillard offers many examples of Black English rules that can trip up White speakers and listeners. For instance, Black English speakers can express a sense of stretched-out or enduring action, which is found in other languages but less familiar to Standard English speakers. They do it by the use of *be*, as in *He be waitin' for me last night*. The *be* indicates that he was waiting a long time or all night. It is not used to express immediate action; one would not say *He be waitin' for me right now*, but rather the nicely condensed *He waitin'*. This rule can be used very subtly. For example, if you say *He be workin' when the boss come in*, you're using the enduring-action form to say that he was working before and during the boss' visit. But to say *He workin' when the boss come in* is to imply he picked up his tools only at the moment the boss arrived, and was presumably shirking off before that. Romance languages allow for a fairly similar distinction between a one-time-only action and one repeated or stretched out. It's very common to hear New York Italians using constructions like *I'm living here all my life* or *I'm working there twenty years*, bending the rules of the Standard English to give an Italianate sense of an action that has been happening for a long time and is still continuing in the present. The Standard English *I have been* approximates but doesn't quite deliver with the same vividness.

On the other side of the scale, Black English often dispenses with verb tenses. In Black English it is permissible to say *He work there twenty years ago* and *He work tomorrow*, where Standard English would demand *worked* and *will work*. This economy shows the deep pidgin roots of Black English. Pidgins, because they must be learned quickly and shared by users of many tongues, often seek the straightest, simplest route to communication. One of the most familiar economies of Black English is the dropped contraction, as in *He runnin'* where a Standard English speaker would say *He's running*. Written records of the speech of Black slaves show them also dispensing with gender distinctions in pronouns, using words like "him" and "her" interchangeably. Some regional variants of Black English retain a similarly relaxed rule on pronoun cases, wherein *She run* and *Her run* are equally accepted and understood. Former slave Georgia Baker, interviewed in the 1930s, routinely said things like, "Us sho' et good, dem days. Now us jus' eats what-some-ever us can git." Another, Teshan Young, told an interviewer, "Ise 'membah one slave dat gits whupped so bad hims neber gits up. Hims died."

A linguist would stress that a variant or dialect of a standard language is not an *inferior* or *incorrect* version of it—not a collection of mistakes and errors accumulated by a social group who do not and cannot understand the rules of the standard form. It's just a variation on the standard; not wrong, just different. This is a very hard concept for most people to accept, because we're taught from the first words we utter that there's one correct way to speak, and every-thing else is to be shunned. This is a social convention. In most cultures, there is a "proper" way of speaking, and how "correctly" one speaks is a sign of one's class, status, education, employability and so on. In England, speaking Cockney is a sign that you were born low-class. In America, speaking Black English has the same function, as does speaking with a pronounced Southern drawl or an Appalachian twang. Black Americans who speak only Black English—who haven't learned how to "switch" to Standard American English when need be—instantly mark themselves to Whites as poorly educated and not well assimilated into the mainstream culture. Their chances of success in the business or professional world will be as low as those of a runaway slave two hundred years ago.

Linguist Stanley Novak writes about the social consequences of language variance:

"There are nonstandard dialects of English distributed by region, ethnicity and social class that are used for everyday communication in informal contexts and referred to as colloquial or vernacular language. These language varieties are often shibboleths, in that they simultaneously unite members of a community around their unique characteristics and differentiate members of separate communities, and in that they are simultaneously symbols of alienness subject to misinterpretation/stereotyping by outsiders and symbols of pride in a shared cultural identity by insiders. Like the Biblical shibboleth whose pronunciation determined whether one would be allowed to pass unharmed, language can open—or close—literal and meta-phorical doors in American society. Humans are extremely social animals, and social interaction is primarily communicative; how we (mis)communicate determines in large part how we are judged, individually or collectively, as (un)intelligible, (un)intelligent, (un)-educable, (un)educated, (un)personable, (un)persons. . . .

"The language variety distinctive of African Americans is nearly as old as Standard American English, but it has often been misinterpreted as defective, has never been standardized, and has always had lower status compared to SAE. . . ."

Novak was writing during the Ebonics controversy, when the differences between Black and Standard English, and what to do about them, were suddenly a very hot topic. Ebonics wasn't a new concept when it exploded into national headlines in December 1996. A Black linguist, Robert Williams, had coined the term in 1973. He derived it from the words "ebony" and "phonics," and offered it as a new variant on such designations as Negro English, Black English and African-American Vernacular English. The term then sat quietly in the halls of academe for a quarter of a century, until the board of education in Oakland, California, inadvertently sparked a giant row about it. The board did that by passing a resolution declaring that Ebonics is the primary language spoken by African-Americans, and is West African in origin and a distinct tongue from Standard American English, "not a dialect of English." For African-American students, then, English is a second language. Thus, the board reasoned, there should be the same sort of federally funded bilingual programs for African-American kids as there are for children from Spanish speaking homes. These should include instructions and lessons translated into their native Ebonics.

The resulting public uproar was instantaneous. Many people, including Black parents and community leaders, misread the board's intention as teaching Black kids in Ebonics *instead* of Standard English. They suffered nightmare visions of Black kids growing up and trying to enter higher education or the workforce unable to speak, read or write English. Some observers denounced the resolution as blatant race-baiting and "playing the ethnic card" in a bid for increased funding. They interpreted the Oakland educators as saying, "Hey, if all these Latin kids are getting federal funds for ESL schooling, Black kids should be getting some, too. We want our fair share." Which, undeniably, was at least some part of the board's agenda and motivation.

Less than a week after the Oakland resolution hit the news, the U.S. secretary of education issued a stern ruling that Ebonics was not in fact a distinct language, and therefore no federal funds would be forthcoming. The U.S. Senate held hearings on the issue. The Reverend Jesse Jackson initially opposed the Oakland resolution, then changed his mind. The media, and White folks in general, had a field day with Ebonics. Jokes about it flashed through the Internet, and were soon so popular and ubiquitous that the Equal Employment Opportunity Commission felt compelled to ban them as a form of workplace harassment.

Some cooler heads tried to be heard in the midst of all the shouting and laughter over Ebonics. Charles J. Fillmore, a Berkeley linguist, summed up the "pedagogically relevant assumptions" behind the resolution in, well, plain English. "The way some African American children speak when they show up in Oakland's schools is so different from standard English that teachers often can't understand what they are saying," he wrote. Instead of treating Ebonics "as simply sloppy or wrong," the proposed program would help kids learn Standard English "by encouraging them to compare the way they speak with what they need to learn in school," which could happen only if "their teachers treat what they already have, linguistically, as a worthy possession rather than as evidence of carelessness and ignorance."

Too bad the people on the Oakland board had not invited Fillmore to write their resolution for them. In less than a month, the chagrined board members issued a revised proclamation. Their new wording softened the original ESL-sounding approach to something more like mainstreaming, "to move students from the language patterns they bring to school to English proficiency." In another and final revision released in May 1997, the word "Ebonics" itself had disappeared from the text.

The public controversy over Ebonics disappeared almost as quickly, but not before it had repercussions that were precisely the opposite of the beleaguered Oakland educators' intent. In 1998, California voters approved Proposition 227, effectively abolishing *all* bilingual programs in the state's schools. Instead, non-English-speaking students or those with "limited English proficiency" would get a year of intensive English lessons and then be mainstreamed. As it turns out, this seems to have been the right course all along: reading-test scores for both Black and Latino students in California have been on the rise since.

The sad thing about the Oakland initiative is that, for all its multiculti one-upmanship and pedagogical ineptitude, it was an attempt to address a problem that had been vexing educators for a long time: the difficulties that children raised in Ebonics-dominated environments face in trying to communicate with their Standard-speaking teachers, and vice versa. The language barrier really can be so broad and deep that young students and their teachers seem to speak two different tongues. The resultant misunderstandings can have a terrible impact on the kids' education. It has not been uncommon for even well-meaning psychologists and education experts studying the problem to come up with horribly condescending and intrinsically racist theories.

The most despicably racist have simply updated social Darwinism to conclude that Blacks are genetically programmed to have lower IQs than Whites, and that's all there is to it. You could dumb down standardized tests and curve the scores all you wanted, but you wouldn't be fooling Mother Nature. It was simply wrong and unfair to expect Black kids to do as well in school as White kids. A softer version of this line of thought perverts Howard Gardner's theory of "multiple intelligences." Gardner, a Harvard education specialist, argues that the IQ test is designed to show only linguistic, mathematical and logical skills, completely missing other types of equally valid intelligence, like the "body intelligence" exhibited by athletes and dancers, the visual-spatial intelligence demonstrated by artists, and the interpersonal intelligence shown by people with good social skills. Modern-day social Darwinists twist this theory along racial lines, claiming that Europeans are genetically more likely to get those linguistic-math-logic skills, while Blacks tend to get the body skills. After all, can't they run faster and dance better than Whites?

A more sympathetic, though still patronizing and wrongheaded, approach said that the kids' problem was not genetic but environmental. Poor Black kids grew up in homes and neighborhoods that were language-deficient and did not encourage them to develop their communication skills. Linguist William Labov summed this up as "the notion of 'verbal deprivation': black children from the ghetto area are said to receive little verbal stimulation, to hear very little well-formed language, and as a result are impoverished in their means of verbal expression. It is said that they cannot speak complete sentences, do not know the names of common objects, cannot form concepts or convey logical thoughts." It was only natural, then, that they would perform poorly in the classroom, on IQ tests and in interviews with psychologists.

Labov conducted tests of his own, and brilliantly showed that the problem was neither in the kids' genes nor in their homes, but *in their interactions with teachers, test-givers and psychologists,* none of whom understood the impact the Black-versus-Standard language barrier could have, not only on how students interacted with them, but on how *they* interacted with the students. As Labov put it, their theories "are based upon the work of educational psychologists who know very little about language and even less about black children. The concept of verbal deprivation has no basis in social reality; in fact, black children in the urban ghettos receive a great deal of verbal stimulation, hear more well-formed sentences than middle-class children, and participate fully in a highly verbal culture; they have the same basic vocabulary, possess the same capacity for conceptual learning, and use the same logic as anyone else who learns to speak and understand English."

Labov was not arguing against the overwhelming evidence that poor Black children were underperforming in schools around the nation. Nor was he denying that learning how to communicate in Standard English was key to any sort of success they might hope to achieve in school and later life. What he was saying was that the onus should be placed not on the kids, their dialect, their parents or their neighborhoods, but on the schools. Which, in its ungraceful way, was all the Oakland board of education was trying to say when it sparked the Ebonics debate.

It should be obvious that the debate raised issues not just of race, but of class as well. In what Greg Tate has dubbed "post-liberation" America—America since the changes wrought by the civil rights movement—many Black Americans speak Standard American English as their "first" language. They are middle-class, educated professionals who have grown up and live in integrated environments where SAE is the norm. They may be able to "flip the script" and speak Black English when they care to, but it is now no more their primary speech. Michael King, a Black commentator who railed against Ebonics in the classroom, admitted that he switched between the two as the situation called for. It's in poor Black homes and neighborhoods that Black English remains the norm. When rap artists proudly and defiantly flaunt Ebonics, they are well aware that they're sending all sorts of messages about race *and* class.

Flipping the script hasn't always been simple. In the 1960s, Black psychiatrists William Grier and Price Cobbs noted that for some Blacks in mainstream society, Black English could be a source of either shame or pride, or even both simultaneously. Grier and Cobbs discussed two Black men who spoke in what struck them as almost theatrically old-fashioned Southern Black English. One had grown up in the rural South, but had long since left it for the big city, where he'd become a highly successful businessman; still, to hear him speak, you'd think he was a nineteenth-century plantation field hand. The other had never even been to the South. He'd grown up in a Northern city, done very well in school, and he was pursuing a Ph.D.—in speech. And yet he, too, mysteriously spoke in what they described as a heavy Southern Black "patois."

How you speak determines how others perceive your individual and social identity. It is also a way to signal how you identify yourself. Both of these men were consciously using their Black speech, but for different reasons. The businessman used it as a way to disarm his white competitors, to mislead them into thinking that he was not the sharp, aggressive businessman he was. It was the linguistic equivalent of the shuckin' and jivin' that Blacks had long used to charm and beguile potentially hostile Whites. The other man, whom Grier and Cobbs call Booker, had more complex and neurotic motivations. On one level, flaunting his Black English even around his university speech professors was an act of defiance, a way of forcing them to accept his Blackness. But on a deeper level it was a way of identifying with his distant and uninvolved father, who had abandoned Booker and his mother when he was a child. Booker both resented this man and yearned to be like him; and his use of Black English was one way to identify with him; Grier and Cobbs reported that Booker's speech was a stunningly accurate impersonation of his father's.

BLACK ENGLISH IS NOT SYNONYMOUS WITH BLACK SLANG. Black English incorporates a wealth of wonderful slang, neologisms, turns of phrase and plays on words. But it is much more than that, as we have seen. Just as Standard American English is more than merely American slang and neologisms, Black English is not just ghetto slang. And yet many people insist on reducing Black English / Ebonics to street slang, thereby allowing themselves to write off the topic as unworthy of serious consideration. Even some Black commentators fell into this knee-jerk mode during the Oakland controversy. In an editorial titled "Ebonics Slang No Substitute for Standard English," Michael King declared, "No matter what the racial warlords may say . . . Ebonics is not a language. All it is is black slang. . . . The race warlords and their intellectual footsoldiers are trying to elevate slang to the status of a language by dressing it up with psychobabble."

This is simply incorrect. Yet even if Black English *were* merely Black slang, there's no denying it has immeasurably enriched the American vernacular, and through it that of the entire English-speaking or -imitating world. In the 1958 *Book of Negro Folklore,* Langston Hughes and Arna Bontemps listed several pages of "Harlem Jive." Much of that hepcat lingo is now archaic or extinct, including the word "hepcat" itself. The shelf-life of slang, like that of other sectors of popular culture, can be cruelly brief. But if we take from Hughes and Bontemps' list what's still in circulation, and update that with some of the words, phrases and usages popularized since, we can build our own admittedly incomplete list of Black idioms currently used or understood by pretty much all Americans, and plenty of other people around the world:

> cat, hip, cool, groove, man, brother, sister (sista), baby, jazz, jive, bad (= good), blues, Casper, crib, split, snatch, fly, lush, dig, drag, blow, stash, cop (v.), den, take a powder, old school, joint, rock and roll, rap, phat, hiphop, high, reefer, newjack, step to, signify, all that, beef, kick(s), gig, mellow, junk(ie), gangbanger, jam, down low, righteous, solid, bling, booty, bug (v.), bumrush, uptight, mad, mack, OG, def, dog (dawg), hincty, dicty, john, dope, wack, word (up), gangsta,

flava, playa, B-boy, rip off, blunt, chronic, chill, ill, bodacious, co-
pacetic, bring it, props, ups, homey, bust a cap, bust a move, blow
your top, get busy, get jiggy, get down, get off

Are these all giant, enduring additions to the canon of civilization? No. They're slang. Yet American culture would not be American culture without some of this slang and the concepts encoded in
it. The words "hep," "hip," "dig" and "jive" all seem to come from the
West African Wolof language: *hepi,* meaning "to see," *hipi,* "to open
one's eyes," *dega,* "to understand," and *jev,* "to disparage or talk
falsely." The concept of cool comes directly from the Yoruban, where
it denotes grace, calm, nobility and strength of character. From the
earliest colonial days, John Leland argues, White Americans have
admired and emulated these concepts, which have helped mold
American culture—the very idea of hipness, he's convinced, could
have come only from America—as well as the American "national
character" of which Constance Rourke wrote.

Nevertheless, it is not uncommon for Blacks, especially young
Blacks (young people universally being touchier than their elders),
to complain that their culture is being mocked or ripped off when
other Americans pick up on Black slang. An editorial in a 2003 issue
of the Howard University *Hilltop* from offers a typical example. The
author did not find it amusing when Whites spoke Black slang,
citing a CNN headline ("What the Dealy Diddy?") and Conan
O'Brien's use of the words "Fo' sheezy my neezy" on his program.

"First of all, he has no business saying 'my neezy,'" the author
huffed. "Sugar coated or not, it is still an offensive and derogatory
term, particularly when coming from someone who is not black.
Second of all, it was a lame and disrespectful attempt to cause
amusement at the cost of making black hip-hop terminology seem
stupid."

One wanted to take this young person aside and advise him

or her to chill. It is unlikely that either the CNN headline-writer or Conan O'Brien's joke-writer intended to make hiphop terminology "seem stupid." Far more likely, both writers were simply trying to sound, you know, hip and down. At the turn of the twentieth century, W. E. B. Du Bois wrote of the Black American's "double-consciousness," a "sense of always looking at one's self through the eyes of others, of measuring one's soul by the tape of a world that looks on in amused contempt and pity." In short, a self-consciousness about how they were perceived by White folks, to the point of defining themselves by or in opposition to White perceptions. Clearly, many Black Americans—especially young ones (young people being infinitely more self-conscious than their elders)—still struggle with this.

Complainers on the other side of the exchange, usually but certainly not always White, have long bemoaned the supposedly coarsening and vulgarizing effects Black slang has on Mother English. Yes, some aspects of Black slang, particularly that popularized by rap and hiphop, are coarse, vulgar, violent, sexist, homophobic and low-class. (It's certainly true, as Debra Dickerson writes, that many rap videos feature women "nearly naked and reduced to the basest pelvic-thrusting vulgarity. The average rap lyric is an ode to misogyny, objectification, and antifemale violence.") That's in the nature of slang. It is a way to mention what's unmentionable in polite discourse. Part of its function is to give a popular name to outré or outlaw behavior and ideas. Darius James reminds us in *Voodoo Stew*, for instance, that "snatch" became a slang term for the vagina in Harlem clubs where the dancing girls were so limber and adroit that they could grab patrons' upheld folding money in their nether lips. Only one of numerous examples. Maybe slang is coarse because the bulk of it (and usually the best) tends to be generated by the "lower orders"—the slaves and swots and *sgobbone*s, the cowboys and criminals, the underclass and outcast—while the educated and professional classes mostly invent just jargon. Compare the juiceless, sexless technoslang of computer hackers with the word list we built above.

At any rate, coarseness and vulgarity are hardly new elements in American popular culture, and it's hysteria to proclaim the End of American Civilization every time a fly girl shakes her booty on MTV. American culture withstood a few centuries of violent and hateful slang from the mouths and minds of White folks. I think it's strong enough to stand up to gangsta rap.

It will have to be. There's no getting around the fact that Whites find Black English in varying measures amusing, confusing, cryptic, poetic, lyrical, colorful, vulgar, low-class, threatening—and irresistible. For all that some Whites have mocked, lampooned and bemoaned Black English, they must like it—they imitate it all the time. Look at how the entirety of White Southernness, the Americans you might think would want least to be identified with Blackness, speak in accents, dialects and dictions heavily influenced by their long intimacy with Southern Black culture. I can remember as a young person in the 1960s hearing White Southern politicians like Lester Maddox and George Wallace ranting against desegregation and "race-mixing" in voices that were as Black as Shirley Q. Liquor can ever hope to sound. What was up with that? Every time one of these characters vowed to defend pure White bloodlines, one itched to go poke around in his genealogical woodpile.

It's no wonder White folks enjoy imitating and absorbing Black speech. Black English is generally more fun to speak than White English. It sounds better. I think that's because Black English is based in orality. It began and developed as spoken language. It has rhythm and poetics. Modern Standard speech is based in literacy, and often apes the cool monotone of the printed page. In other words, we learn to both speak and read Standard English at basically the same time, and when trying to speak "well," we often reach for the oral equivalent of literature. There's no canon of written Ebonics, unless you count Negro-dialect literature. It has always been passed on orally, and it still is today, through rap.

Black English is active, where Standard is passive. It can be wonderfully direct and concise, where Standard often meanders and obfuscates. William Labov was especially on point in noting how verbose and obtuse middle-class Standard speech can be, compared with the economy of Black speech. One only has to think of the appallingly dull and evasive language of government and corporate America, those two massive employers of the middle classes, to know he's right. Yet Black English is also intrinsically mischievous and playful, coded and subversive in ways that make Standard English seem as dull-witted and flatfooted as the stereotypical White folk who speak it.

Growing up and living in Baltimore, a very chocolate city, I often heard unadulterated Southern Black English, especially from older folks. Standing in line at an inner-city fried-chicken place one night, I heard an old Black man ask for his order to be made "eckta kipsy." It took me a few seconds to understand that he was saying "extra crispy." Ever since, I have preferred the "eckta kipsy" variant. It simply sounds more edible, crunchier, more tasty, where "extra crispy" now strikes me as cold and clinical-sounding.

One afternoon in the 1970s, a friend and I got lost wandering around in the southwest Baltimore neighborhood where one of Edgar Allan Poe's houses has been preserved as a museum, the Poe House. We were stoned, we both had long hair and were dressed in raggedy hippie outfits. The neighborhood was very poor and very black. Thoroughly confused, we stopped on the sidewalk below a porch where an elderly Black man sat in a folding chair, eyeing us carefully but impassively. His attention was not unfriendly, though he was clearly wondering what the hell these two long-haired White boys were doing strolling around in his very not-White part of town.

"Excuse us, sir," we called up to him. "Can you tell us how to get to the Poe House?"

He gazed at us with exquisitely deadpan features, examining our threadbare clothes and unkempt hair for the space of five, ten, fifteen heartbeats. Finally he said, in a voice rich with his Deep South upbringing and inflected with the most eloquently subtle hint of derision, "Oh, you keep goin' the way you is. You git to de Poe House by an' by."

I understand that The Wise Old Negro Who Sets the Silly White Folk Straight with His Choice Words of Wisdom is a stereotype who inhabits a good half of the books and movies I've discussed. All I can tell you is that this really happened. Some stereotypes are extrapolations from life.

I can also say his response remains one of the funniest things a stranger has ever said to me. The sly genius of the "Poe House" / "po' house" pun collapsed the entire social universe of our exchange—privileged, young, idiotic, slumming White boys meet poor, aged, world-wearied, slum-dwelling Black man—into two brilliant syllables. On top of that, his words were both a crushing put-down and the literal truth: We kept goin' the way we was, and we did in fact come to the Poe House by and by. His reply had been both flawlessly, politely civil and insidiously, subversively ridiculing. It was as though he'd encapsulated the entire history of Black and White American communication in that single utterance, freighted with all the coded meaning of the servant's double-edged courtesy to his ostensible social betters. Molière couldn't have sketched it more ingeniously, economically or poetically.

In the book *Life Turns Man Up and Down,* Kurt Thometz documents a culture that arrived quite recently at another crossroads of African orality and English literacy. In the eastern Nigerian (Biafran) market town of Onitsha, a fabulous blooming of African publishing began just after World War II and thrived until the tragic fiasco of the Biafran War. After centuries of colonial and slave-trade influence from the British, the Igbo people of eastern Nigeria were starting to develop their own literature in the borrowed English language. It was a wholly new literature, written by Africans for Africans *in English*, at a time when both author and reader were only just learning to read and write it.

And what a vibrant, sexy, crazy-quilt literature it is. Like Elizabethan pamphleteers who operated under very similar conditions, the Onitsha writers and publishers were making it up as they went. Publishers mixed typefaces and graphic designs with zestful abandon—a drawing by a local artist here, a photo of Pat Boone ripped from an American magazine there. Typos abound. The authors were similarly loose with grammar and syntax, often using commas and quotation marks more as decoration than punctuation, being freely creative with spelling, mixing metaphors and inventing words. The writing often reads like surrealist work or *Finnegans Wake*, and can demand just as much full-immersion commitment from the reader accustomed to Standard English. Thometz dubs it "Mad English."

In a creolizing process, authors mixed English words with Igbo idioms; they took Western (mostly American paperback) publishing forms—crime and mystery novels, romances, how-to and advice books—and adapted them to local customs and situations. There are bodice-rippers about sex-craved nymphettes (*Mabel the Sweet Honey That Poured Away*), there's Nigerian noir, and there's how-to advice for the Igbo man in the big city, with magnificently sage titles like *Why Harlots Hate Married Men and Love Bachelors, How to Avoid Corner Corner Love and Win Good Love from Girls* and the eminently wise *Money Hard To Get But Easy To Spend*.

Here's the opening passage of *Rosemary and the Taxi Driver*, a lusty tale of love amid high-life juke joints:

"If there was a prize to be awarded for falling in love at first blush, Rosemary should be given the richest golden medal," She has been chasing around the romantic seaport of Lagos, with her flareful flush of romance. Her voilet gown with vibrant colours and heavenly patterns vested below her knees. She wore a dazzling gold neck-lace, shiny ear rings and a botanical veil, stained all over with jet colours. . . .

The sun flickered over her canon-ball-head, with the hairs on her forehead, heightened like onboard type of shaving. She resoluted to follow the train at the earliest declining hour of the day. At down, She got ready to march with all the guts of the times, besides her ro-mantic love. She sang many love poems to them, while they twist, wiggle waggle and utter many love incantations, worthy of marring all the lively zests of any woman folk.

A kind of aleatoric (or alchemical?) Joyceanism abounds through-out this literature, as West meets East, they embrace, copulate and spawn a mixed-culture poetics.

They felt like cavalries, led into an Indian hotel, where beauty sparks itself, amidst kindness.

It was a total below me down, as he didn't feel his hands cold, before he caught him in the tough position of life.

Startled were the leaves around, mourning under the roary wind.

That's as beautiful a line of English poetry as was ever written by any Westerner, of any ethnicity, ever.

Maybe Americans should take the Igbo (a very old and wise cul-ture, after all) for a model regarding our own cross-pollination of African orality and English literacy. Let the Anglophiles bemoan the erosion of Standard English. Let the Afrocentrists and multiculturalists fret about the dilution of Black culture in the mainstream. Meanwhile, the rest of us should just get down with the creolizing. Let Whites stop fighting their very evident natural inclination to enjoy and envy the felicities of Black speech. Let Blacks stop feeling offended and ripped off when Whites adopt it. Let us all chill.

10

PIMP JIM CROW
Wiggaz, Niggaz & a Wonky

I'm now reading your account of nights in Paris and I'm struck again by your apparent assumption that you have somehow crossed the color line. Have you done something to yourself? Why are you the only white man that all your negro friends will tolerate? You say, "They (the whites) mix with the negroes about like oil and water." I'm not trying to pull any white jingo stuff on you here, but I'm curious. I wonder if you're really as hip as you seem to think you are, or just deluded. In other words, are you just another one of these nigger-loving liberals, or have you found that secret bridge that Mailer keeps looking for?

—Hunter S. Thompson in a letter
  to his friend Paul Semonin

Real black men die; soft niggaz become white women.

—Norman Kelley

So now we come back to the first decade of the twenty-first century. It's been roughly four hundred years since the first African slaves were shanghaied to North America; going on two hundred since the first blackface minstrels became stars; roughly a hundred fifty since the end of slavery; a little more than a hundred since the coon song; half a century since the great victories of the civil rights movement.

Looking around American pop culture, what do we see?

Over here, a giant concert hall is packed with an audience of almost entirely White youth. The young man on stage dresses, moves and sounds Black, and performs to Black music, but he's White: Eminem, whom historian W. T. Lhamon has aptly dubbed the T. D. Rice of our time.

On TV, a young Black man cavorts and preens in a $10,000 designer suit, his neck, fingers, ears and teeth sparkling with many tens of thousands of dollars' worth of gold, silver and diamonds. Surrounded by a harem of nearly naked young Black women gyrating and contorting with a lasciviousness rarely seen outside a sex club in previous generations, he recites dazzling rhymes, boasting of his sterling talents as a killer, a sex god and a high-roller. He is any of several dozen popular rap and hiphop artists, and he is instantly recognizable as Zip Coon. One rap group has even put out a CD titled *The Minstrel Show.*

The audience for both the White and the Black rapper includes a large number of young White males, who emulate their hiphop heroes by dressing, talking and even walking in ways they think are authentically Black. They don't actually blacken their faces (except perhaps when attending the odd frat party), but their dress and demeanor can be called a kind of virtual blackface—blackface as lifestyle. And yet for very many of them, their only contact with actual Black people or Black culture is in the stereotyped images of Blackness they receive through hiphop lyrics and videos. Call them wiggers, wiggaz, White Negroes, they are the direct descendants of the rowdy young audiences who cheered on the original blackface minstrels.

Go back to the TV, and flip to Comedy Central, where young Black comedians Chris Rock and Chris Tucker go through those routines that some critics have denounced as nothing more than modern coon-show antics, grinnin' and shuckin' for de White folk. And British comedian Tracey Ullman performs what is in effect a one-woman vaudeville revue, a cornucopia of gender and ethnic cross-dressing and racial caricatures that incorporate not only twenty-first-century blackface but jewface, gayface, yellowface and arabface as well. Flick to one of the movie channels, and there are the Wayanses in whiteface, satirizing the Paris Hiltonizing of upper-class White culture. Or perhaps Eddie Murphy in an old *Saturday Night Live* skit or one of his mid-career movies, also working out neo-vaudevillian impersonations of Whites, Jews, Italians or entire families of Black folk.

On the WB network and UPN, we have seen so many all-Black sitcoms that witty Black skeptics dubbed them the We Black and the Us People Network. Trafficking in fantasies of a sanitized, "white-washed" Black culture that is entirely middle-class, college-educated, professional and upwardly mobile, these shows are distinguishable from old-fashioned TV sitcoms only in that the formerly all-White casts have been supplanted by all-Black ones. They relate to actual Black culture in contemporary America no more than *Father Knows Best* and *Ozzie and Harriet* reflected actual White culture in the 1950s. As stereotypes go, this generation of programs is arguably no less offensive than *The Amos 'N' Andy Show*. The most Black thing about them is the way they have been ghettoized on second-rate channels, where no White viewers need see them.

Over on Court TV we find Michael Jackson, a Black man who took up whiteface not merely as a performance mode, but as a lifestyle. He goes beyond simple Uncle Tomism or Eurocentrism or buppyism. He represents the flip side of the White Negro—the Black Caucasian. His need to assume Whiteness seems as pathological, or at least as deeply neurotic, as the urges that drove the most base blackfaced White performer in the heyday of minstrelsy and the coon song. Certainly his permanent whiteface mask is as monstrous a caricature of Whiteness as the most loathsome blackface that ever parodied true Blackness. It's all the more mystifying and tragic to re-member that Michael Jackson conquered pop culture as a young Black man; he was the undisputed King of Pop, the most successful

Black pop star ever, the biggest star since Elvis and the Beatles, adored by White, Black and Other fans without cavil or equivocation. Only at the pinnacle of success did he begin his terrifying transformation to Whiteness. By the 2000s, as Norman Kelley, author of *The Head Negro in Charge Syndrome,* points out, he had retreated so far from his Blackness that he identified himself as Black only when he thought it would buy him some sympathy for his bizarre behavior. Thus he "played the race card" and attached himself to the Barnumesque Reverend Al Sharpton in his unseemly public spat with Sony, and complained that authorities investigating his alleged pedophilic habits were "racist." Let's call him a Wonky, or Wannabe Honky. Starring in his own personal adventure across the color line, his own *White Like Me.*

Let's listen to our favorite rock & roll songs. There may never be a resolution to the decades-old argument over whether rock & roll was simply Black music ripped off by Whites (as Black music writers like Greg Tate and, more cautiously, Kelley have tended to agree) or a truly American mongrel of Black and White—an inextricable mix of blues, country, jazz, folk and Tin Pan Alley balladry, wherein songwriters White and Black wrote transposably for performers Black and White, and Black performers copped from White ones just as often as White ones imitated Black ones. What is undeniable is that to the extent that White rockers consciously tried to sound and move like Black ones—Elvis and Mick Jagger being merely the most obvious of many, many examples—they were engaged in a revival of blackface minstrelsy. In Fred Goodman's book *The Mansion on the Hill,* singer Peter Wolf of the J. Geils Band recalls how the band's manager, Dee Anthony, rigorously trained him in the "Al Jolson theory of showbiz." That Wolf (né Blankfield) was a Jewish entertainer carrying on the Jolson tradition seals the argument.

In the bookstore, there's a new wave of popular paperback novels variously known as "urban fiction," "hiphop lit" and "gangsta lit." They are written and published by and for young Blacks steeped in hiphop language and imagery, and have titles like *Gangsta, A Hustler's Wife* and *Road Dawgz*. They feature stock gangsta and ho characters, and plots filled with sex and gore that have been appropriated straight out of Iceberg Slim's books, In Da Hood and Blaxploitation movies, and rap lyrics. They are thick enough with hiphop jargon and street slang that readers not in the know must find them all but inscrutable. Perhaps inevitably, White hiphop fans have their own corollary, a guilty-White-liberal genre of "wigger lit" with titles like *Bomb the Suburbs* and *Angry Black White Boy*. Taken together, these two genres clearly represent a new twist on Negro-dialect literature.

In antique stores, on eBay and in souvenir shops throughout the South, Negrobilia, both authentic and in reproduction, is bigger and more expensive than ever.

Shirley Q. Liquor continues to record and, fitfully, give live performances of her blackface routine. Bobby Berger is still celebrating Al Jolson in his Baltimore restaurant. Amateurs continue to put their jobs or educations on the line by engaging in a little prankish blackface.

Everywhere we look, in short, we can see examples of W. T. Lhamon's lore cycles—those bits of popular culture that hide or mutate to survive changing times—operating with a vengeance and fully in the open. Old modes of expression and representation that were driven underground, suppressed or banned by well-intentioned and right-thinking social engineers refuse to die, *unless the social conditions and the functions they served in the culture disappear with them*. Otherwise, they resurface a generation or two later, often in new guises, but still recognizable to anyone who knows a bit of history.

MORE THAN EVEN ROCK WAS IN MICK JAGGER'S THICK-lipped, drawling heyday, hiphop has been widely critiqued as a modern-day resurfacing of minstrel-show stereotypes and attitudes. Depending on who was counting, 2004 was either the twenty-fifth anniversary of hiphop, starting with the seminal 1979 recording "Rapper's Delight," or the thirtieth, because DJs and MCs first appeared on the streets of the Bronx around 1974. Some sticklers preferred to date the culture to 1973, when Afrika Bambaataa founded the Universal Zulu Nation, cornerstone of the movement.

There was no disagreement over one fact: Hiphop in 2004 bore little resemblance to its original form. Hiphop and rap began as Black youth culture on the streets of the Bronx, as kids with little money but lots of ingenuity began mixing bits of recorded music on portable turntables and reciting their own poetics over the beats. By 2004, this music had long since blown up from its do-it-yourself roots in the Bronx into a global entertainment conglomerate. Some people celebrated this as a success story for Black youth culture. Others, as Greg Tate wrote, "have been so gauche as to ask, What the heck are we celebrating exactly?" Drawing explicit parallels between the nineteenth-century coon show and twenty-first-century hiphop, Tate glumly asserted that "the Negro art form we call hiphop wouldn't even exist if African Americans of whatever socioeconomic caste weren't still niggers," seen by Whites as "sexy beasts on the order of King Kong."

For good or ill, no one could deny that by 2004 rap and hiphop dominated pop music around the world, while the more broadly defined hiphop culture—the baggy clothing, the gaudy jewelry, the elaborate lingo, the lifestyle and attitudes—had become a leading mode (some argued *the* leading mode) of global youth-culture expression. Writing in *Vibe* magazine in 2002, Fab 5 Freddy, one of the founding fathers of hiphop culture, described how, disillusioned with the music's crass commercialization in the States, he traveled to Brazil to find hiphop being appropriated by revolutionary rappers from the desperately poor *favelas* of Rio de Janeiro. To Fab, this use of hiphop to convey political and social messages felt much closer to the Black youth culture he'd helped create than to any hiphop being created in the United States in the twenty-first century.

In *Where You're At,* published in Britain in 2003 and the United States in 2004, British hiphop fan Patrick Neate took similar journeys around the world to find evidence of hiphop culture everywhere "from New York to Nairobi, the Rio *favelas* to the townships of South Africa," and was emboldened to announce, "It's a hiphop planet." Looking for a global culture, he found that hiphop was in fact "glocalized"—global, but with its meaning and uses adapted to specific social environments. Visiting with rappers and DJs in New York, he saw how becoming a multibillion-dollar media industry had transformed the original street culture into branded merchandise and off-the-rack attitude. Hiphop began as "a grassroots, bottom-up expression of who you were and where you came from" and its language was "arcane and inaccessible to the mainstream," he writes. "Now hiphop is the mainstream and its language . . . is the language of marketing and media."

Still, Neate wandered the planet, hoping to find places where hiphop meant more than sneaker brands and bling. In Tokyo he encountered crowds of louche B-boys and those cornrowed *ganguro* girls who artificially darken the skin of their faces at tanning salons or with makeup. "Hiphop here? It's like they read it from a book," a Black American expat scoffs. Probing further, though, Neate concluded that hiphop fashion was one way for Japanese youth to assert some individuality in a maniacally conformist society. In Rome and Rio, he also found youth ingeniously appropriating hiphop forms to express political dissent and social discontent.

Conversely, in France—the world's second-largest market for hiphop—the music had mutated from an underground voice of alienation to virtually a state-sanctioned art form. It was heavily subsidized by the French Music Bureau, a joint government–industry agency, as part of the government's mandate to promote Francophone music and combat the corrupting influence of Anglophone (i.e., American) imports. In South Africa, Neate learned that young people were in many ways as racially fragmented—Black, White and "Colored" (mixed-race)—as they had been during apartheid. Borrowing styles of language, attitude and dress from American hiphop stars, Neate concludes, helped them build something like a common culture.

Neate's guarded optimism probably struck other fans, like Tate, as naive. In the view of many, hiphop had traveled a familiar trajectory in American popular culture, from authentic popular expression to big business, and had sold its soul along the way. Like minstrelsy, jazz, race films and rock & roll, it had been transformed into a formulaic set of stereotypes as mass entertainment.

And many critics easily recognized those stereotypes as old and familiar.

"Images of black youth seen on MTV, BET, or VH1," Stanley Crouch wrote, "are not far removed from those D. W. Griffith used in *Birth of a Nation*. . . . This is the new minstrelsy. The neo-Sambo is sturdily placed in our contemporary popular iconography."

In 2004, *The Atlanta Constitution-Journal* ran an article that began:

Minstrel performers in black-face became huge stars in the 19th century by singing about blacks fighting with razors, stealing chickens and visiting whorehouses.

Hip-hop stars follow the same script for stardom today.

A growing number of blacks say that hip-hop artists are the new minstrels. Their celebration of booty and bullets recycles 300-year-old stereotypes of blacks as oversexed and inherently violent.

"Stepin Fetchit couldn't have done a better job," says Fred Robinson, a 39-year-old Lithonia [Georgia] pastor and father of three. "It's normalized a subculture that is destructive to the well-being of the black community."

The New Republic drew the same historical parallels, stating that "hip-hop and coon comedy both commodify black stereotypes and pass them off as an expression of racial authenticity. Thus, a century after Bert Williams and George Walker formed Two Real Coons, rap group N.W.A. produced a song called 'Real Niggaz.'"

That's an interesting point. Nineteenth-century minstrels prided themselves on the accuracy of their "Ethiopian delineations," even when trafficking in the most rank stereotypes—Zip Coon, Sambo, Tambo, Bones. Rappers routinely boast of "keeping it real," even as they, too, adhere to a rigidly limited set of degrading stereotypes: gangsta, pimp, ho. In both eras, the performers could easily say that they were merely living up to the expectations of their predominantly, though not entirely, White audiences. "We wear the mask," they shrug on the way to the bank. Or, as one MC put it to a reporter in 2004, "If an artist makes more money talking about being a thug and his realness in the street, then he's going to do more of that because that's where the success is. . . . They will do what sells."

In other words, some rappers pay such lip service to keeping it real because they're painfully aware they're anything but real. Just as White minstrels in blackface were nothing like "authentic Ethiopians," many rappers, especially by the 1990s, had never been anywhere near a real ghetto, had never run with the Crips, and had certainly never pimped out a stable of fine bitches. As the worldwide demand for rap and hiphop recordings grew, the music industry recruited ever-growing armies of new talent to fill its maw. It was inevitable that the talent pool of "authentic" gangstas who could rap would be used up, and a new generation of posing "wanksters" would arise who could talk the talk, even if they'd never walked the walk. In a real sense they were no more authentically "ghetto" than the wiggers who bought their CDs.

The urge to demonstrate that they're real gangstas has been so compelling that some have been willing to kill and be killed to prove it. Thus the surprising reprise of gangsta rap, and attendant gunplay, in the 2000s. This new generation of hardcore types was spearheaded by 50 Cent, who, as MTV.com breathlessly reported, "lived everything most rappers write rhymes about but never actually experience: drugs, crimes, imprisonments, stabbings, and, most infamously of all, shootings." That his much-publicized "beefs" with other rappers seemed curiously well timed to promote his latest releases did not go unnoted. That he was lofted to stardom by Eminem adds a level of irony that requires no further comment.

Norman Kelley offers a fascinating comparison of Michael Jackson's headlong flight into White with 50 Cent's headstrong determination to prove his Blackness:

"Jackson's descent into Whiteness is emblematic of how Blacks have internalized the perceived essence of Whiteness, which may underscore the psychic job that Whites have performed on Blacks: getting them to either hate or reject themselves as humans. A 'king of pop' has to be White, since Whiteness is the transcendent universality that is supposedly beyond color. That many African Americans support Jackson may well show that the very concept of Blackness, at least as articulated in the 1960s and 1970s, no longer holds any authentic or conceptual validity even within Black America.

"The last battle for true Blackness is the hyper-masculinity of a Tupac Shakur—revolutionary thuggery—or the return of the Bad Nigger Syndrome as expressed by the apolitical 50 Cent. This school of hyper-masculine Blackness could be seen as a rejection of the 'Soft Blackness' that an alabaster Jackson represents, all with the deadly consequences that have led to Tupac's death and the mythology of 50 Cent being shot many times. Real black men die; soft niggaz become white women."

Many commentators place the blame for the reduction of hiphop to a set of crude, self-destructive stereotypes squarely on White culture: It was all the fault of those young White men who make up the bulk of hiphop's audience, and the older White men who control the music industry. Public Enemy's Chuck D: "The endorsement of thugs is white people's fantasy of what they want us to be." Music and film critic Armond White: "What poor blacks do in society's margins—having just enough room to destroy themselves—makes for a pitiful white fantasy of power. It's merely a source of decadent delectation." Norman Kelley: "It's interesting that gangsta rap is supposed to be so Black and authentic, but purchase-wise, it's controlled by young White people—suburban youth. Sometimes I think Black folks are still on the plantation. Once upon a time you came here and sold your labor power. Now you sell your cultural power."

Repeated often enough, urban legend will be accepted as fact. No facts or figures back the assertion that it is hiphop's White fans alone who drive rap toward its violent, thuggish imagery. To argue that the entire hiphop industry is made up of Black puppets dangling from strings held by Evil White Men is both college-campus cant and as much an insult to Black culture as the most "racist, classist, misogynist" joke in Shirley Q. Liquor's repertoire. It negates the spectacular cultural and aesthetic achievements of global hiphop. Like all victimology, it infantilizes and disempowers the very people it intends to champion. The frequent use of terms like "slavery" and "the plantation" in these arguments suggests a perverse nostalgia for a time when Blacks truly were powerless victims—and therefore could not be held responsible for their actions.

On one level, it is tautological to say that White youth control the actions of rappers because they predominate among hiphop's American consumers. Hiphop is a vibrant, sexy, "dangerous" form of youth music positively guaranteed to upset the listener's parents. *Of course* White youth went for it in a big way. So did Black, Asian, Hispanic and Other youth. *Of course* White hiphop fans outnumber Black ones—it's a function of simple demographics, not the sign of an insidious plot by White youth to co-opt yet another cultural creation of Black youth.

Positioning hiphop as a victim culture also flies in the face of the fact that it is the first Black cultural product in which not only the entertainers but also many of the most successful entrepreneurs and impresarios are Black. Russell Simmons, Sean Combs and Damon Dash are the ubiquitously cited examples, but many successful hiphop artists—including Nelly, Lil Jon, and several authentic "thugz" like 50 Cent—have proven to be extremely gifted business-men. (50 Cent has so cannily coordinated the timing of his CD and movie releases and his bullets-flying arguments with other rappers that *Slate* called him "a pioneer of the hip-hop beef as postmodern marketing strategy.") Stanley Crouch argues that much hiphop is created "primarily for the material enrichment of black entertain-ers, producers, and directors, not present-day whites, who would be run off the planet if they—like the creators of nineteenth-century minstrelsy—were responsible for the images, the ideas, and the con-tent." The business end of hiphop culture has diversified far beyond the entertainment industry into real estate, fashion, housewares and other interests only the accountants in charge of the portfolios can enumerate.

IF HIPHOP CAN BE SO EASILY DENOUNCED AS MODERN-day minstrelsy, it should also be possible to defend it on some of the same grounds as I used to defend early minstrelsy in chapter 3. And in fact I think it can be. It should be remembered that hiphop—at least early hiphop, before its mass marketing—was an authentic youth music, and like all youth music since early minstrelsy, it of-fended and alarmed the adults who make up the cultural, social and political establishment. That's part of why youth music exists, from minstrelsy through early jazz to rock & roll and punk and hiphop and raves—to upset adults. In both the White and the Black com-munities, preachers, politicians and the graybearded guardians of cul-ture have excoriated hiphop's corrupting effect on the morals of America's youth, using terms remarkably similar to those with which the same types in different eras condemned "Jump Jim Crow," the waltz and the Charleston, Elvis' pelvis and "God Save the Queen."

Social historians have a term for this kind of hue and cry: "moral panic." It turns out that civic leaders, the cultural elite and the upper classes have been worrying about the power of mass entertainment to corrupt youth ever since the invention of mass entertainment. In the 1820s and 1830s, as the stepped-up pace of urbanization and industrialization concentrated large populations of poor and working-class youth in slum areas like Manhattan's Five Points and London's East End, low-cost, "low-class" variety theaters (called "penny gaffs" in England) sprang up to entertain them with cheap theatricals and blackfaced minstrels. Very soon, the middle and upper classes were in a panic that these entertainments would incite the youth of the lower orders to acts of licentiousness and lawlessness that they presumably would not have gotten up to had they not attended these shows.

Around the same time, advances in printing technology began to make possible the wholesale distribution of cheap fictions aimed at entertaining the lower orders. They were called "dime novels" or "half-dime novels" in America, "penny dreadfuls" in England. (They were also called "penny bloods." Sadly, there was no rival literature called "penny crips.") Written by both slumming professional authors and barely literate hacks, these precursors of the dime-store paperback trafficked in simple, formulaic tales of crime and passion, featuring bold highwaymen, fallen ladies, unrepentant murderers and swaggering outlaws of the Wild West. Civic and religious leaders denounced these books for glorifying the lives of criminals, thieves, murderers and prostitutes. When actual criminals were brought to trial, prosecutors often claimed that youthful consumption of this "dreadful" literature had started them on the road to vice and violence.

As soon as movies became mass entertainment in the early twentieth century, there were charges from above that they were deleterious to the morals of the lower classes. In the early 1930s, Hollywood churned out dozens of gangster movies like *Scarface, Little Caesar* and *The Public Enemy*. Once again, newspaper editorials and prose-cuting attorneys made broad claims that violent young criminals were imitating activities they saw glorified in these films. The public outcry prompted Hollywood studios to establish the self-censoring Hays Code in 1934. Soon dime-store paperbacks of "pulp fiction" purveying similar tales of crime and lust sold in the millions of copies, and were similarly condemned.

In the early 1950s, both comic books and rock & roll were said to be leading youth astray. The last quarter of the century, a period of high anxiety in American culture, saw wave after wave of moral panic sweeping through the media, the middle class, the courts and Congress. The moral fiber of America's youth was under attack from all directions. There was violence on television and, again, in the movies. Congress held hearings on the explicit lyrics and hedonistic messages in rock music. Satanists were running the day-care centers and indoctrinating young followers through heavy metal music. There were violent computer and video games. By the late '90s, a cor-nucopia of pornography was being piped directly into kids' bedrooms through their Internet connections, also the avenue through which pederasts and snuff-film makers preyed on them. In the 1990s, kids' TV shows like *Teletubbies* and *SpongeBob SquarePants* were scruti-nized for their crypto-homosexual messages. And there was rap and hiphop. One awaits the outcry as gangsta lit increases in popularity and market penetration.

Along with the tone of apocalyptic dread, one other thing is con-sistent through all these eras: No reputable documentation—no po-lice reports or court dockets, no sociologists' or psychologists' studies, no congressional hearings—has ever proven a link between the violent, sexy, politically incorrect entertainments young people gleefully devour and the widespread behavior of young people. Not one. As we have seen, the social and economic factors in poor urban neighborhoods that encourage youth to join street gangs existed long before, and continue to exist utterly independent of, gangsta rap. As Norman Kelley and others have argued, the wholesale flight of upwardly mobile, suburbia-bound professionals from poor urban neighborhoods leaves a leadership vacuum far more pernicious and pervasive in its influence on the morals of urban youth than any influence 50 Cent could ever hope to exert. Young people experienced homosexual urges millions of years before the Teletubbies ever waddled across a TV screen. American baby boomers, raised in an environment rich with violent media and loaded down with toy guns and other weapons of mayhem, grew up to become antiwar protesters and hippies. Whites among them were raised among a panoply of blackface images, Aunt Jemima cookie jars, *Amos 'N' Andy* programs and nigger jokes, and marched in Selma anyway. There are *no* documented trends toward increased violence in America, despite the immersion of today's youth in bloody video games, horror movies and gangsta rap; the truth is, America—both in its entertainments and in reality—is far less violent today than it ever was.

One final aspect all these moral panics seem to have in common: While claiming to voice fear *for* the morals of youth, what they actually seem to be expressing is a fear *of* youth, especially lower-class "ethnic" youth, from the young Irish "thugs" who prowled New York's ghetto streets in the 1830s to the Crips and Bloods and other "thugz" in our ghettos today.

WATCHING SHIRLEY Q. LIQUOR PERFORM ON THE BOWERY in 2004, I was only a few blocks away from those original Bowery and Five Points variety houses where blackface minstrels had first shot to international stardom almost two centuries earlier. American society and culture are vastly different now from what they were then, and yet blackface, that strange, often tasteless and cruel combination of mockery and mimicry, still exists, and its influences and spin-offs, for better or worse, can still be seen all over American culture.

During the course of writing this book, I went for a walk one fine afternoon in Brooklyn, where I live. At one point I passed through a gaggle of junior high school students, boys and girls, visibly of several ethnic backgrounds, lounging and laughing on the sidewalk. One of the boys was wearing a hooded sweatshirt, XXL jeans and new Vans on his feet. As I passed he gave me his best, most menacing get-out-my-way glare from under his hoody, a glower clearly learned from hiphop videos and painstakingly practiced in the bathroom mirror. I thought of the Black girl in Charles Chesnutt's 1901 *The Marrow of Tradition,* still in "the chip-on-the-shoulder stage." But this was a hundred years later, and this kid was White, and the school he hung out in front of is one of the best and most exclusive prep schools in the country.

A few blocks farther on, I was crossing at an intersection, in the crosswalk, obeying the "Walk" sign, when a sporty little car turned onto the street, going much too fast, and came flying into the crosswalk. It squealed to a halt with its front bumper not six inches from my leg. Had the driver been a half-second slower on the brakes, I would certainly have been crippled.

Then, adding insult to barely averted injury, the driver blew the horn at me.

I reacted the way I hope any self-respecting, law-abiding pedestrian would: I stood my ground in the middle of the crosswalk, and flipped the driver the bird.

The driver's window slid down, and a very attractive twenty-something Black woman stuck her head out. For a split second, my thinking clouded by adrenaline and maybe by her neat, businesslike, middle-class appearance, I expected her to apologize for almost maiming me.

Instead, she glowered at me and shouted, "Fuck you, White trash! Get out of the street!"

Well. As Shirley Q. Liquor might say, that was just ignunt.

Brooklyn drivers are notorious. You can't follow the local news without reading of one, two, sometimes three or four pedestrians killed by lousy Brooklyn drivers every single day. I figured myself lucky and moved on.

I did, however, wonder what might have happened if the situation had been reversed—if I had been driving, had almost broken her legs, and then had leaned out to shout some racial slur. I also wondered what she yells when she almost knocks down a Black pedestrian, or an Asian, or a Hasidic Jew.

For hundreds of years, the unrestrained freedom to shout racist slurs on crowded streets was the sole prerogative of White Americans, and Blacks were their favorite (though hardly only) targets. Today, for a Black person to yell a racist slur at a White person is, at worst, an ugly social gaffe; for the White person to do the same would be freighted with very different social, moral and possibly legal implications.

Turnabout is fair play. Generations of Whites shouted racial slurs with impunity, because they could; it signified their dominance and power over Blacks and others. It's only fair that a Black woman in the twenty-first century feels empowered to return the insult with equal impunity. Sometimes payback really is a bitch. In a sporty little car.

I'm not calling that young woman a racist. I prefer to think she was just, well, a New Yorker. Shouting insults at strangers in public, especially when you know you're the one at fault, is a cherished local pastime. No one in the world is ignunt like New Yorkers can be ignunt.

Still, she did drop instantly to the bottom line. She didn't yell, "Fuck you, asshole!" She went straight and instinctively to race. And ultimately that's the significance of our little exchange.

Despite several decades now of *bien-pensant* social engineering, disapproved attitudes about race and ethnicity persist in America—

among Americans of all races and ethnicities. Bad attitude comes in all colors and sizes. We can all be ignunt in America. We pretty much expect it of one another. In a stew of multiple ethnicities, nationalities, regionalities, religious and political affiliations, Americans can still be like those first Europeans and Africans meeting in the 1400s— we often key on our differences rather than our commonalities.

And our popular culture, our mutt culture, reflects that. Centuries of effort by social engineers, guardians of taste, preachers and teachers, multiculturalists and nativists have failed to produce an American culture of which any of them could approve. Crudeness and rudeness, vulgarity and violence, and all manner of insults and jokes at the expense of our neighbors are at play as we continue the project of creating our own Omni-American culture. We both mock and mimic one another, are by turns attracted to and repulsed by one another, sometimes love and sometimes hate one another, sometimes fight and sometimes embrace. We are as quick to offend as to be offended. It is a culture no high-minded purist could love, and no wishful forgetfulness will amend. No doubt all this will continue for as long as America is America, and Lhamon's lore cycles will go on spinning into the distant future.

On my way home that afternoon I stopped at my local deli for a pack of cigarettes. The deli is owned by a Korean couple, younger than I am, who don't speak a whole lot of English but speak a lot more English than I do Korean. They must have been prospering, because they had just hired two Egyptian helpers. (I knew they were Egyptian because I'd gone in there a few days earlier with a half-Egyptian friend and they'd all bonded.) The Korean wife and one of the Egyptian men were having great fun teaching each other a few simple words in their respective languages. They were giggling and laughing at each other's struggling mispronunciations, and they saw me smiling, and when I spoke my few words of Arabic that my half-Egyptian friend had taught me, we all laughed and had a grand time.

Now, if the President of the United States had at that moment declared war on Egypt, or the President of Egypt had declared war on South Korea, and thousands of people had been killed or horribly mangled as a result, I do not know that our few moments of frivolity would have had any impact on that. But then again, for a fleeting few minutes it felt like there was nothing a pair of knotheads called the President of This and the President of That could have done to prevent us from enjoying those few moments of culture-swapping. And maybe in the end that feeling, and the possibilities it suggests, as implausible as they are, are all and everything the American experiment means.

AFTERWORD

Trickin' the Paddies with Uncle Aglio e Olio

by Darius James

Uncle Al was Uncle Al not because his name was Uncle Albert. Uncle Al was Uncle Al because his name was *Aloysius*—Aloysius *Nixon,* to be precise— but in my mouth, his name atomized into a mule's bray sizzled in oil, garlic and fresh basil: Uncle *Aglio e Olio.* So I sufficed with "Uncle Al."

Uncle Al was married to my great-aunt Maggie. (Her name was *Amelia,* not Margaret.) Aunt Maggie was the sister of my paternal grandfather. (His name, incidentally, was Albert. However, we called him Dooley.) Uncle Al was my absolute favorite uncle. He looked like the Cream of Wheat chef. Eliminate his gold-capped tooth, my uncle was his identical twin. And given that he was both hustler and rascal, I have no doubt Uncle Al's likeness is, in fact, the original model for that innocuous Negro on the cereal box. Uncle Al was 'bout a *blip.*

In the 1940s, Uncle Al was a local promoter on New Haven's chitlin circuit. Mounting shows with national headliners like Duke Ellington, Count Basie and Cab Calloway on ballroom tours, he catered to the wartime crowds of Lindy-Hoppin' jitterbugs. He also acted the fool and cut the coon in blackface. He once showed me a publicity photo of himself standing on a stage built on the carnival grounds of West Haven's Savin Rock. He was blacked-up in mule-mouthed greasepaint. He also wore bold-striped baggy-legged zoot pants with a tuxedo jacket and a cravat. Scantily costumed dancing girls stood behind him in risqué poses. His curious grin, I suppose, was a consequence of performing with a chorus of curvaceous and thick-thighed *white* women in a era of Jumpin' Jim Crow. How he escaped the noose with *that* spectacle of "blackface" I'll never know.

In his later years, he collected bets for the then illegal lottery. Once, a crowd of onlookers watched him evade police by expertly racing through the streets of New Haven on his sleek three-speed bicycle. A flurry of numbers slips trailed behind him in the wind like swirls of confetti. Thereafter, his popularity soared. And his clientele grew.

Eventually, he was taken hostage by age and arthritis. His legs had gotten bad. He could no longer ride his bicycle. So he stopped collecting numbers. And he was confined to the apartment he shared with my aunt in a noisy New Haven slum. Despite his affliction, however, Uncle Al had not lost his ability to spin a yarn of ludicrous weave.

During my visits, which were frequent, he would beguile me with tales that kept me amused for hours. He told me, for instance, how he once shot a game of craps with Stepin Fetchit with a pair of *haunted* dice ("Them dice rose up in the air an' circled like two *ghosts*! They was movin' slower than that bald-headed fool did in his movies!"). And how he got drunk with Mantan Moreland in his dressing room ("That was one man who couldn't hold his liquor! He started talkin' in Chinese! Callin' me his number-one son! Shoved two chopsticks up my nose! Tried to rub my head! Said we had to go out an' solve the mystery of *Who Put the High Yalla in Fredi Washington?*").

Uncle Al told me about old-time characters in the funny papers like Krazy Kat and Ignatz. And how people used to listen to *The Shadow, Fibber McGee and Molly, Lights Out* and *The Jack Benny Show* on the radio. He even said *Amos 'N' Andy* was really two white men pretending to be colored. (Now, I knew that was one of Uncle Al's lies because I watched *Amos 'N' Andy* on TV. Any fool could see Amos 'n' Andy was real colored people.) Once, describing the mischief of his youth, he explained how he used to trick the paddies (that's white folks in early-twentieth-century Negro talk) into eating *dogshit.*

"That's *mean,* Uncle Al! Why you want to do that? They get sick and die!"

"What kind of Uncle Tom Negro are you? Ain't you *hep* to what that crazy redhead Negro is sayin' down in Harlem? White folks been makin' us eat *crap* for years!"

He had me there. "Okay, so what you do?"

"We'd scrape fresh dog doo-doo off the street, spread peanut butter and chocolate on two pieces of bread and mash the dog doo-doo between the two slices. When we were done, we'd wrap 'em up and put 'em in a bag. Then we'd have these other sandwiches just made up of peanut butter and chocolate. We'd go out with the doo-doo bag, stand on a street corner eatin' the *plain* sandwiches and carry on like they was the most delicious thing that ever was. Soon enough, them paddies come rollin' along, see us eatin' them *plain* sandwiches with just the peanut butter and chocolate.

"Now, paddies don't like to see colored folks have *nothin'.* Even sandwiches made out of *dog shit.* They'd get so mad seein' colored folks with somethin', their faces turn red and scrunch up like they was suckin' lemons. They'd barge up, barkin' like policemen.

"'Where you get them sammiches?'

"Since we were colored, they thought we stole 'em. We'd point to the doo-doo bag on the ground.

"'Gimme one!'

"'That's five cents.'

"'WHAT? I can see that you all is niggers but I didn't know you all was crazy, too!'

"'Cost a nickel.'

"'I ain't got no nickel for no sammiches been nigger-lipped by niggers wit' nigger lips! Niggers don't know how to spend a nickel no way!'

"So we didn't stud them paddies. We just kept cuttin' up an' carryin' on like before, eatin' our plain peanut butter and chocolate sandwiches. We did a little dance. Whistled a little tune. Rolled our behinds. Them paddies just stood there gettin' madder and madder. Eyeballs gettin' bigger by the minute. Drool slobberin' down their chins. We just kept on dancin' an' rollin' our behinds.

"Finally, we wore 'em out. They couldn't take it no more. Watchin' us enjoy somethin' they didn't have. They'd throw a fist full of pennies at us."

"'Here's your goddamned nickel! Don't know why you niggers need money, anyway! Niggers like to steal everything they got!'

"We'd pick up the pennies, reach into the bag and give them their 'sammich.' It was neatly wrapped in plain brown paper. '*Thank you and enjoy your sandwich, sir.*'

"We grinned. Our teeth were whiter than they were."

Uncle Al told this story the summer of my seventh birthday. It was the last such story I would hear him tell. I was away on a two-week holiday with relatives on the New Jersey shore when he died that summer. I miss him. He was my living familial link to both the *orality* of African-American comic tradition and the vanished world of blackface entertainment, both topics explored by John Strausbaugh in this book.

Uncle Al's stories were as far-fetched and outrageous as any trickster tale found in folklore. They taught me how to laugh at racist perceptions. And how to laugh at the ridiculousness of people, black and white (and red and brown and yellow and piebald). How to laugh at myself, period. Most important, he taught me how to transmute my anger into laughter. This was how a black man of the Jim Crow generation in the arena of blackface performance endured. And I was fortunate to have learned these lessons from him.

Uncle Al was, as Constance Rourke writes of the blackface min-strel, "irreverent wisdom [with] an underlying note of rebellion." He was the traditional African griot transformed by the American experience. Uncle Al's attitude toward blackface performance in the 1940s also reflected the origins of American minstrelsy.

As John points out, American blackface has roots in the fact that blacks on the plantations found white folks funny. White folks didn't get that the joke was on them. And a comedy of cultural er-rors has ensued for, well, the next 387 years. Funnier still is the fact that popular, broad-based culture and entertainment in America, the foundation of our current global mediascape of superfluous thought, began with Africans on the plantation parodying the be-havior of the white upper classes through song and dance. So, essen-tially, it started with a routine that Richard Pryor later legitimized in the 1960s but that had been a perennial joke within the black community from the beginning—mimicking the constipated gait of stiff-butt white folks.

Missing the joke but recognizing a dynamic new form, the virtual darkies of the traveling minstrel show crisscrossed the country, giv-ing America its first truly successful form of popular entertainment. Blackface minstrels were the radio and TV of their time. Through the comic malapropism of a "stump speaker," they disseminated at-titudes, ideas and opinions that gave birth to a national worldview in America. They introduced the popular songs of the day. And had everybody in the country dancing to fiddle-driven tunes like "Coons on the Moon." ("Oh, happy day! My bale o' cotton done flown away! It's de lak ob grabo fashanul pull! But Newton still can't 'splain why my hair am made o' wool!") Perversely, the minstrel's function in those times was not dissimilar to Chuck D's explanation of hiphop in the 1980s: "Rap is the ghetto's CNN!" ("Ethiopian Delineators are white America's *real Herald Tribune!*")

Despite its performers' grotesque caricaturing, the confounding irony of the minstrel show is that it also reflected a growing acceptance by the general public of African-derived forms of music and dance—forms that became, in time, uniquely *American*. The public of the minstrel years wanted the *spectacle* of black people without having to bear the actual presence of black people. It was this irony that drove Bert Williams to his early grave. And why Gosden and Correll, instead of the pioneering comedy team of Miller and Lyles, came to produce the radio show *Amos 'N' Andy*. And prompted Sam Phillips to say, "Find me a white man that *shakes* like a nigga . . ." Eventually, the acceptance of African-derived polyrhythms led to a more general acceptance and recognition of African-American people.

BLACKFACE, IN TRUTH, DIDN'T BEGIN WITH THE MINSTREL show. It began with the kidnapping, drugging and *tanning* of poor white Europeans who were then shipped off to the American slave market. These people, too, were so traumatized they also didn't know who the fuck they were or where they came from. They woke up in America as confused by the sudden appearance of a dark complexion as Godfrey Cambridge in *Watermelon Man*. Maybe that's what being an American really means. Waking up confused in the morning.

Many of these European hostages were Irish. They were thrown together with the Africans. The Irish couldn't speak the language of the Africans. The Africans couldn't speak the language of the Irish. So guess what? The Irish danced a jig. The Africans answered with their own distinctive set of movements. The two tribes *blended*. The result? *Tap dancing.*

And believe it or not, "white niggers" have been around longer than hiphop videos on MTV. White niggers have been vocal at least since the publication of Carl Van Vechten's *Nigger Heaven*. Or Mezz Mezzrow's *Really the Blues*. ("That nigga can't play a lick!" many jazz musicians said in his time. "But *goddamn!* His reefer is the *bomb!*")

In fact, I've known black cultural nationalists in my life who've embraced Mark Twain as a white nigger. ("Yeah, Huck Finn! He my nigga!") I suspect the phenomenon started with musicians, growing more pronounced in the bebop era of the 1940s.

The Beats are another wave of so-called white negroes. But how did that play itself out? Where are the significant discussions about poets Bob Kaufman, Ted Joans and Jayne Cortez? The exoticizing of black life by the Beats didn't constitute an *understanding* of black spirituality.

However, by criticizing the beats, I'm *certainly* not sayin' there aren't *down* white people. There are plenty of them. One of the most amazing nights I've ever spent in this life was with a woman I was cattin' with in Milan. On this night, there were cultural celebrations of Italy's African population throughout the city. This woman and I were hanging out in a squat. And an African dance troupe was there, doing their thing. And do you know them Italians started dancin' with the Africans and put their negroidal hindpots to shame? I saw it happen with my own two eyes! A whole bunch of assumptions were flushed down the toilet that night. So, yeah, there are a lot of white niggers. Find them in the *strangest* places.

ONE OF THE UNIQUE ASPECTS OF *BLACK LIKE YOU* IS THAT John doesn't approach the subject of blackface entertainment with a discussion of Eminem (who is a seriously funny muthafucka). Or the Beastie Boys (some other seriously funny muthafuckas who built their career on precedents set by Mel Brooks in *Blazing Saddles*, a contemporary urban blending of the Borscht Belt and the Chitlin Circuit). Nor does John bother until the last chapter with the *zomboid suburban wiggers* of MTV. Instead, he approaches blackface through a subject rarely addressed in American pop culture: queer performance. Though he compares early blackface entertainment with the adolescent rebellions of rock and roll, and the media-orchestrated shenanigans of gangsta rap, his story begins with the controversy surrounding snap queen Shirley Q. Liquor—a Southern cracka in blackface and a dress whose routines are really no different in character from the stand-ups on BET or on *Def Comedy Jam*.

Shirley Q. presents a *double* mask. It is not the classic masks of comedy and tragedy but the masks of race and gender. What is the meaning and purpose of these masks? And what does this say about Americans and our history?

Queer history is a history intimately connected with the evolution of blackface, church music, blues (Peachtree Payne, anyone?), jazz, r&b, and rock and roll in America. Minstrel shows were primarily a boy thing. A whiteboy thing. People comment on the deleterious effects of blackface on the black population in America but very few comment on the fact that female impersonation was also a big part of this show. White boys as the black and female Aunt Jemima. Shirley Q. has history and tradition.

The foundation of much American music is the church. Listen to early country spirituals and you'll notice there are no racial differences in the singers' voices. In other words, it's clear both blacks and whites are singing to the same god.

Gays often found refuge in the church. Esquirita, for example, played organ for traveling preacher Brother Joe May. Then he left. Put on some high-heeled Cuban stomps. And *frolicked,* as Professor Longhair was fond of saying, in the fields of after-hours spots, r&b joints and *wrestling* arenas.

In New Orleans, there was once a club called the Dew Drop Inn. It was famous for its "baby doll" acts as much as it was for featuring the nation's leading r&b headliners. It was also the club where Bumps Blackwell first heard Little Richard sing "Tutti Frutti." It has long been my contention that the *theatricality* of rock and roll is a direct result of the subculture of southern black gays.

When blackface shows declined in popularity, the female impersonator replaced blackface. According to a conversation I once had with a *male* impersonator, a woman well into her seventies living at the Chelsea Hotel, traveling drag shows had been touring the country since the 1920s. Wesley Brown, in his charming novel *Darktown Strutters,* suggests male impersonators in the minstrel troupe go as far back as the days before the Civil War.

EMERGING FROM THE UNDERGROUND AT ROSA-LUXEMBURG Platz here in Berlin on a mild Sunday evening, I walked a short distance through Berlin Mitte, and climbed the stairs leading to the entrance of the Volksbühne theater. That night, the theater was hosting a presentation by the esteemed American pop critic, cultural historian and author Greil Marcus. His appearance had been announced only days before by e-mail. And for reasons unknown but fortuitous, I was on the theater's e-mail list for the event.

I was a bit wonderstruck by the e-mail's arrival. Greil had been on my mind for some time. Months before I abandoned the high cost of Manhattan for the low rents of Berlin, I received a phone call from my friend Mark Jacobson. Mark, with the novels *Gojiro* and *Everyone and No One* under his belt, and his writing about his adventures as a New York cabbie, which in turn inspired the long-running television series *Taxi,* is one of the secret chiefs of American humor.

"Guess what?" he said.

"What?"

"Greil Marcus read your book, man!"

"Which one?"

"*That's Blaxploitation!*"

"What did he say? "

"He seemed a little baffled by it."

"How do you know?"

"It's in the updated edition of *Mystery Train*. He mentions it in the back."

I rushed to Tower Books and examined a copy. My book was referenced in the appendix under the chapter heading "Sly Stone: The Myth of Staggerlee."

Then, knowingly or unknowingly, a few years later, in his column "Real Life Rock Top 10," Greil *bitch-slapped* a puppet-opportunist *Village Voice* writer who had written a faulty and wrongheaded review of *That's Blaxploitation!* His review was based on the assumption that I was a brat from a family of booshie-academics (in fact, I'm a brat from a family of working-class *bohemians*). Greil yawned over this writer's collection of scribbles by saying I had previously covered similar territory in my book, only better. So I wanted to thank Greil and give him editions of my work published in Germany. Unfortunately, I had no direct way to contact him.

Then, suddenly, as if evoked by magic, there he was in Berlin. In recent years, as I've been investigating the link between creativity, magic and the divine, these episodes happen with such uncanny frequency that these occurrences have become outright *bizarre*. New Orleans piano man and Hoodoo true-believer Dr. John summed it up best, when, after a series of unsuccessful attempts to arrange an interview with him through his management, I bumped into him on the street by pure happenstance.

"There are no accidents in life, son," he said, listing on his feathered cane.

Greil started the evening by plying the trade of Berlin's unemployed: spinning records. In Berlin, everyone and his drunken, currywurst-gobbling cousin is a fucking DJ. You got a record collection, you got a gig providing audio atmosphere for scenes of reptilian debauchery. I've even *had* to fucking DJ in order for my former manager to book gigs for a reading tour. So, sitting in the auditorium's back rows, I amused myself with the thought that Greil's DJ

Dustbin of History persona was probably one of his tour's contractual preconditions. In addition to Sam Cooke's "A Change Is Gonna Come," his set included a parody off the National Lampoon *Radio Dinner* album.

It was then that I realized the eighty-odd Germans present were not going to get this guy *at all.*

The purpose of Greil's visit was to promote the recently published German-language edition of *Like a Rolling Stone: Bob Dylan at the Crossroads,* his meditation on the cultural, social, political and historical impact of Dylan's Top 40 musical accident of 1965. I must confess that even if Black Panther defense minister Brotha Huey, according to Black Panther chairman Bobby, was diggin' Dylan, and relatin' his lyrics to how they were applicable to the liberation of black people and all oppressed peoples in general, wherever they might be, I was never an enthusiastic Dylan fan. I was a child when Dylan became a presence on the radio in the early 1960s. Bob Dylan, in my mind then, was that whiny guy the conscientious young psychiatric aides who worked with my mother in the nuthouse listened to in their off hours. How could that be *real* music, I reasoned, if it didn't have fast drums and loud guitars? You couldn't dance to Dylan. So what was the point? Arthur Lee he was not.

Naturally, as I was born one year before Rosa Parks refused to unglue her high-yalla buttcheeks from an Alabama bus seat, I identified, out of self-interest, with the goals of the civil rights movement. They let us eat that $1.98 turkey with canned peas, mashed potato and gravy dinner at Woolworth's in New Haven. Why not Birmingham? In New Haven, I learned de white folks could let de cullids hab dey "equal rights" and could still be a bunch of fucking racists. As Buckwheat said to Porky in the very last chapter of the *Our Gang* serial, "*White folks am a bitch!*"

And I was also deeply traumatized by those images broadcast on television of angry faces contorted by hate, of demonstrators washed away by high-pressure fire hoses and mauled by snarling dogs. But the March on Washington wasn't exactly exciting must-see TV for an eight-year-old. So I wasn't hip to the fact Dylan plucked his protest guitar on behalf of Martin Luther King and the other Negroes amassed in D.C.

I did have some interest in Dylan in high school, though. My interest, however, was a product of erroneous adolescent thinking. I owned a doorstopper titled something like *The Complete Bob Dylan Songbook*. Quoting Dylan, I thought, might help me get my freak on with some quasi-mystical suburban hippie chick lounging in the grass of my high school's quadrangle. Otherwise, I had no idea what that muthafucka was talkin' about. Shit made no sense to me.

DJ Dustbin ended his set of '60s Top 40. And Greil walked out from the wings and stood behind a lectern, looking professorial and beatific under the lighting. There was polite applause.

With the exception of a few English-speaking expats like myself (including Ed Ward, a rock journalist with an entertaining and informed blog called "BerlinBites"), the audience was composed of serious and earnest Germans who had grown up under the influence of the '68 generation. Generally, "the '68 generation" refers to the student protest movement that swept throughout Western Europe in the late 1960s, emblematized by the student strikes in Paris, May '68. However, the movement of the '68 generation began earlier in Germany. Its beginnings coincide with the beginnings of the Berkeley Free Speech movement. And the release of Dylan's "Blowin' in the Wind." That is why the selection Greil read that evening was an interesting choice.

What he read had less to do with the making of "Like a Rolling Stone" than with the transformation America underwent in those years: the extraordinary challenges faced by civil rights workers; the growing opposition to an escalating war in Vietnam; the Watts riots.

Stirred by memories his text invoked, I realized baby boomers were the spawn of men and women who fought the good fight of World War II—the fight against Fascism, the fight for democracy, the fight for a world where every person mattered, a world where everyone had a voice. Our parents' antifascist values mattered then. They matter now. Suffering through economic depression and war, our mothers and fathers had instilled a vision of a so-called free world—mothers and fathers who had derived a spiritual strength (in my case) from a people who had endured and triumphed over the hardships of American slavery. *How the fuck did they do that?*

Greil's discussion that night gave me insight into an answer. He did so by reaffirming the importance of spirituals, gospel and the blues. And that I come from a people who derived strength, power, from something as simple as a fucking *song.* "Sometimes we be all singin'," Little Richard told me in 1995, describing memories that could have also been scenes in that film by King Vidor, *Hallelujah.* "My mother be out in the backyard washin' clothes with a washboard. Everybody be singin'. You see Mr. Willie over there singin'. You hear my mama over there. An' you hear Miss Bessy there. It be a big choir. The whole neighborhood singin'. Everybody back there washin' clothes."

That was what Greil and cats like Jim Dickinson, Robert Palmer, Mark Jacobson, Nick Tosches and Dr. "Black Like Bob" Thompson was talking about. How a fucking song has the magical and spiritual power to change. Old white mofos talkin' some deep *AFRICAN* shit.

An extraordinary thing happened that night as Greil spoke. I don't fault the Germans for not catching the thing that happened. It required an ear particularly sensitive to the nuances of spoken American English. Accustomed as I am to the antics of so-called spoken-word artists (antics I am also certainly guilty of), I heard something I had never heard before at a public reading. As Greil stood at the lectern, reading his text, voices emerged I recognized and knew. It was subtle, but clearly those voices were there. His cadences echoed the rhythms of Martin Luther King, Malcolm X, Walter Mosley and Stanley Crouch. They all spoke through his text. And Greil brought these voices to his reading without sacrificing their integrity or his own.

This was not an act of racial mimicry. This wasn't "cultural theft." It was the opposite of the blackface mask. It was Elvis swaying in the pews of a sanctified black church in Tupelo, Mississippi. And recognizing that its power was also his own. It was a blend of diverse American influences solidified into a single voice. Greil's writing—*Greil's voice*—was the result of a life sincerely engaged by the full spectrum of American experience.

I waited until the auditorium emptied of autograph-seekers. I paused before I approached and introduced myself.

"Mr. Marcus, my name is Darius James."

He smiled. "Yes, the author of that fabulous book. It's a pleasure to meet you."

We shook hands. I was struck by the sensitivity in his eyes.

Greil's reading was a demonstration of an underacknowledged fact in American life, that, as John Strausbaugh has written here, himself invoking Albert Murray: *"The so-called black and so-called white people of the United States resemble nobody else in the world so much as they resemble each other."*

NOTES

CHAPTER 1

page 11 "reactionary hipness": Justin Driver, "Black Comedy's Reactionary Hipness: The Mirth of a Nation," *The New Republic,* June 11, 2001.

page 12 "That's what makes it so hard" Candace Lunn, "A Commentary on Shirley Q and Minstrelsy," *Washington Square News,* March 3, 2004.

page 12 Some feminists have argued: Kelly Kleiman, "Drag = Blackface," *Chicago-Kent Law Review,* 75, no. 3 (2000); also "Dragging Women Down," *In These Times,* March 2004.

page 14 The word "nigger" . . . "the N-word": Randall Kennedy, *Nigger* (New York: Pantheon, 2002).

page 15 "delighted the subject": Robert Lipsyte, "Comedy Central," *The New York Times,* May 30, 2004.

pages 15–16 "a mock phone call"; "'I'm not sure'": Willie P. Richardson; Richard Burgess, "Comedian Still Gets Laughs," *The Daily Advertiser* (Lafayette, LA), July 10, 2004.

page 16 This includes the musicians, and quotations following: Darren Keast, "The Real Shock Rock," *Houston Press,* October 16, 2003.

page 17 In 1978, Bobby Berger: Arthur Hirsch, "The Ever-Shifting Color of Blackface," *The Baltimore Sun,* November 12, 2000.

page 20 In the 2000s, blackface has appeared: Joe Connolly, "Blackface Makes Its Way to College Campuses," *The Daily Orange* (Syracuse University), November 14, 2003.

page 20   Blackface incidents . . . date back to the mid-1980s: Manning Marable, "Along the Color Line," *The New York Beacon*, May 3, 1995.

page 22   In the Broad Channel community: Maggie Haberman, "3 Axed in Bias Gag Win 300G from City," New York *Daily News*, December 1, 2004.

page 22   In 1999, Missouri governor Mel Carnahan: Norm Parish, "Furor over Carnahan in Blackface Revisits '60s Culture and Tumult," *St. Louis Post-Dispatch*, November 2, 1999.

page 22   In 2004, a Louisiana judge: "Louisiana Judge Suspended for Wearing Blackface," UPI, December 14, 2004.

page 22   That same year . . . University of Central Florida: Kevin Meehan, "Wigged Out at UCF," *The Orlando Sentinel*, April 2, 2004.

page 23   In 1995, the Club Med . . . of Dakar: M. J. McCollum, "Club Med Being Sued for Putting On Minstrel Show," *The Philadelphia Tribune*, July 14, 1995.

page 23   At around the same time, Japanese: Benjamin Genocchio, "For Japanese Girls, Black Is Beautiful," *The New York Times*, April 4, 2004.

page 23   anti-Black attitude in Japan: Patrick Neate, *Where You're At* (New York: Riverhead, 2004).

page 23   Cape Town . . . Coon Carnival: Jacki Lyden, "Some Find South African New Year Celebration Offensive," National Public Radio, January 16, 1994.

page 25   "lore cycles": W. T. Lhamon, Jr., *Raising Cain* (Cambridge, MA: Harvard University Press, 1998).

page 26   three dominating figures of an "American type": Constance Rourke, *American Humor* (New York: Doubleday, 1931).

page 26   Portentously, Thomas Jefferson: James Olney, "'I Ain't Gonna Be No Topsy' Because 'Paris Is My Old Kentucky Home,'" *The Southern Review*, January 2001.

page 28   Many of Rourke's ideas: Adam Kirsch, "The Star, the Born-Again Sinner, and the Gangster," slate.com, March 31, 2004.

page 29   Boston University anthropologist Peter Wood: *Diversity: The Invention of a Concept* (San Francisco: Encounter, 2003).

page 29   "victimization": Shelby Steele, *A Dream Deferred* (New York: HarperCollins, 1998).

page 30   "The prevalence of race": Greg Tate, *Everything But the Burden* (New York: Broadway, 2003).

page 33   "no qualities of any sort": Stanley Crouch and Playthell Benjamin, *Reconsidering the Souls of Black Folk* (Philadelphia: Running Press, 2002).

page 33   "Identity is best defined": Albert Murray, *The Omni-Americans* (New York: Outerbridge & Dienstfrey, 1970).

CHAPTER 2

page 35   In 1441, a Portuguese trading ship: James Pope-Hennessy, *Sins of the Fathers* (London: Weidenfeld & Nicolson, 1967).

page 36   One thing the two sides had in common: William D. Piersen, *Black Legacy* (Amherst: University of Massachusetts Press, 1993).

page 37   "Almost everything the white man": Ibid.

page 38   Whiteface made it to the legitimate theater: Douglas Turner Ward, *Happy Ending and Day of Absence* (New York: Dramatists Play Service, 1994).

page 39   One imprudent king: Pope-Hennessy, *Sins of the Fathers*.

page 39   "So ever since then": Zora Neale Hurston, *Mules and Men* (Philadelphia: J. B. Lippincott, 1935).

page 40   Today . . . accusations of Uncle Tomism: Richard Laurence, and James B. Lowe, *The American Directory of Certified Uncle Toms* (Chicago: Lushena, 2002).

page 40   Those first Africans kidnapped to Portugal: Pope-Hennessy, *Sins of the Fathers*.

page 42   "a signal for wild and almost indiscriminate slaughter". Ibid.

page 43   "nothing inside the 'pure' African vision": Stanley Crouch and Playthell Benjamin, *Reconsidering the Souls of Black Folk* (Philadelphia: Running Press, 2002).

page 45   "One reads of live Eskimos" and the following several paragraphs are derived from essays collected in Bernth Lindfors, ed., *Africans on Stage* (Bloomington: Indiana University Press, 1999).

page 46   "African hermaphrodite": Ricky Jay, *Extraordinary Exhibitions* (New York: Quantuck Lane, 2005).

page 48   "It was not the lonely": Jan Hennop, "Mbeki Calls 19th Century Europeans 'Barbarians' at 'Hottentot Venus' Funeral," Agence France-Presse, August 9, 2002.

page 48   LoBagola and Farini: see Lindfors, *Africans on Stage*.

page 49   "living exhibits of Turks and Arabs": Laura L. Behling, "Reification and Resistance," *Women's Studies in Communication*, September 2002.

page 50 "cultures" and Culture: James Buzard and Joseph Childers, "Victorian Ethnographies," *Victorian Studies*, 41, no. 3 (1998).

page 50 Americans, at least those who wrote for the papers: Lindfors, *Africans on Stage.*

page 52 Along with the savages . . . another subset of humanity: Behling, "Reification and Resistance."

page 53 real, live Aunt Jemima: Marilyn Kern-Foxworth, *Aunt Jemima, Uncle Ben, and Rastus* (Westport, CT: Greenwood, 1994).

page 53 Great Ethnological Congress: Lindfors, *Africans on Stage.*

page 54 eleven-volume encyclopedia, and quotations following: Howard Benjamin Grose, ed., *Our Wonder World*, vol. 1 (Chicago: Geo. L. Schulman, 1914).

page 55 In the fine arts . . . portraits of Black Americans: Guy C. McElroy, *Facing History* (San Francisco: Bedford Arts, 1990).

CHAPTER 3

page 57 "When American life": Ralph Ellison, *Shadow and Act* (New York: Random House, 1964).

page 57 "Unfurl a white man": Greg Tate, "The King of Coonology," *The Village Voice*, December 31, 2004.

page 61 One traveler claims to hear: Marshall W. Stearns, *The Story of Jazz* (London: Oxford University Press, 1956).

page 62 Blackface in European folk and legitimate theater: Robert Hornback, "Emblems of Folly in the First *Othello*," *Comparative Drama*, March 2001.

page 63 "Darkie Day": Matt Pengelly, "Fighting to End Darkie Day in Cornwall, England," *Day to Day*, National Public Radio, March 8, 2005.

page 63 The blackfaced Moor: Hornback, "Emblems of Folly in the First *Othello*."

page 63 Blackface theater in early America: Dale Cockrell, *Demons of Disorder* (Cambridge, England: Cambridge University Press, 1997).

page 64 "the black man sympathetically": Eileen Southern, *The Music of Black Americans* (New York: W. W. Norton, 1983).

page 65 The most famous was Ira Aldridge: Bernth Lindfors, "Mislike Me Not for My Complexion," *African American Review*, Summer 1999.

page 66 a tragic capitulation to the racism: Eric Lott, *Love and Theft* (New York: Oxford University Press, 1993).

page 66   a canny way of turning the tables: Nicolas M. Evans, "Ira Aldridge: Shakespeare and Minstrelsy," *American Transcendental Quarterly,* September 2002.

page 66   touring theater troupes who ventured: Constance Rourke, *American Humor* (New York: Doubleday, 1931).

page 67   Blackface folk rituals also crossed: Cockrell, *Demons of Disorder.*

page 69   in the West African cultures . . . the poet-singer griot: Alan Lomax, *The Land Where the Blues Began* (New York: Pantheon, 1993).

page 70   Blacks and Whites admired and picked up: Southern, *The Music of Black Americans.*

page 71   mass-produced guitars: John Leland, *Hip: The History* (New York: HarperCollins, 2004).

page 72   early minstrelsy . . . as an outbreak of rebellious youth culture: W. T. Lhamon, Jr., *Raising Cain:* (Cambridge, MA: Harvard University Press, 1998).

page 73   The very instruments on which the music: Cockrell, *Demons and Disorder.*

page 78   "coon" . . . rural White: David R. Roediger, *The Wages of Whiteness* (New York: Verso, 1991).

page 78   "Zip" was short for Scipio: Ibid.

page 82   "By most accounts the indenture's unfreedom": Roediger, *The Wages of Whiteness.*

page 84   "filthy, lazy, ignorant": Quoted in John W. Blassingame, *The Slave Community* (New York: Oxford University Press, 1972).

page 84   "the biggest con job": Stanley Crouch and Playthell Benjamin, *Reconsidering the Souls of Black Folk* (Philadelphia: Running Press, 2002).

page 84   numerous mixed-race tribes: Michael Kolhoff, "Fugitive Communities in Colonial America," *The Early America Review,* Summer/Fall 2001.

page 85   "The proximity of unfree whites and Black": Roediger, *The Wages of Whiteness.*

page 85   "One hates to say it": Cockrell, *Demons of Disorder.*

page 85   mongrel underclass . . . in lower Manhattan: Lhamon, *Raising Cain.*

page 85   From its very inception: Mark Caldwell, *New York Night* (New York: Scribner, 2005).

page 85   "the cradle of the gangs"; "Thousands eked out": Herbert Asbury, *The Gangs of New York* (New York: Alfred A. Knopf, 1927).

page 86 "a common world"; "court reports are filled": Cockrell, *Demons of Disorder.*

page 86 Free Blacks held small businesses: Tyler Anbinder, *Five Points* (New York: Plume, 2002).

page 87 This mostly male environment: Lott, *Love and Theft.*

page 88 the Chatham . . . an abolitionist chapel: Anbinder, *Five Points.*

page 88 The entertainments continued: Asbury, *The Gangs of New York.*

page 90 White workers . . . were struggling: Roediger, *The Wages of Whiteness.*

page 91 "*Low-browed* and *savage*": Ibid.

page 94 how much more outrageous: Cockrell, *Demons of Disorder.*

page 96 Historians who argue that minstrelsy was unrelievedly racist: Annmarie Bean, James V. Hatch, and Brooks McNamara, eds., *Inside the Minstrel Mask* (Hanover, NH: Wesleyan University Press, 1996).

page 98 Dixon . . . fared less well: Cockrell, *Demons of Disorder.*

CHAPTER 4

page 101 Edwin P. Christy and Daniel Decatur Emmett: Dale Cockrell, *Demons of Disorder* (Cambridge, England: Cambridge University Press, 1997); W. T. Lhamon, Jr., *Raising Cain* (Cambridge, MA: Harvard University Press, 1998).

page 102 "novel, grotesque" . . . "entirely exempt": Edward Rice, *Monarchs of Minstrelsy* (New York: Kenny, 1911).

page 104 Ben and Lew Snowden: Norm Cohen, "Way Up North in Dixie," *American Music,* Spring 1995; John Leland, *Hip: The History* (New York: HarperCollins, 2004).

page 104 As with traveling circuses: Eileen Southern, *The Music of Black Americans* (New York: W. W. Norton, 1983).

page 104 "No band ever sounded": A. J. Liebling, *Back Where I Came From* (New York: Sheridan House, 1938).

page 104 "set within a ritual": Constance Rourke, *American Humor* (New York: Doubleday, 1931).

page 105 usually dancing the cakewalk: Marshall W. Stearns, *The Story of Jazz* (London: Oxford University Press, 1956).

page 106 followed by a short one-act burlesque: Full texts of plays cited are found in Gary D. Engle, *This Grotesque Essence* (Baton Rouge: Louisiana

State University Press, 1978), and Annmarie Bean, James V. Hatch, and Brooks McNamara, eds., *Inside the Minstrel Mask* (Hanover, NH: Wesleyan University Press, 1996).

page 107   rough and eccentric edges: Cockrell, *Demons of Disorder.*

page 111   Minstrels stooped to new lows: Bean, Hatch, and McNamara, *Inside the Minstrel Mask.*

page 114   "Before the Civil War": Quoted ibid.

page 118   "While it contains a certain irony": Matthew R. Martin, "The Two-Faced New South," *The Southern Literary Journal,* March 1998.

page 122   According to one legend . . . "Jump Jim Crow": Southern, *The Music of Black Americans.*

page 123   Master Juba: Edward Thorpe, *Black Dance* (Woodstock, NY: Overlook, 1990); Southern, *The Music of Black Americans.*

page 124   Other Black dancers: Bean, Hatch, and McNamara, *Inside the Minstrel Mask.*

page 124   The Georgia Minstrels: Southern, *The Music of Black Americans.*

page 125   "At the height of his fame": Ibid.

page 126   New York City had ten: Engle, *This Grotesque Essence.*

page 126   Sheet music for minstrel-show hits; "Representations of upstanding": Stephanie Dunston, "The Minstrel in the Parlor," *American Transcendental Quarterly,* December 2002.

page 127   "Oh, well, there's one thing": "They Will Use Burnt Cork," *Brooklyn Eagle,* December 18, 1893.

page 128   "The stage performances": Hartley Davis, "In Vaudeville," *Everybody's Magazine,* August 1905.

page 129   "where an honest belief": Ibid.

page 130   "For the benefit of those who have never": B. F. Keith, "The Vogue of the Vaudeville," *National Magazine,* November 1898.

page 131   "The Irish characters are drunk": Lawrence E. Mintz, "Humor and Ethnic Stereotypes in Vaudeville and Burlesque," *Melus,* December 1996.

page 132   the earliest European explorers to Africa: William D. Piersen, *Black Legacy* (Amherst: University of Massachusetts Press, 1993).

page 132   So did the Indians: Ann Maydosz, "A Study in Red and Black," *The Journal of Negro History,* September 2000.

page 132   Universities today routinely champion: Peter Wood, *Diversity: The Invention of a Concept* (San Francisco: Encounter, 2003).

page 138   One of the saddest stories; W. C. Fields: David Hinckley, "Bert Williams in Blackface," New York *Daily News,* April 15, 2004.

page 139   T.O.B.A. circuit: Simi Horwitz, "Rollin' On," *Backstage,* April 1999.

page 139   Toby shows: Dawn Larsen, "The Canvas Cathedral," *Theater History Studies,* June 2001.

page 140   During the Depression, the WPA: Arthur Jarvis, "Opportunity, Experience, and Recognition," *The Journal of Negro History,* September 2000.

page 140   "the white boy who stole the blues": John Leland, *Hip: The History* (New York: HarperCollins, 2004).

page 142   slipping subversive ideas in among the coon songs: David Krasner, "Parody and Double Consciousness in the Language of Early Black Musical Theatre," *African American Review,* June 1995.

page 144   Emmett Miller: Nick Tosches, *Where Dead Voices Gather* (New York: Little, Brown, 2001).

page 144   Lincoln Perry and Dewey "Pigmeat" Markham: Champ Clark, *Shuffling to Ignominy* (New York: iUniverse, 2005).

page 145   During World War II, the USO sent: Joseph Boskin, *Sambo* (New York: Oxford University Press, 1986).

page 145   How-to guidebooks: Harry L. Newton, *Laughland: A Merry Minstrel Book* (Chicago and Minneapolis: T. S. Denison, 1909). Anonymous, "Gentlemen, Be Seated," unpublished manuscript (Toronto [?], n.d.).

page 148   student minstrel show: Michael D. Yates, "Minstrel Show," *CounterPunch,* September 2003.

CHAPTER 5

page 151   "I'm gwine ter larn you," and subsequent quotations: Joel Chandler Harris, *Uncle Remus: His Songs and His Sayings* (New York: Appleton, 1881).

page 152   White Americans tried to capture: J. L. Dillard, *Black English* (New York: Random House, 1972).

page 152   "Americans savored them in almanacs": Walter Blair and Raven I. McDavid, Jr., eds., *The Mirth of a Nation* (Minneapolis: University of Minnesota Press, 1983).

pages 152–153   Davy Crockett; Charles H. Smith; Alfred Henry Lewis: Ibid.

page 153   new waves of European immigrants: Holger Kersten, "Using the Immigrant's Voice," *Melus,* December 1996.

page 153   White writers who passed themselves off: Robert Fikes, Jr., "Adventures in Exoticism," *The Western Journal of Black Studies,* March 2002.

page 154   "condescending . . . literary slumming": Ibid.

page 154   "The Gold-Bug": *The Complete Tales and Poems of Edgar Allan Poe* (New York: The Modern Library, 1938).

page 154   *The Yemassee,* a novel, and quotations following: William Gilmore Simms, *The Yemassee* (New York: Harper & Brothers, 1844).

page 156   *Uncle Tom's Cabin,* and quotations following: Harriet Beecher Stowe, *Uncle Tom's Cabin* (Boston: John P. Jewett, 1852).

page 157   "In one memorable instance": Kendra Hamilton, "The Strange Career of Uncle Tom," *Black Issues in Higher Education,* June 2002.

page 159   The National had been founded: Mark Caldwell, *New York Night* (New York, Scribner, 2005).

page 161   when his father took him: Edward Rice, *Monarchs of Minstrelsy* (New York: Kenny, 1911)

page 162   "fifty people saw": Hamilton, "The Strange Career of Uncle Tom."

page 163   Historian Ernest Allen: Ibid.

page 165   a meteoric postwar boom in the magazine industry: Pamela Price Kabak, "The Black Man in Late Nineteenth-Century Literature," Yale–New Haven Teachers Institute, 2004.

page 166   best-known story collection, and quotations following: Thomas Nelson Page, *In Ole Virginia, or Marse Chan and Other Stories* (New York: Charles Scribner's Sons, 1887).

page 167   stories of the Tar Baby: Roger D. Abrahams, ed., *Afro-American Folktales* (New York: Pantheon, 1985).

page 169   "Indeed, for generations black southerners": Jennifer Ritterhouse, "Reading, Intimacy, and the Role of Uncle Remus in White Southern Social Memory," *The Journal of Southern History,* August 2003.

page 172   He wrote against lynching: Ibid.

page 172   "my purpose has been": Harris, "Introductions," *Uncle Remus.*

page 174   Maria Howard Weeden, and quotations following: Howard Weeden, *Bandanna Ballads* (New York: Doubleday & McClure, 1899).

page 176   a kind of gentleman's pastime to record: Abrahams, *Afro-American Folktales.*

page 176   *Diddie, Dumps and Tot:* Louise Clarke-Pyrnelle, *Diddie, Dumps and Tot* (New York: Harper & Brothers, 1882).

page 176   *Dialect Tales:* Sherwood Bonner, *Dialect Tales* (New York: Harper & Brothers, 1883).

page 176   *The Clansman:* Thomas Dixon, Jr., *The Clansman* (New York: Doubleday, Page, 1905).

page 178   Poems by Dunbar: Paul Laurence Dunbar, *The Complete Poems* (New York: Dodd, Mead, 1913).

page 179   he could adopt a rather distant stance: William M. Ramsey, "Dunbar's Dixie," *The Southern Literary Journal,* September 1999.

page 183   A number of their stories: James Mellon, ed., *Bullwhip Days* (New York: Weidenfeld & Nicolson, 1988).

page 184   Passages from Chesnutt: Charles W. Chesnutt, *Stories, Novels, and Essays* (New York: Library Classics, 2002).

page 186   "by noting [his] role as a subversive voice": Henry B. Wonham, "The Curious Psychological Spectacle of a Mind Enslaved," *Mississippi Quarterly,* December 1997.

page 186   "I shall write for a purpose": Matthew R. Martin, "The Two-Faced New South," *The Southern Literary Journal,* March 1998.

page 186   *Mules and Men;* "Well, you know": Zora Neale Hurston, *Mules and Men* (Philadelphia: J. B. Lippincott, 1935).

page 187   "Ah didn't want": Ibid.

page 187   "continually needed to defend her work": Donna M. Williams, "Our Love/Hate Relationship with Zora Neale Hurston," *The Black Collegian,* January 1994.

page 188   Whether this usage is proper or appropriate: William Dahill-Baue, "Insignificant Monkeys," *Mississippi Quarterly,* June 1996.

page 188   *Ol' Man Adam,* and quotations following: Roark Bradford, *Ol' Man Adam an' His Chillun* (New York: Harper & Brothers, 1928).

page 190   "It is now evident": Donald Bogle, *Toms, Coons, Mulattoes, Mammies, & Bucks,* 3rd rev. ed. (New York: Continuum, 1996).

page 191   Octavus Roy Cohen: Octavus Roy Cohen, *Florian Slappey Goes Abroad* (Boston: Little, Brown, 1928); and *Florian Slappey* (New York: D. Appleton-Century, 1938).

page 192   emboldened Van Vechten: Carl Van Vechten, *Nigger Heaven* (New York: Alfred A. Knopf, 1926).

page 193   "catering to the voyeurism of whites": Fikes, "Adventures in Exoticism."

page 194   *Black Like Me*: John Howard Griffin, *Black Like Me* (Boston: Houghton Mifflin, 1961).

page 195   "Yeah, we got our troubles": Albert Murray, *The Omni-Americans* (New York: Outerbridge & Dienstfrey, 1970).

page 196   as Eric Lott and others have pointed out: Eric Lott, *Love and Theft* (New York: Oxford University Press, 1993).

page 197   Ralph Ellison noted: Ralph Ellison, *Shadow and Act* (New York: Random House, 1964).

page 197   "Tom said he slipped": Mark Twain, *The Adventures of Huckleberry Finn* (New York: Charles L. Webster, 1884).

page 198   "Twain fitted Jim": Ellison, *Shadow and Act.*

CHAPTER 6

page 202   Black film caricatures . . . five archetypes: Donald Bogle, *Toms, Coons, Mulattoes, Mammies, & Bucks*, 3rd rev. ed. (New York: Continuum, 1996).

page 202   Political scientist Michael Rogin: Michael Rogin, *Blackface, White Noise* (Berkeley: University of California Press, 1996).

page 208   "*The Birth of a Nation* is not bad": Roger Ebert, "Birth of a Nation," *Chicago Sun-Times,* March 30, 2003.

page 210   "In 1950, there were renewed outcries": Bogle, *Toms, Coons, Mulattoes, Mammies, & Bucks.*

page 211   chapter of the NAACP flipped: David Heitz, "NAACP Uses Film to Fight Racism," *Quad-City Times* (Davenport, IA), July 10, 2004.

page 211   a "feeble" effort: John Rockwell, "Can't Wash Politics out of Art, but You Can Avoid a Hard Sell," *The New York Times,* July 30, 2004.

page 215   *The Jazz Singer* is at least: Rogin, *Blackface, White Noise.*

page 216   Rogin, for example, insists: Ibid.

page 225   *Pick 'n' Pat:* Joseph Boskin, *Sambo* (New York: Oxford University Press, 1986).

page 229   "if you were a Black actor": Melvin Van Peebles, narration to Mark Daniels' documentary film *Classified X.*

page 230   Many studio bosses: Bogle, *Toms, Coons, Mulattoes, Mammies, & Bucks.*

page 231   Lincoln Perry/Stepin Fetchit: Mel Watkins, *Stepin Fetchit* (New York: Pantheon, 2005); Champ Clark, *Shuffling to Ignominy* (New York: iUniverse, 2005).

page 236   "an all-seeing, all-hearing, all-knowing": Bogle, *Toms, Coons, Mulattoes, Mammies, & Bucks.*

page 240   about a third of the cartoons . . . blackface, coon or mammy: Christopher P. Lehman, "The New Black Animated Images of 1946," *Journal of Popular Film and Television,* Summer 2001.

pages 243–244   George Pal and Jasper: Ibid.; Richard Neupert, "Trouble in Watermelon Land: George Pal and the Little Jasper Cartoons," *Film Quarterly,* Fall 2001.

page 246   not Sidney Poitier: Clark, *Shuffling to Ignominy.*

CHAPTER 7

page 247   history of Black filmmaking: Donald Bogle, *Toms, Coons, Mulattoes, Mammies, & Bucks,* 3rd rev. ed. (New York: Continuum, 1996); Manthia Diawara, ed., *Black American Cinema* (New York: Routledge, 1993).

page 252   "He was important to Black filmmaking": Quoted in Diawara, *Black American Cinema.*

page 253   "What had happened was that": Melvin Van Peebles, narration to Mark Daniels' documentary film *Classified X.*

page 253   Hollywood . . . often went overboard: Bogle, *Toms, Coons, Mulattoes, Mammies, & Bucks.*

page 254   "mama on the couch" dramas: George C. Wolfe, *The Colored Museum* (New York: Grove Weidenfeld, 1988).

page 255   "a European art film set in Watts": Nelson George, *Blackface* (New York: Cooper Square, 2002).

page 261   hoodoo conjure men . . . two-headed: Zora Neale Hurston, *Tell My Horse* (Philadelphia: J. B. Lippincott, 1938).

page 267   "carpetbagging Afrocentrists": Debra J. Dickerson, *The End of Blackness* (New York: Pantheon, 2004).

page 269   "the most egregious example": Ralph Luker, "The Year When We Got Caught," History News Network, December 30, 2002.

page 269   "Afro-fascist"; "sort of rancid fairy tale": Quoted in Bogle, *Toms, Coons, Mulattoes, Mammies, & Bucks.*

page 269   "rawest opportunism": Quoted in Diawara, *Black American Cinema.*

page 269   "the black Spielberg": Bogle, *Toms, Coons, Mulattoes, Mammies, & Bucks.*

page 269   brilliant performance art: Andrew Sarris, "Spike Lee on Race and the Idiot Box," *The New York Observer,* October 9, 2000.

page 270   "He regularly ripped": Nelson George, *Blackface* (New York: Cooper Square, 2002).

page 270   Interviewed about *Bamboozled:* Andy Seiler, "Lee Will Not Be Bamboozled," *USA Today,* October 5, 2000.

page 271   trafficking in modern minstrel-show humor: A. O. Scott, "Can Black People Fly? Don't Ask 'Soul Plane,' " *The New York Times,* June 13, 2004.

page 272   "a surprisingly standard drag comedy": Carla Meyer, "Omigod! They Totally Believe We're Women—Haven't They, Like, Seen 'Tootsie' a Million Times?" *San Francisco Chronicle,* June 23, 2004.

page 272   "Think of 'White Chicks' ": Stephen Hunter, "Great White Hopeless," *The Washington Post,* June 23, 2004.

CHAPTER 8

page 275   Blacks began appearing as commercial icons: Marilyn Kern-Foxworth, *Aunt Jemima, Uncle Ben, and Rastus* (Westport, CT: Greenwood, 1994).

page 277   Clarence Thomas: George E. Curry, "We Were Too Kind," *Emerge,* November 11, 1996.

page 278   Gladys Knight: Martin Evans, "Singer Gladys Knight Hired as Spokeswoman for Aunt Jemima," *The Los Angeles Sentinel,* September 22, 1994.

page 278   Condoleezza Rice: J. R. Ross, "Sly Apologizes for Calling Rice 'Aunt Jemima,' " *Wisconsin State Journal* (Madison), November 23, 2004.

page 279   Sambo: Joseph Boskin, *Sambo* (New York: Oxford University Press, 1986).

page 282   entire kitchen . . . in Negro-themed items: Jan Lindenberger, *Black Memorabilia for the Kitchen* (Atglen, PA: Shiffer, 2003).

page 282   Toys and games: Boskin, *Sambo.*

page 283 Picture postcards: Ibid.

page 285 Famous and successful Blacks: Mark Lowery, "Collecting Our History," *Black Enterprise,* June 1, 1995.

page 285 how-to articles: Fern Gillespie, "Black Collectibles—Just a Click Away," *Essence,* December 1999.

page 285 "Many White collectors": Lynn Casmier-Paz, "Heritage, Not Hate?" *Southern Cultures,* March 2003.

page 285 "Collectors have come to realize": Chrisena A. Coleman, "Collectors of the Black Experience," *The Record* (Bergen, NJ), February 13, 1992.

page 285 Harvard convened: Catherine Fox, "Harvard Panel Ponders Role of Offensive Art," *The Atlanta Journal-Constitution,* March 19, 1998.

page 286 "For as long as black memorabilia": Casmier-Paz, "Heritage, Not Hate?"

CHAPTER 9

page 291 Others refused to acknowledge: J. L. Dillard, *Black English* (New York: Random House, 1972).

page 292 Jack Maddox; Tom Hawkins: Quoted in James Mellon, ed., *Bullwhip Days* (New York: Weidenfeld & Nicolson, 1988).

page 293 "Is thought secreted": Marilyn Kern-Foxworth, *Aunt Jemima, Uncle Ben, and Rastus* (Westport, CT: Greenwood, 1994).

page 293 Nat Turner: Joanne Grant, ed. *Black Protest* (New York: Fawcett, 1969).

page 293 Black English follows rules, and examples: J. L. Dillard, *Black English* (New York: Random House, 1972).

page 295 Georgia Baker; Teshan Young: Quoted in Mellon, *Bullwhip Days.*

page 296 "There are nonstandard dialects": Stanley M. (Ben) Novak, "American Shibboleth: Ebonics," Cambridge Scientific Abstracts, September 2000.

page 298 "pedagogically relevant assumptions": Charles J. Fillmore, "A Linguist Looks at the Ebonics Debate," Center for Applied Linguistics, January 1997.

page 300 "the notion of 'verbal deprivation'"; theories "are based": William Labov, "Academic Ignorance and Black Intelligence," *The Atlantic Monthly,* June 1972.

page 301 Michael King . . . admitted: Michael King, "Ebonics Slang No

Substitute for Standard English," The National Center for Public Policy Research, August 2002.

page 301 William Grier and Price Cobbs noted that: William H. Grier and Price M. Cobbs, *Black Rage* (New York: Basic Books, 1968).

page 303 "No matter what": King, "Ebonics Slang No Substitute for Standard English."

page 303 several pages of "Harlem Jive": Langston Hughes and Arna Bontemps, eds., *The Book of Negro Folklore* (New York: Dodd, Mead, 1958).

page 304 The words "hep," "hip," "dig" and "jive"; White Americans have admired: John Leland, *Hip: The History* (New York: HarperCollins, 2004).

page 304 The concept of cool: Robert Farris Thompson, *Flash of the Spirit* (New York: Random House, 1983).

page 304 An editorial in a 2003 issue: "Black Slang in the Mouths of Whites," *The Hilltop* (Howard University), February 21, 2003.

page 305 women "nearly naked": Debra J. Dickerson, *The End of Blackness* (New York: Pantheon, 2004).

page 305 "snatch" became a slang term: Darius James, *Voodoo Stew* (Berlin: Verbrecher, 2002).

page 308 a culture that arrived . . . at another crossroads: Kurt Thometz, ed., *Life Turns Man Up and Down* (New York: Pantheon, 2001).

CHAPTER 10

page 313 "I'm now reading your account": Hunter S. Thompson, *The Proud Highway* (New York: Ballantine, 1998).

page 313 "Real black men die": Norman Kelley, *The Head Negro in Charge Syndrome* (New York: Nation Books, 2004).

page 316 "Al Jolson theory of showbiz": Fred Goodman, *The Mansion on the Hill* (New York: Times Books, 1997).

page 316 In the bookstore . . . titles like: K'wan, *Gangsta* (Columbus, OH: Triple Crown, 2002); Vikki Turner, *A Hustler's Wife* (Columbus, OH: Triple Crown, 2003); K'wan, *Road Dawgz* (Columbus, OH: Triple Crown, 2003).

page 317 "wigger lit": William Upski Wimsatt, *Bomb the Suburbs* (New York: Soft Skull, 2001); Adam Mansbach, *Angry Black White Boy* (New York: Three Rivers, 2005).

page 318 "have been so gauche": Greg Tate, "Hiphop Turns 30: Whatcha Celebratin' For?" *The Village Voice*, January 4, 2005.

page 318 Fab 5 Freddy...described how: Freddy Brathwaite, "Brazil, a Hiphop Revolution," *Vibe,* November 2002.

page 319 "from New York to Nairobi," and quotations following: Patrick Neate, *Where You're At* (New York: Riverhead, 2004).

page 320 "Images of black youth": Stanley Crouch, *The Artificial White Man* (New York: Basic Books, 2005).

page 320 "Minstrel performers in black-face": John Blake, "Hip-Hop's Celebration of Booty and Bullets Lambasted," *The Atlanta Journal-Constitution:* September 30, 2004.

page 320 "hip-hop and coon comedy": Justin Driver, "Black Comedy's Reactionary Hipness: The Mirth of a Nation," *The New Republic,* June 11, 2001.

page 321 "If an artist makes more money": Glenn Gamboa, "30 Years of Hiphop," *Newsday,* October 8, 2004.

page 324 "a pioneer of the hip-hop beef": Jody Rose, "The Genius of Beef," slate.com, March 24, 2005.

page 324 "primarily for the material enrichment": Crouch, *The Artificial White Man.*

page 325 "moral panic": John Springhall, *Youth, Popular Culture and Moral Panics* (New York: St. Martin's, 1998).

page 327 American Baby Boomers: Harold Schechter, *Savage Pastimes* (New York: St. Martin's, 2005).

BIBLIOGRAPHY

Abrahams, Roger D., ed. *Afro-American Folktales.* New York: Pantheon, 1985.

Anbinder, Tyler. *Five Points.* New York: Plume, 2002.

Asbury, Herbert. *The Gangs of New York.* New York: Alfred A. Knopf, 1927.

Bean, Annmarie, James V. Hatch, and Brooks McNamara, eds. *Inside the Minstrel Mask.* Hanover, NH: Wesleyan University Press, 1996.

Behling, Laura L. "Reification and Resistance," *Women's Studies in Communication,* September 2002.

"Black Slang in the Mouths of Whites" *The Hilltop* (Howard University), February 21, 2003.

Blair, Walter, and Raven I. McDavid, Jr., eds. *The Mirth of a Nation.* Minneapolis: University of Minnesota Press, 1983.

Blake, John. "Hip-Hop's Celebration of Booty and Bullets Lambasted," *The Atlanta Journal-Constitution,* September 30, 2004.

Blassingame, John W. *The Slave Community.* New York: Oxford University Press, 1972.

Bogle, Donald. *Toms, Coons, Mulattoes, Mammies, & Bucks,* 3rd rev. ed. New York: Continuum, 1996.

Bonner, Sherwood. *Dialect Tales.* New York: Harper & Brothers, 1883.

Boskin, Joseph. *Sambo.* New York: Oxford University Press, 1986.

Bradford, Roark. *Ol' Man Adam an' His Chillun.* New York: Harper & Brothers, 1928.

Brathwaite, Fab 5 Freddy. "Brazil, a Hiphop Revolution," *Vibe,* November 2002.

Burgess, Richard. "Comedian Still Gets Laughs," *The Daily Advertiser* (Lafayette, LA), July 10, 2004.

Buzard, James, and Joseph Childers. "Victorian Ethnographies," *Victorian Studies,* 41, no. 3 (1998).

Caldwell, Mark. *New York Night: The Mystique and Its History.* New York: Scribner, 2005.

Casmier-Paz, Lynn. "Heritage, Not Hate?" *Southern Cultures,* March 2003.

Chesnutt, Charles W. *Stories, Novels, and Essays.* New York: Library Classics, 2002.

Clark, Champ. *Shuffling to Ignominy: The Tragedy of Stepin Fetchit.* New York: iUniverse, 2005.

Clarke-Pyrnelle, Louise. *Diddie, Dumps and Tot.* New York: Harper & Brothers, 1882.

Cockrell, Dale. *Demons of Disorder.* Cambridge, England: Cambridge University Press, 1997.

Cohen, Norm. "Way Up North in Dixie," *American Music,* Spring 1995.

Cohen, Octavus Roy. *Florian Slappey.* New York: D. Appleton-Century, 1938.

———. *Florian Slappey Goes Abroad.* Boston: Little, Brown, 1928.

Coleman, Chrisena. "Collectors of the Black Experience," *The Record* (Bergen, NJ), February 13, 1992.

Connolly, Joe. "Blackface Makes Its Way to College Campuses," *The Daily Orange* (Syracuse University), November 14, 2003.

Crouch, Stanley. *The Artificial White Man.* New York, Basic Books, 2005.

———, and Playthell Benjamin. *Reconsidering the Souls of Black Folk.* Philadelphia: Running Press, 2002.

Curry, George E. "We Were Too Kind," *Emerge,* November 11, 1996.

Dahill-Baue, William. "Insignificant Monkeys," *Mississippi Quarterly,* June 1996.

Davis, Hartley. "In Vaudeville," *Everybody's Magazine,* August 1905.

Diawara, Manthia, ed. *Black American Cinema.* New York, Routledge, 1993.

Dickerson, Debra J. *The End of Blackness.* New York: Pantheon, 2004.

Dillard, J. L. *Black English.* New York: Random House, 1972.

Dixon, Thomas, Jr. *The Clansman.* New York: Doubleday, Page, 1905.

Driver, Justin. "Black Comedy's Reactionary Hipness: The Mirth of a Nation," *The New Republic,* June 11, 2001.

Dunbar, Paul Laurence. *The Complete Poems.* New York: Dodd, Mead, 1913.

Dunston, Stephanie. "The Minstrel in the Parlor," *American Transcendental Quarterly,* December 2002.

Ebert, Roger. "Birth of a Nation," *Chicago Sun-Times,* March 30, 2003.

Ellison, Ralph. *Shadow and Act.* New York: Random House, 1964.

Engle, Gary D. *This Grotesque Essence.* Baton Rouge: Louisiana State University Press, 1978.

Evans, Martin. "Singer Gladys Knight Hired as Spokeswoman for Aunt Jemima," *The Los Angeles Sentinel,* September 22, 1994.

Evans, Nicolas M. "Ira Aldridge: Shakespeare and Minstrelsy," *American Transcendental Quarterly,* September 2002.

Fikes, Robert, Jr. "Adventures in Exoticism," *The Western Journal of Black Studies,* March 2002.

Fillmore, Charles J. "A Linguist Looks at the Ebonics Debate," Center for Applied Linguistics, January 1997.

Fox, Catherine. "Harvard Panel Ponders Role of Offensive Art," *The Atlanta Journal-Constitution,* March 19, 1998.

Gamboa, Glenn. "30 Years of Hiphop," *Newsday,* October 8, 2004.

Genocchio, Benjamin. "For Japanese Girls, Black Is Beautiful," *The New York Times,* April 4, 2004.

"Gentlemen, Be Seated," unpublished manuscript, Toronto (?), n.d.

George, Nelson, *Blackface.* New York: Cooper Square, 2002.

Gillespie, Fern. "Black Collectibles—Just a Click Away," *Essence,* December 1999.

Goodman, Fred. *The Mansion on the Hill.* New York: Times Books, 1997.

Grant, Joanne, ed. *Black Protest.* New York: Fawcett, 1969.

Grier, William H., and Price M. Cobbs. *Black Rage.* New York: Basic Books, 1968.

Griffin, John Howard, *Black Like Me.* Boston: Houghton Mifflin, 1961.

Grose, Howard Benjamin, ed. *Our Wonder World,* vol. 1. Chicago: Geo. L. Schulman, 1914.

Haberman, Maggie. "3 Axed in Bias Gag Win 300G from City," New York *Daily News,* December 1, 2004.

Hamilton, Kendra. "The Strange Career of Uncle Tom," *Black Issues in Higher Education,* June 2002.

Harris, Joel Chandler. *Uncle Remus: His Songs and His Sayings.* New York: Appleton, 1881.

Heitz, David. "NAACP Uses Film to Fight Racism," *Quad-City Times* (Davenport, IA), July 10, 2004.

Hennop, Jan. "Mbeki Calls 19th Century Europeans 'Barbarians' at 'Hottentot Venus' Funeral," Agence France-Presse, August 9, 2002.

Hinckley, David. "Bert Williams in Blackface," New York *Daily News*, April 15, 2004.

Hirsch, Arthur. "The Ever-Shifting Color of Blackface," *The Baltimore Sun*, November 12, 2000.

Hornback, Robert. "Emblems of Folly in the First *Othello*," *Comparative Drama*, March 2001.

Horwitz, Simi. "Rollin' On," *Backstage*, April 1999.

Hughes, Langston, and Arna Bontemps, eds. *The Book of Negro Folklore*. New York: Dodd, Mead, 1958.

Hunter, Stephen. "Great White Hopeless," *The Washington Post*, June 23, 2004.

Hurston, Zora Neale. *Mules and Men*. Philadelphia: J. B. Lippincott, 1935.

———. *Tell My Horse*. Philadelphia: J. B. Lippincott, 1938.

James, Darius. *That's Blaxploitation! Roots of the Badasssss 'Tude*. New York: St. Martin's, 1995.

———. *Voodoo Stew*. Berlin: Verbrecher, 2002.

Jarvis, Arthur. "Opportunity, Experience, and Recognition," *The Journal of Negro History*, September 2000.

Jay, Ricky. *Extraordinary Exhibitions*. New York: Quantuck Lane, 2005.

Kabak, Pamela Price. "The Black Man in Late Nineteenth-Century Literature," Yale–New Haven Teachers Institute, 2004.

Keast, Darren. "The Real Shock Rock," *Houston Press*, October 16, 2003.

Keith, B. F. "The Vogue of the Vaudeville," *National Magazine*, November 1898.

Kelley, Norman. *The Head Negro in Charge Syndrome: The Dead End of Black Politics*. New York: Nation Books, 2004.

Kennedy, Randall. *Nigger*. New York: Pantheon, 2002.

Kern-Foxworth, Marilyn. *Aunt Jemima, Uncle Ben, and Rastus*. Westport, CT: Greenwood, 1994.

Kersten, Holger. "Using the Immigrant's Voice," *Melus*, December 1996.

King, Michael. "Ebonics Slang No Substitute for Standard English," The National Center for Public Policy Research, August 2002.

Kirsch, Adam. "The Star, the Born-Again Sinner, and the Gangster," slate.com, March 31, 2004.

Kleiman, Kelly. "Drag = Blackface," *Chicago-Kent Law Review*, 75, no. 3 (2000).

———. "Dragging Women Down," *In These Times*, March 2004.

Kolhoff, Michael. "Fugitive Communities in Colonial America," *The Early America Review*, Summer/Fall 2001.

Krasner, David. "Parody and Double Consciousness in the Language of Early Black Musical Theatre," *African American Review*, June 1995.

K'wan. *Gangsta*. Columbus, OH: Triple Crown, 2002.

———. *Road Dawgz*. Columbus, OH: Triple Crown, 2003.

Labov, William. "Academic Ignorance and Black Intelligence," *The Atlantic Monthly*, June 1972.

Larsen, Dawn. "The Canvas Cathedral," *Theater History Studies*, June 2001.

Laurence, Richard, and James B. Lowe. *The American Directory of Certified Uncle Toms*. Chicago: Lushena, 2002.

Lehman, Christopher P. "The New Black Animated Images of 1946," *Journal of Popular Film and Television*, Summer 2001.

Leland, John. *Hip: The History*. New York: HarperCollins, 2004.

Lhamon, W. T., Jr. *Raising Cain: Blackface Performance from Jim Crow to Hip Hop*. Cambridge, MA: Harvard University Press, 1998.

Liebling, A. J. *Back Where I Came From*. New York: Sheridan House, 1938.

Lindenberger, Jan. *Black Memorabilia for the Kitchen*. Atglen, PA: Shiffer, 2003.

Lindfors, Bernth. "Mislike Me Not for My Complexion," *African American Review*, Summer 1999.

———, ed. *Africans on Stage: Studies in Ethnological Show Business*. Bloomington: Indiana University Press, 1999.

Lipsyte, Robert. "Comedy Central," *The New York Times*, May 30, 2004.

Lomax, Alan. *The Land Where the Blues Began*. New York: Pantheon, 1993.

Lott, Eric. *Love and Theft: Blackface Minstrelsy and the American Working Class*. New York: Oxford University Press, 1993.

"Louisiana Judge Suspended for Wearing Blackface," UPI, December 14, 2004.

Lowery, Mark. "Collecting Our History," *Black Enterprise*, June 1, 1995.

Luker, Ralph. "The Year When We Got Caught," History News Network, December 30, 2002.

Lunn, Candace. "A Commentary on Shirley Q and Minstrelsy," *Washington Square News*, March 3, 2004.

Lyden, Jacki. "Some Find South African New Year Celebration Offensive," National Public Radio, January 16, 1994.

Mansbach, Adam. *Angry Black White Boy*. New York: Three Rivers, 2005.

Marable, Manning. "Along the Color Line," *The New York Beacon*, May 3, 1995.

Martin, Matthew R. "The Two-Faced New South," *The Southern Literary Journal*, March 1998.

Maydosz, Ann. "A Study in Red and Black," *The Journal of Negro History*, September 2000.

McCollum, M. J. "Club Med Being Sued for Putting On Minstrel Show," *The Philadelphia Tribune*, July 14, 1995.

McElroy, Guy C. *Facing History*. San Francisco: Bedford Arts, 1990.

Meehan, Kevin. "Wigged Out at UCF," *The Orlando Sentinel*, April 2, 2004.

Mellon, James, ed. *Bullwhip Days*. New York: Weidenfeld & Nicolson, 1988.

Meyer, Carla. "Omigod! They Totally Believe We're Women—Haven't They, Like, Seen 'Tootsie' a Million Times?" *San Francisco Chronicle*, June 23, 2004.

Mintz, Lawrence E. "Humor and Ethnic Stereotypes in Vaudeville and Burlesque," *Melus*, December 1996.

Murray, Albert. *The Omni-Americans*. New York: Outerbridge & Dienstfrey, 1970.

Neate, Patrick. *Where You're At: Notes from the Frontline of a Hip-Hop Planet*. New York: Riverhead, 2004.

Neupert, Richard. "Trouble in Watermelon Land: George Pal and the Little Jasper Cartoons," *Film Quarterly*, Fall 2001.

Newton, Harry L. *Laughland: A Merry Minstrel Book*. Chicago and Minneapolis: T. S. Denison, 1909.

Novak, Stanley M. (Ben). "American Shibboleth: Ebonics," Cambridge Scientific Abstracts, September 2000.

Olney, James. "'I Ain't Gonna Be No Topsy' Because 'Paris Is My Old Kentucky Home,'" *The Southern Review*, January 2001.

Page, Thomas Nelson. *In Ole Virginia*. New York: Charles Scribner's Sons, 1887.

Parish, Norm. "Furor over Carnahan in Blackface Revisits '60s Culture and Tumult," *St. Louis Post-Dispatch*, November 2, 1999.

Pengelly, Matt. "Fighting to End Darkie Day in Cornwall, England," *Day to Day,* National Public Radio, March 8, 2005.

Piersen, William D. *Black Legacy: America's Hidden Heritage.* Amherst: University of Massachusetts Press, 1993.

Poe, Edgar A. *The Complete Tales and Poems of Edgar Allan Poe.* New York: The Modern Library, 1938.

Pope-Hennessy, James. *Sins of the Fathers.* London: Weidenfeld & Nicolson, 1967.

Ramsey, William M. "Dunbar's Dixie," *The Southern Literary Journal,* September 1999.

Rice, Edward. *Monarchs of Minstrelsy.* New York: Kenny, 1911.

Ritterhouse, Jennifer. "Reading, Intimacy, and the Role of Uncle Remus in White Southern Social Memory," *The Journal of Southern History,* August 2003.

Rockwell, John. "Can't Wash Politics out of Art, but You Can Avoid a Hard Sell," *The New York Times,* July 30, 2004.

Roediger, David R. *The Wages of Whiteness.* New York: Verso, 1991.

Rogin, Michael. *Blackface, White Noise.* Berkeley: University of California Press, 1996.

Ross, Alex. "Nausea," *The New Yorker,* August 3, 2004.

Ross, J. R. "Sly Apologizes for Calling Rice 'Aunt Jemima,'" *Wisconsin State Journal* (Madison), November 23, 2004.

Rourke, Constance. *American Humor.* New York: Doubleday, 1931.

Sarris, Andrew. "Spike Lee on Race and the Idiot Box," *The New York Observer,* October 9, 2000.

Schechter, Harold. *Savage Pastimes.* New York: St. Martin's, 2005.

Scott, A. O. "Can Black People Fly? Don't Ask 'Soul Plane,'" The New York Times, June 13, 2004.

Seiler, Andy. "Lee Will Not Be Bamboozled," *USA Today,* October 5, 2000.

Simms, William Gilmore. *The Yemassee.* New York: Harper & Brothers, 1844.

Southern, Eileen. *The Music of Black Americans.* New York: W. W. Norton, 1983.

Springhall, John. *Youth, Popular Culture and Moral Panics.* New York: St. Martin's, 1998.

Stearns, Marshall W. *The Story of Jazz.* London: Oxford University Press, 1956.

Steele, Shelby. *A Dream Deferred: The Second Betrayal of Black Culture in America.* New York: HarperCollins, 1998.

Stowe, Harriet Beecher. *Uncle Tom's Cabin.* Boston: John P. Jewett, 1852.

Stringer, Vickie M. *Let That Be the Reason.* New York: Upstream, 2001.

Tate, Greg. "Hiphop Turns 30: Whatcha Celebratin' For?" *The Village Voice,* January 4, 2005.

———. "The King of Coonology." *The Village Voice,* December 31, 2004.

———, ed. *Everything But the Burden.* New York: Broadway, 2003.

"They Will Use Burnt Cork," *Brooklyn Eagle,* December 18, 1893.

Thometz, Kurt, ed. *Life Turns Man Up and Down: High Life, Useful Advice, and Mad English.* New York: Pantheon, 2001.

Thompson, Hunter S. *The Proud Highway.* New York: Ballantine, 1998.

Thompson, Robert Farris. *Flash of the Spirit.* New York: Random House, 1983.

Thorpe, Edward. *Black Dance.* Woodstock, NY: Overlook, 1990.

Tosches, Nick. *Where Dead Voices Gather.* New York: Little, Brown, 2001.

Turner, Vikki. *A Hustler's Wife.* Columbus, OH: Triple Crown, 2003.

Twain, Mark. *The Adventures of Huckleberry Finn.* New York: Charles L. Webster, 1884.

Van Vechten, Carl. *Nigger Heaven.* New York: Alfred A. Knopf, 1926.

Ward, Douglas Turner. *Happy Ending and Day of Absence.* New York: Dramatists Play Service, 1994.

Watkins, Mel. *Stepin Fetchit.* New York: Pantheon, 2005.

Weeden, Howard. *Bandanna Ballads.* New York: Doubleday & McClure, 1899.

Williams, Donna M. "Our Love/Hate Relationship with Zora Neale Hurston," *The Black Collegian,* January 1994.

Wimsatt, William Upski. *Bomb the Suburbs.* New York: Soft Skull, 2001.

Wolfe, George C. *The Colored Museum.* New York: Grove Weidenfeld, 1988.

Wonham, Henry B. "The Curious Psychological Spectacle of a Mind Enslaved," *Mississippi Quarterly,* December 1997.

Wood, Peter. *Diversity: The Invention of a Concept.* San Francisco: Encounter, 2003.

Yates, Michael D. "Minstrel Show," *CounterPunch,* September 2003.